The Perfect Dictatorship

Also by Stein Ringen

Nation of Devils: Democratic Leadership and the Problem of Obedience (2013)

The Korean State and Social Policy: How South Korea Lifted Itself from Poverty and Dictatorship to Affluence and Democracy (with Huck-ju Kwon, Ilcheong Yi, Taekyoon Kim, and Jooha Lee, 2011)

The Economic Consequences of Mr. Brown: How a Strong Government Was Defeated by a Weak System of Governance (2009)

The Liberal Vision and Other Essays on Democracy and Progress (2007)

What Democracy Is For: On Freedom and Moral Government (2007)

Citizens, Families and Reform (1997 and 2005)

The Possibility of Politics: A Study in the Political Economy of the Welfare State (1987 and 2006)

The Perfect Dictatorship

China in the 21st Century

Stein Ringen

Hong Kong University Press
The University of Hong Kong
Pokfulam Road
Hong Kong
www.hkupress.org

ISBN 978-988-8208-93-7 (*Hardback*)
ISBN 978-988-8208-94-4 (*Paperback*)

British Library Cataloguing-in-Publication Data
A catalogue record for this book is available from the British Library.

Digitally printed

'A new interpretation of the Chinese party-state—shows the advantage that derives from a comparative theorist looking at the Chinese system.'

—**Tony Saich**, Harvard University

'China is a complex country, and there is a range of reasonable interpretations of its political system. Professor Ringen's interpretation is different than my own, but China watchers need to engage with his thought-provoking and carefully argued assessment. If current trends of repression intensify, less pessimistic analysts will need to recognise that Ringen's analysis may have been prescient.'

—**Daniel A. Bell**, Tsinghua University

'Inspirational and trenchant. Stein Ringen's book is a must-read to understand China's politics, economy, ideology and social control, and its adaptability and challenges under the CCP's rule, especially in the 21st century.'

—**Teng Biao**, Harvard Law School and New York University

'Stein Ringen's insights as a prominent political scientist enable a powerful examination of the Chinese state in a penetrating analysis that reaches strong conclusions which some will see as controversial. The book is scholarly, objective, and free from ideological partiality or insider bias. Whether one ultimately wishes to challenge or embrace his findings, the book should be read.'

—**Lina Song**, University of Nottingham

A friend who has written an excellent book about modern China says in his preface that he wishes China well. For my part, I wish the Chinese well. I dedicate this book to the Chinese people and to their freedom, happiness and prosperity.

Contents

Preface

This book has been some time in the making. Some main conclusions were reached quite early in the project and have been confirmed in subsequent developments.

I early on found that the workings of the complicated mixed command and market economy have caused an exaggerated view of China's economic strength. There has without question been strong economic growth, and the Chinese economy is obviously a very big one, but China has not advanced economically, and hence in strength generally, to the extent the leaders have boasted and the world has mostly accepted. In part official statistics have overstated growth, and in part weaknesses and costs in the socialist market economy have gone unaccounted. By 2015, accumulated weaknesses in the economy burst through the surface of pretence, manifested in the mid-year stock market crash, and rattled the confidence of the regime, its people, and international markets.

I also found that the political system is better described as harshly dictatorial than as mildly authoritarian. That conclusion I had reached by the time of the last change of leadership, in 2012–13. This leadership has subsequently cracked down upon real and imagined oppositional forces with much brutality. However, I do not think it would be correct to say that Xi Jinping and his allies brought dictatorship back to China. There is a continuity of political dictatorship during economic opening up. What the new leaders have done is to put to effective use the apparatus that was ready for them when they came into office. I think we should be clear and straight in language and that China analysis should be grounded in an undisguised awareness that we are dealing with a dictatorial state.

The regime uses an intricate combination of legitimacy and control to maintain its highly prized stability. It has bought legitimacy with the spreading of economic rewards and by fostering a reputation of effective governance. It has exercised control with the help of propaganda, thought work, and brute repression. However, under Xi Jinping's leadership there has been a shift in the mode of governance. With the pace of economic growth sliding downwards, the regime turned more strongly to the use of controls, as if it lost confidence in its ability to purchase legitimacy. It intensified repression, reverted to Maoist traditions of propaganda and political education, streamlined and centralised the structures of power, and extended the role of the party. It scaled back collective leadership for a new kind of one-person rule, complete with a touch of person cult around the supreme leader. It brought ideology back in more strongly than at any time since Mao, albeit a new brand of ideology, under Xi's label of a nationalistic China Dream. This shift has happened step by step but systematically enough to establish the Xi regime as radically different from that of Deng Xiaoping and his followers.

The present Chinese regime, then, in my interpretation, is less strong, more dictatorial, and more of its own kind than the world has mostly wanted to believe.

I started this reflection by thinking that I would probably find in China much of what I had seen previously in South Korea, only writ large.[1] It has been a journey of surprise, and I have not at all found what I expected.

I have found the reading of China less difficult than I had thought. In much of what is written about China, the country and people continue to be seen as inscrutable and mysterious. The Chinese claim to be a uniquely ancient civilisation, and those who look in from the outside sometimes buy into their host's mythology. Non-Chinese writers bring tribute by underlining how very foreign, for them, China is and how difficult it is to understand. It's a big country, and for that reason a complicated one, not least in its governance, but inscrutable it is not. What for me makes China fascinating is less its history than how very different from anything else known to humankind its system is *today*.

Much is also in admiration of China and of its model of development. I had expected to fall into that fold. China's development is indeed impressive. I am not squeamish about authoritarianism, having seen effective governance in the hands of autocratic rulers in South Korea and in the main lauded that form of rule as progressive for the Korean people. But as I have worked along, not only has that expectation been dashed but also my interpretation of the Chinese case has become ever darker. The Chinese party-state is different from any other kind of state. The dictatorship is relentless, determined, and unforgiving, sophisticated in how it does it but uncompromising in what it does. The fact of dictatorship tends to be skirted over a bit, and there is a tendency to play it down by resorting to the more moderate language of 'authoritarianism'. But I have seen authoritarianism at work elsewhere, and what I am seeing in China is different. The state of rule is hard, and, confounding Western expectations, the direction of rule is not towards the softer.

The job I found myself having taken on with this book was to get inside and dissect a system that is unlike any other, a dictatorship that works to perfection, so well that it in some ways does not even look dictatorial, and a dictatorship that grows harder

1. In Ringen et al., *The Korean State*.

within a setting of economic progress. This is counterintuitive for someone like me, with a background in democracy analysis. Dictatorships are supposed to be crude; the Chinese one is not. Economic progress is supposed to make dictatorship less necessary; that is not the way it is seen in China.

I am grateful to colleagues and friends in China who have helped and guided me with much generosity and forbearance. I have relied on many of them for information, in everything from the big questions to tedious and technical details. I have met officials, central and local, and have always been received with generosity. I have met many students at lectures and seminars and have benefitted greatly from stimulating and enlightening discussions with them. Chinese governance is a convoluted business, and there are no doubt remaining mistakes in my descriptions. There are fewer mistakes than there would have been without help from Chinese friends and contacts. Those that remain are entirely my own responsibility.

My conclusions have become critical of the Chinese model, in the end very critical, so much so that I think it is not necessarily in the interest of Chinese friends that I associate them with this book. Some I have not maintained contact with, and I know that some think I have turned my back on them, something I deeply regret and for which I here apologise to those concerned. I would have liked to thank helpers by name but have decided not to. It is not that I believe any single book matters that much. But things are hard in China now. A man or a woman who has entertained a critical outsider might find himself or herself in difficulty with some authority, of which there are many that are able to cause trouble whether they have reason to or not, and in that case even an innocent association with a foreign work, even if itself not very significant, might become another weapon in the hands of another villain.

I do not name Chinese friends and colleagues, nor do I name non-Chinese ones. There are many who have helped with ideas, perspectives, criticism, and inspiration, and I thank all who have engaged in exchange and discussion.

I am grateful to St Antony's College and its Centre for Asian Studies for giving this project a home and to colleagues there and in the splendid wider community of China studies at the University of Oxford for support and encouragement in many ways.

At Hong Kong University Press, I am grateful to my acquisitions editor, Yuet Sang Leung, and publisher, Malcolm Litchfield, for their warm encouragement and support for the project, to Sherlon Ip and Carol Zhong for their firm hand in the copyediting and production of the book, and to Winnie Chau, Jenifer Lim, and Felix Cheung for their engagement, from a very early stage, for its promotion.

Introduction

A Good Regime?

In a retrospective on the Spanish Civil War, George Orwell, master wordsmith, and a volunteer in a faction on the republican side, said that what had been at stake, as he saw it, was 'the cause of the common people'. My question in this book is whether the reformed Chinese state is doing the common people's work. It should be: It calls itself a people's republic and the leaders boast that they are. But is it and are they?

It is not impossible that the Chinese state is on its way to becoming a good regime of its own kind. Many outside observers have come to accept that it is.[1] Inside believers are not naïve. They know of the regime's blemishes but will argue that it deals with the problems and that people are better off. They may compare it with India, the other big Asian nation, which is democratic but where governance has not delivered, and people have suffered for it.

I will take it as a serious proposition that the Chinese model is special in such a way that it is indeed serving the cause of the common people. In 2012, with the new leadership, the People's Republic moved into a new phase of its historical march. It is possible that the previous phase, that of Deng Xiaoping and his disciples, was an interim in which the Chinese house was put in order and that the new phase, that of Xi Jinping, is about building on that order for the benefit of the Chinese people.

If they are doing the people's work, they are doing it in their own way. Their institutions have 'Chinese characteristics'. When they claim to be democratic, or a market economy, or a rule-of-law system, they add 'with Chinese characteristics'.[2] The Chinese system has been and is different from any other. It has to be understood on its own terms and not, for example, as a soviet regime that has miraculously survived or as a new member of the family of capitalist nations. There is a deep-rooted misunderstanding outside of China that as the country grows economically it will also become 'normal' socially and politically, meaning, from a Western, capitalistic, democratic vantage, more like us. But China is not and is not becoming ordinary; it is and will remain *different*. Under the new leadership, which has radically changed

1. A recent sophisticated, if critical, voice for this interpretation is Bell, *The China Model*.
2. In a speech about multiculturalism and minority rights to UNESCO in Paris in early 2014, Xi Jinping even embraced 'Buddhism with Chinese characteristics'.

both the substance and forms of governance, China is now even different from its own previous reformed self.

China is the country and empire that sits on the territory over which the rulers in Beijing claim control. It is an empire in that it embraces vast non-Chinese lands, such Tibet, Xinjiang, and parts of Mongolia (although the notions of 'Chinese' and 'non-Chinese' thus used are ambiguous). It is a country in the sense that the whole empire is contained within one set of borders. It is a nation with a long history and a strong awareness of its own greatness. Always, the governing of China is a national project, one of national greatness.

China today is almost as big as the empire has ever been. The Qing dynasty in the 18th century claimed more territory, including all of Mongolia and swathes of Kazakhstan and south and east Russia, and Korea and Vietnam as vassal states. Central control is possibly stronger than ever but is still, as it has always been, tenuous. Beijing may be able to hold the country together but is far from directing developments in the provinces. The country is not only big but also diverse, the regions vastly different from one another in development, economy, tradition, culture, language, ethnicity, religion, and in many other ways.

This is the rising power in the world: big, bureaucratic, undergoing ferocious economic growth, assertive, much admired, and much feared. It is the ultimate state-led country, the country as strong as the state is strong. How and where is this state leading its country?

To know a state—what kind it is, what it is about—we need to dissect what its leaders say, how the machinery of government is built up, how they work it, and what comes out of it. All regimes must present themselves to their people and to the world and explain and justify their hold on and use of power. To be obeyed at home and respected abroad, the leaders need a narrative to help them attract that obedience and respect. An effective regime must then have the capacity to act. It must have a machinery through which intentions can be translated into doings. How the leaders are able to do that is determined in part by the shape of the administration at their disposal. But since leaders differ in how well they are able to use their bureaucracies, we do not finally know a state until we can see how intentions and actions flow through to consequences out there among the people, in society, and in the world.

China will never be a beautiful utopia, but it could be on the way to making itself as benevolent an autocracy as is possible in the Chinese context, given the country's history and contemporary complexity. It could be making itself a regime that is progressive for the Chinese people and that presents itself to them, at this time in their history, as the best they could realistically have.

While pondering this question, a second one emerges—a question about ideology. Since Deng Xiaoping, the great modern reformer, the Chinese leaders have been seen to have worked pragmatically and unburdened by ideology. But as I try to get inside this state, the question puts itself in front of me of whether it might look pragmatic but still be ideological. It was an ideological state in Mao's time. Has it now shed ideology, or is it remaking itself into a new ideological state on non-Maoist terms? As there is no understanding of the Chinese state other than as a party-state, there may be no good understanding of the party-state that does not include ideology.

Two questions stand against each other. In which way is China leaning, towards a permanently pragmatic state, or towards a new version of its original self, an ideological state? The tug of war between these two views underlies the following discussions to the end, and beyond.

Chapter 1
Leaders

The Chinese state is not just a state; it is a party-state. That sets it apart. It is not a democracy, obviously, but nor is it a bog-standard dictatorship in which typically a military junta holds power with force on behalf of itself or, say, a class of landowners.

A party-state is more than a one-party dictatorship. It is a system with two overpowering bureaucracies, side by side and intertwined. The state controls society, and the party controls the state. There is a double system of control. Control is this state's nature. If it were not for a determination to control, there would be no rationale for the double system. And once there is a party-state, the determination to control is a given. The double system is an awesome structure, all the more so when in the hands of able leaders. The current leader, Xi Jinping, the general secretary of the party, the president of the nation, and the commander-in-chief of the armed forces, now China's strong and domineering leader, is using the apparatus available to him with force and determination. A big and powerful country, a strong state, an ambitious and shrewd leader—that adds up to a force to be reckoned with. The rest of us had better understand what is going on.

Party-states are dictatorships. All the known ones in history have been dictatorships, and the remaining ones, including China, are dictatorships.[1] Communist rule in China was dictatorial before the communists were in control of all of the country, established itself as a brute dictatorship nationally in 1949, and continued to be a deadly dictatorship under Mao.[2] China today is a sophisticated dictatorship in which citizens are allowed many freedoms but only up to a point. At that point, when necessary, and often enough that no one is in doubt, the party-state clamps down, sometimes in crude and sometimes in subtle ways, and with whatever force is necessary. It bears being set down at the start and then not forgotten that the regime

1. There are now only a few party-states left in the world. The old fascist ones are gone, as are the communist ones in Europe and the former Soviet Union, the African ones that tried to make themselves party-states, and the Ba'atist ones in Iraq and (probably) Syria. In addition to China, there is only North Korea, Vietnam, Laos, Cuba, and possibly Eritrea. Even in this family, China stands out. It is big, strong, effective, and economically successful.
2. On the early People's Republic, see Dikötter, *The Tragedy of Liberation*.

that presents itself to the world as reformed is one that still rules, ultimately, by fear, intimidation, violence, and death.

However, although it is true that China remains a dictatorship, the term 'dictatorship' is still not adequate as a description of the current system. For now, 'dictatorship' will do, and I will stick with that, but I will come back to a more faceted explanation of the particular brand of dictatorship that has come to operate in China.

Everyone knows that China is a party-state, but this is one of those knowns that are so obvious that it is often overlooked. And if you do overlook it, and look to China as just another state, you will understand nothing and misunderstand everything.[3]

Priorities

Three ghosts of fear haunt the Chinese leaders. The first is the memory of the century of humiliation. Going into the 19th century, China was the world's biggest economy and the leading power in technology and administration. Then followed a century of catastrophic decline. The country was subjugated by foreign powers that established colonies and bases on Chinese territory, sometimes under the label of 'concessions', and took control of much of China's foreign trade. The imperial regime eventually collapsed, central control was lost, and the nation disintegrated into warlordism and civil war. Large parts of the country were invaded and occupied.[4] China's leaders, and probably Chinese people, had been used to thinking of their country as the 'middle kingdom' at the centre of the world with other countries and peoples around it, more or less distant from the centre and with lesser and possibly barbarian civilizations. The loss of position corresponding to that self-understanding was a calamity. The view persists that China has a rightful place in the world, which belongs to it by natural justice, and that that place is at the centre. The reclaiming of the nation's rightful place is on the leaders' minds, and probably something they are under intense pressure from below to pursue. The century of humiliation proved that China's rightful status is not assured and that the nation and its strength need to be always nurtured and protected. When the communists took power in 1949, Mao declared that China had

3. A terminological warning on two terms that will appear with more repetition than I would have wanted: The Chinese are ruled through a vast party, state, military, security, central, and local bureaucratic network. I will often refer to that network as 'the system' and occasionally as 'the regime'. A crucial and recurrent issue for this system is its 'legitimacy', by which I mean its sanding in the eyes and minds of the Chinese people, or some of them, or of outsiders for that matter, and the degree to which it commands their genuine acceptance and loyalty.

4. As usual, there are nuances in the literature on the magnitude of catastrophe. Chang, in *Empress Dowager Cixi*, argues that economic and administrative modernisation was well underway during the imperial regime. Mitter, in *A Bitter Revolution* and *China's War with Japan*, argues that the nationalist regime in the 20th century was more effective than has generally been acknowledged. However, the prevailing view within China, and certainly in official historiography and in official terminology, is that the period from the opium wars to the communist revolution was a 'century of humiliation'. Regime decline may well have started earlier, but foreign imperialistic influence made itself seriously felt as of the early to mid-19th century.

risen again and since then, with some setbacks in the process, the leaders have seen themselves as working for resurrection in the world. This is, in the current official terminology, the 'rejuvenation' of the nation.[5]

The second ghost is the memory of Mao's destructive excesses. After 1949, the country was under central control and gaining in strength and economic prowess. This was all scarified by the Great Leap Forward (1958–60) and the Cultural Revolution (1966–76). These were disasters, for the Chinese people first of all but also for the regime itself. They were self-inflicted catastrophes by a regime that had allowed a single supreme leader absolute authority. This experience proved that the party-state has in itself the capacity to self-destruct. The lesson for subsequent leaders has been that protections need to be built into the procedures of the party-state and its system of management against its in-built propensity to excess.

And the third ghost is the memory of the gradual decline and eventual collapse of the Soviet Union, the regime on which communist China had modelled itself. The Soviet leaders, as it looked from Beijing, starting with the denouncement of Stalin, neglected their own system, denied its continuity, allowed the economy to falter, and relaxed controls. They made great claims on the obedience of their people but failed to reward them with prosperity. This experience proved that a great communist power, constituted as a party-state, can implode if it is not protected and managed with strength and wisdom. Two main lessons have been drawn in China from the Soviet failure. One is about the importance of controls and that they must never be allowed to erode. But as important is a second lesson, that even solid controls are not enough. There must also be reward: something tangible and economic in it for the people, or at least for enough of them. Deng Xiaoping made the understanding accepted that the rulers, in their own interest, must reward the ruled with the experience that they are in a trajectory of prosperity.

The reformed regime took to governing by rewards. That was productive. However, the question now is whether, under the new leadership, the pendulum is swinging back towards more government by ideology. If so, that could be a shift of great consequence for the Chinese people—and for the world.

For the party-state, there is one single supreme determination: its own perpetuation. The regime that has been in power since 1949 has taken it to be imperative that it shall continue to hold power. Today's rulers insist that their regime is the one that came into being with the communist victory in the civil war in 1949 and that the Chinese Communist Party, the CCP, by definition embodies the continuation of that regime. They claim the right to rule by having liberated the country through revolution and lifted it out of humiliation, and by having shown themselves able to hold it together and under control. The new leaders slotted themselves into an ancient

5. As is brilliantly on display in the exhibition of 'the rejuvenation of the nation' in the National Museum in Beijing.

tradition in which Chinese thinkers and holders of power have seen the advancement of national strength as their great project and the strong state as the instrument of that project.

This determination is absolute. When the chips are down, the inescapable bottom line is the preservation of the regime and its power. That was put on display in 1989, when the People's Liberation Army (PLA) was turned on the people. There were nationwide uprisings with broadly based protest movements across the country and with serious revolts in many cities—80 or more it is sometimes said, sometimes 130, sometimes many more, as usual we do not know—fuelled by discontent and animated by a demand for democracy. These were not mere incidents, which the regime is deft at managing; it was revolt. Accommodation proved impossible. Those within the regime who were inclined to political opening up and compromise were sidelined. The regime—and this was in its modern incarnation—reasserted itself with force even though that put at risk its whole project of reform and opening up, a project the subsequent salvaging of which was touch and go.

The nature of the crackdown in 1989 is not well remembered, neither in China nor in the world.[6] The challenge to the regime was not from students protesting but from a popular revolt with broad support in the population and with participation by various groups of citizens: workers, even officials, even soldiers, for a few days in Beijing, and possibly elsewhere, even journalists in state media, under a banner that they were fed up with lying. In Beijing, it was not an event contained in Tiananmen Square but revolt and retaliation that spread through the city. It was not a Beijing event but a national uprising. Nor is it well remembered what was cracked down upon. The 1980s were years of hope. Young people thought they had a future in an increasingly open society. What was killed, in addition to an unknown number of persons, was hope itself, replaced overnight by hopelessness and empty space where there should be idealism. The people were told that free lives is something they have no business hoping for and that they should just forget, and it was made clear to them that if they were to demand more than is available, the state would stop them. This was earth-shattering for an optimistic generation and a turning point in recent Chinese history. Dictatorship was reasserted and the Chinese told it would persist. Overnight, the only available reality for anyone not intent on being a martyr became one of accommodation. The effects have been lasting and can be seen in the nihilistic materialism, moral corruption, cynicism, disaffection, and confusion of identity that are now prevalent in Chinese culture and social life.

Nor may we always remember just what is new and not new in the new 'model'. China is admired for its turnaround and the resulting economic growth. Reform and opening up is seen as a transformation of the Chinese system, a transformation

6. As explained elegantly in Lim, *The People's Republic of Amnesia*. For the persistence of amnesia, see Paulson, *Dealing with China*, published in 2015, in which the June 4th massacre is reduced to the language of 'incident'.

brought about by a new understanding that the country needs economic growth more than it does ideological purity. It is thought that Deng Xiaoping and his allies regeared the system into one single-mindedly dedicated to economic growth and that China was being edged on to a path of becoming an ordinary country. There has hardly been a more used phrase among the commentariat than the tiresome 'single-mindedly dedicated to economic growth', or some version thereof.

But this regearing never happened. The opening up that Deng launched in 1978 was to be economic and no more.[7] There has been much political reform, but not for political opening up. Far from promising soft governance, Deng stressed from the start that political management must 'seize with both hands' the joint emphasis on economic development and political propaganda and thought work. He did not turn his back on the project of national glory but famously advised the country 'for now to hide its capacity and bide its time'. The regime has not been and is not single-mindedly dedicated to economic growth. It is single-mindedly dedicated to its own preservation. It is certainly dedicated to economic growth, but not for the sake of growth or the blessings that may follow for the common people. Economic growth is not an end; it is a means. The regime is dedicated to economic growth because the leaders know or believe that, without growth and the distribution of rewards that growth allows, they and their edifice would be in danger. That is a strong dedication, but it is not what the leaders are, finally, in business for.

The regearing that happened on Deng's watch was from revolution to gradualism but not away from party-state control. Deng laid down 'the four cardinal principles': to uphold the socialist path, to uphold the people's democratic dictatorship, to uphold the leadership of the Communist Party, and to uphold Mao Zedong Thought and Marxism-Leninism.[8] He made clear in decidedly non-reformist language what was not up for debate, and did so in order to have the backing to stop any political movements that could evolve to threatening the perpetuation of the regime. There were experiments with political liberalisation, for example with elections higher up the line than in villages, but these were reined in on the fear that once let loose they would be unstoppable. In 1987, Hu Yaobang, the nominal head of the party, who was seen to be a voice for liberal political reform, was purged from his post. When the dust had settled after the crackdown in 1989, the next party leader, Zhao Ziyang, also seen to be soft, was the next to be purged, stripped of all his positions at the Fourth Plenum of the 13th Central Committee on 23–24 June of that year, to spend most of his next sixteen years under house arrest, until his death in 2005 at age eighty-five.

7. Recent critical biographies dismiss any notion of Deng as a liberal political reformer and show him in both experience and outlook be entirely a party man wedded to party loyalty. See Vogel, *Deng Xiaoping and the Transformation of China* and Pantsov and Levine, *Deng Xiaoping: A Revolutionary Life*.

8. These cardinal principles are enshrined in the constitution of the Communist Party as 'the foundation on which to build our country. Throughout the course of socialist modernisation we must adhere to the Four Cardinal Principles and combat bourgeois liberalisation.'

Since that definition of normality in 1989, the trend in state-society relations has been towards tightening with stronger controls from above rather than more opening up from below. The leadership that came in in 2012–13 speaks a forceful language of reform. Some of that is no doubt being turned into action, but how much is yet to be seen. There are many things Xi and Co. say they *intend* to do; what they *have* done is to reinforce Leninism within the party and state control in society more broadly.

Mao left a destroyed economy, and it is sometimes thought that it was this destruction that Deng and his allies reacted to. The economy was indeed in dire straits, but Mao's legacy was also a destroyed polity, and the political system was arguably even more damaged than the economic system was. The reforms responded to both these destructions under a double agenda, to both reform the economy and to rebuild the political machinery of control, both in party and administration.[9] The economy has, as everyone knows, been reshaped. But there has been as much political work as well, on this side in the form of reform and restitution rather than reform and opening up. Far from China being made ordinary, it has been reaffirmed as different.[10]

Aligned to the supreme determination to self-perpetuation is a second super-concern, which grows out of China's historical self-image and experience and which is nearly as absolute: to maintain and protect what is seen as the nation's territorial integrity and security.[11] That means, on the one hand, to prevent any part of the empire from falling out from under the control of Beijing. The sensitive areas are in the west, in Tibet and Xinjiang (the name the Qing dynasty imposed on the ancient home of the Muslim Uighurs, meaning 'new territory' or 'new frontier'). If this were a regime single-mindedly dedicated to economic growth, it would shed much of the western provinces, which are a huge economic burden for it, but that is inconceivable—although an idea Mao himself flirted with while waiting to ascend to national control.[12] Any question of conceding autonomy in a real meaning to, say, Tibet, is not on the agenda and is something that the current rulers just would not contemplate. (And Tibet does have at least one important resource: water, and good water at that.) Instead, they are busy eradicating ethnic cultures and wasting resources by colonising the western provinces with Han officials and migrants in order to integrate these lands irrevocably into the country (a colonising strategy that is incidentally also followed, quietly and under the radar, in Hong Kong). They are investing enormous efforts into the promotion of their own story of Tibet worldwide, including by bullying

9. See, for example, Shambaugh, *China's Communist Party* and Yang, *Remaking the Chinese Leviathan*.
10. The failure of political opening up has been referred to as a 'stalled transition', inspired by, for example, Pei, *China's Trapped Transition*. My interpretation is that although there has been much political-administrative reform and although there have been ups and downs in the direction of political reform, political reform in the sense of political opening up was never decisively on the official agenda; hence, there was no political opening up that subsequently stalled.
11. See Nathan and Scobell, *China's Search for Security*.
12. According to Snow, *Red Star over China*.

anyone who wants to be on good terms with them away from any official contact or exchange with the Dalai Lama, one of the great spiritual leaders of our times.[13] (Anyone they can, that is, which effectively seems to mean everyone except the Americans and Indians, and even the American president now tiptoes about meeting His Holiness, recently by refraining from publishing photos from a meeting of theirs. When Mr. Obama exchanged greetings with the Dalai Lama at the annual National Prayer Breakfast in Washington on 5 February 2015 and said he was a 'good friend', a Chinese Foreign Ministry spokesman retaliated: 'We oppose any foreign country allowing the Dalai Lama to visit, and oppose any country using the issue of Tibet to interfere in China's internal affairs.' The official news agency, *Xinhua*, said that the president's action was to 'drive a nail' into the heart of the Chinese people.)

It also means the consolidation of territorial integrity where it is not yet settled. The reintegration of Hong Kong and Macao into China in 1997 and 1999 were seen as milestones in the rebuilding of the nation. The rulers are determined that also Taiwan is to be reintegrated. They may be patient about the timing, and possibly flexible about the terms, as they were for Hong Kong and Macao, at least as a transition, but in principle the status of Taiwan, as of Tibet, is not negotiable. Their version of the one-China policy is a principle of respect that foreign leaders who wish to be on collaborative terms are routinely coerced into kowtowing to, for example in communiqués after official meetings. (In the World Bank's *China 2030*, which was produced in collaboration with the Development Research Center of China's State Council, Taiwan is consistently referred to as 'Taiwan, China'.) There are unsettled border disputes with India, and potentially with Pakistan in Kashmir. Much of the long China-India border between Bhutan and Myanmar is contested. Here, from time to time, these two great powers rub up against each other, sometimes in outbursts of bad temper (as, for example, in September 2014, during Xi Jinping's official visit to India, possibly in a Chinese mini-incursion—so it was claimed in Indian media—possibly in disregard of Xi's order to draw back, sufficiently to derail the intended friendship-building) and sometimes in incursions, as in early and mid-year 2013, when Chinese troops without warning or explanation moved south for a while into what they call South Tibet (or South Xizang). In 2011, Tajikistan ceded 1,142 square kilometres of territory to China in an agreement that settled the border between these two countries. The final border demarcations with both Russia and Vietnam were in 2009.

There are dangerous issues with Japan and Vietnam in particular, but also with the Philippines, Malaysia, Brunei, probably Indonesia, indirectly India, and possibly

13. It is a sad observation that they are winning this battle hands down. In the fall of 2014, the South African government let the Dalai Lama know that he would not be allowed to enter the country for a meeting of Nobel Peace Prize laureates, the third time he was denied a visa to the country. A spokesman for the Chinese Foreign Ministry said that 'China highly commends the firm support that the government of South Africa has shown to China on issues regarding China's sovereignty and territorial integrity'. The peace gathering in South Africa was cancelled after the other laureates pulled out.

South Korea over territories and islands, some tiny rocks, in the East and South China Seas, which are a source of conflict. China's claims to its various remote territories, even to Tibet and Xinjiang, even to Taiwan, are based on humbug history, but that does not matter.[14] One would think that civilised neighbours in the modern world would find a way of negotiating such petty disagreements, but there is no sign that China is so inclined or inclined to negotiate except from strength.

Around and following the leadership transition in 2012–13, the Chinese position hardened, and its claims were classified as 'core interests', which is seen as a declaration that China would not agree to any settlement by mediation, all backed up by increasing civil and military presence and infrastructural construction on and around contested islands and waters, in an apparent strategy of gradually establishing it is a practical fact that these rocks and waters and their resources are Chinese and for Chinese use. The Chinese leaders are off and on conciliatory in language, but their activities in the waters go on.[15] The foreign minister, Wang Yi, took the opportunity of a press conference during the 2014 meeting of the National People's Congress to reconfirm the hardening of China's position. To a question from a Japanese reporter on the deteriorating relations between China and Japan, he answered, 'on the issue of principle—history and territory—there is no room for compromise', and added on the Chinese position that 'there will not be any change'. The official policy is repeated on every opportunity, such as by the defence minister, Chang Wanquan, in an exchange with US Defense Secretary Chuck Hagel in Beijing on 8 April 2014, the official policy being 'no compromise, no concession, no treaty'. When US Secretary of State John Kerry was in Beijing on 16 May 2015, Wang Yi said at their news conference that the Chinese claims in the South China Sea were 'unshakable', and China's 'determination to safeguard our own sovereignty and territorial integrity as firm as a rock'. On 26 May 2015, at a Foreign Ministry briefing, a spokeswoman warned the Philippines that 'a small country can't constantly make unreasonable protests'. Official maps (even in Air China's in-flight magazine, even in the weather map in the official English language *China Daily*, even on the map of China's ethnic geography in the Shanghai Museum, although there is no ethnicity at all in the sea areas) include all of the South China Sea, up to neighbouring countries' shores, as Chinese territory, within a sea border known as the 'nine dash line' which allocates 3 million of the South China Sea's 3.5 million square kilometres to China. This aggression is cheered on by China's navy, that wants to expand, by the state-owned China National Offshore Oil Corporation that wants access to likely petroleum resources in the area, and by fantasists in high and low circles who dream of national glory, play with romantic

14. See, for example on Xinjiang, Holdstock, *China's Forgotten People*.
15. That includes the dredging up of artificial islands on tiny reefs, on which are constructed bases, sometimes with airstrips, with potential military use. For aerial video footage, search 'artificial Chinese islands' on *YouTube*.

visions of war, and hate Japan and the Japanese. There is a menacing undertone in China's dealings with its neighbours of 'might is right', a view which in my experience is shared broadly by Chinese people, including those who are educated and familiar with the ways of the world and otherwise non-jingoistic. When China's foreign minister, Wang Yi, gave the Australian foreign minister, Julie Bishop, a public and conspicuously undiplomatic dressing down in Beijing in December 2013, for Australia's criticism of China's unilateral establishment of an 'air defence zone' in the East China Sea between Taiwan and Japan, there was an instant flurry of chauvinistic support on the Chinese Internet (although one never knows how much of such flurry from below is orchestrated from above). It all harkens back, no doubt, to a tradition of China expecting 'tribute' from those on its borders, and is an indication of how the leaders think of themselves and their country. It does not help, of course, that official Japan is responding with its own rhetoric of nationalism and militarism.

China has not been an imperialistic power in the world and is not, say the leaders, making itself an expansionist one today—although they may have some difficulty persuading the peoples of Central Asia, or of parts of Africa, or others who are sensitive to the spreading of a state-sponsored Chinese diaspora to the far corners of the globe.[16] The regime takes pride in its model of governance and development but does not seem intent on imposing it on others. It wants clout and respect, including respect for its economic interests wherever they reach, and to some degree subservience, in particular from neighbours. It is an insecure state and near paranoid about being treated with the respect the leaders believe is due. A common complaint in official commentaries over misbehaviour by others is that not showing Chinese authorities due respect is to offend the Chinese people. It has laid down the threat of war to neighbours such as India (invaded in 1962) and Vietnam (invaded in 1979). It easily takes offence from any form of rebuke and is alert on border issues and to anything the leaders see as a threat to its territorial integrity. When David Cameron, the British prime minister, met with the Dalai Lama in 2010, he found official relations with China interrupted and had to cancel a planned visit. When he was later able to undertake the visit, late in 2013, it was on the understanding of cringing servility in behaviour and speech, at least in public, about human rights in general and Tibet in particular. It is a bullying state—towards neighbours and towards anyone who causes it grief, even in small matters. Ahead of Premier Li Keqiang's visit to Britain in June 2014, his planners complained officially to Downing Street that the intended red carpet for his arrival at Heathrow was three metres too short.[17] When the Norwegian Nobel Committee in 2010 awarded the peace prize to Liu Xiaobo, a prominent opposition figure who was then, and still is, in prison, the government of this small

16. On China's diaspora expansion, see Cardenal and Araújo, *China's Silent Army*. On Central Asia, see Laurelle and Peyrouse, *The Chinese Question in Central Asia*.
17. As revealed by the *Financial Times*, 20 June 2014.

country, which has no control over the decisions of the Nobel Committee, found itself punished by all official relations being cancelled, so completely so that the Norwegian ambassador in Beijing was not invited to diplomatic events, a display of pettiness that persisted for an unusually long time (although the Norwegian government may have improved its position in early 2014 by denying the Dalai Lama, a Nobel Peace Prize laureate, the customary official reception while on a visit to the country that was labelled 'private' and made him enter the parliament building through a side door). But the leaders are possibly truthful in their insistence that China does not represent a threat to anyone in the world who does not oppose its self-defined 'core interests' and who is otherwise co-operative, in particular in economic matters, and treats it with that all-important respect.

On the other hand, it is becoming a very powerful state, including militarily, and is displaying behaviour that is to play with fire. The People's Liberation Army is stronger than ever and remains a factor in the machinery of governance. The combination of insecurity and assertiveness is a danger in any state, all the more so in one that is increasingly nationalistic, has great military might, and is hypersensitive to respect from others.[18] The leaders see their country as being in contention for world leadership and insist on being treated accordingly. They are under the pressure of chauvinism, nationalism, and militarism from below and from within the establishment. Their behaviour towards neighbours is aggressive and provocative, in ways that also pull tertiary powers into the disputes. What the leaders want is unknown; possibly they have no clear design in mind, but they may, as have powerful leaders before them, find that they are unleashing forces which they may be unable to control.

The rulers have good reasons to be concerned over territorial integrity. Through its history, the ability of the central authorities to control what they have claimed has been much wanting. A promise of the Republic of China, as of 1912, was territorial consolidation, which it however was unable to deliver, and a core claim on the right to rule by the current regime is that it has succeeded in unifying the country and is steadfast in territorial matters. But they hardly have defensive reasons for turning to nationalism and aggression.

These are the regime's number one and two concerns that trump all others. Then there are some additional determinations and cautions that are built into the model of governance as it is now configured. The first sub-determination we have already visited: economic growth. The regime is determined to deliver economic growth because it believes, no doubt rightly, that there is an expectation of economic betterment in the population, which it has itself stimulated, and that it cannot successfully claim legitimacy for its rule without rewarding that expectation and delivering growth, and a great deal of it. That makes growth a strong determination, but, again,

18. In *The China Challenge*, Christensen makes the point that China is a country with 'a historical chip on its national shoulder' and no genuine allies in the world (except for the troublesome friendship of North Korea).

not a determination that stands above all else. If the regime again had to put economic growth at risk to preserve itself, it would. It is conceivable that it might accept great economic sacrifice in a mission of protecting its own definition of territorial integrity, and even for the promotion of national glory. East Asia is an area of dangerous tensions. China's economy is integrated with those of neighbouring countries for trade and investments. Self-interest would suggest co-operation, but nations do not always act according to rational calculus; indeed, war often comes about when rationality is overtaken by recklessness or misadventure. In a given situation, the regime might be willing to sacrifice, or be trapped into sacrificing, economic development for a greater national cause. War is not unthinkable. If it were to break out, for example between China and Japan, part of the blame would lie with the Chinese leaders for not having taken care to contain dangers they were aware of.

The regime has learned, through its own and others' painful experience, that it serves itself best by governing with caution. A first caution is in adaptability. Mao was dogmatic and as a result destructive. The Soviet Union failed to adapt, and collapsed. The Chinese model is in constant movement. Governance is reformist, step by step, by trial and error. The central leaders know that their capacities are limited. Or one hopes they know. There has been a radical shift in the mode of governance under the post-2012 leadership, in a relentless concentration of power to the centre: from civil society (such as it is) to the state, from local government to Beijing, within the party-state from state to party organs, and in the party to the general secretary personally. In mid-2015, a centralisation was announced in the military structures of command. Whether more control will deliver for the leaders is an open question. If they remove caution and start to expect perfection they will probably find that trying too hard is a sure avenue to failure.

A second caution is in collective leadership. Governance under Mao was initially successful, if ugly, until he was personally able to wield uncontested authority, when it became, in addition to being ugly, catastrophic. Deng left the principle of collective leadership as one of his legacies. It might happen that collective leadership again falls by the wayside in another swing of the pendulum that would take the system back towards one-person rule. Xi Jinping has, step by step, concentrated ever more bureaucratic power in his own hands, has demonstrated an aggressive willingness to use these powers, including by purging deviants and real or imagined opponents in party and administration, and is allowing elements of cult around his person. He could possibly attain a new emperor-like position and is possibly so doing.[19] So far, the procedures of collective leadership seem to be maintained, but Xi's brash top-down approach deviates from the incrementalist style that emerged in the reform period. If this is to pull China back to a more rigid command system, that might look like

19. 'Xi is not *primus inter pares* like Jiang and Hu, he is simply *primus*.' Roderick MacFarquhar in the *New York Review of Books*, 13 August 2015.

forceful governance but is also, in the context of China's bigness and complexity, a high-risk strategy.

And a third and crucial caution is to maintain control. This is a system that has programmed the determination to control into its DNA. It controls because it must, because control is what it does. The Soviet Union, as seen from China, imploded not only because it allowed itself to grow sclerotic but also because, after Stalin, it neglected the party-state's system of control, the unity of party and military, and the apparatus of internal security. The Chinese system is milder than it has been in its control over society, or rather more sophisticated, but make no mistake about it: The controls are still there and are maintained, perfected, and used.

State and Economy

A recent book by Ronald Coase and Ning Wang purports to explain 'how China became capitalist', but that is to explain something that never happened. The Chinese economy is *exactly* what the Chinese leaders say it is: a socialist market economy. It is a socialist economy in which market mechanisms are used to a significant degree, and a market economy with extensive state ownership and controls.[20]

Market mechanisms operate, firstly, through private ownership. About half of the economy, as measured by production, is in private ownership, mostly in small- and medium-sized family firms.[21] This is the battlefield of naked and raw capitalism that is easily visible to visitors who then go home to spread the story that China has gone not only capitalist but ultra-capitalist. Furthermore, even non-private firms are embedded in some kind of market context. State enterprises have been relieved of their previous welfare responsibilities and are mostly subjected to profit expectations. This, along with the effects of rationalisation—a massive shedding of smaller enterprises and the pushing of legions of workers into unemployment—brought the state-owned sector into high profitability. From the late 1990s, the majority of state-owned firms were profitable, and their profits outstripped the losses of the loss-makers.[22] The market has been allowed an increasing role in the setting of prices, and it is the leadership's intention, they say, that marketisation is to continue. One price

20. An important reference on the political economy is *China 2030*, co-produced by the World Bank and the Development Research Center of the State Council. It is big, thorough, detailed, fact-packed, and critical. It is also informative in that it is co-produced by an official state research centre and hence shows the scope of officially sanctioned criticism of policy. See also Knight and Ding, *China's Remarkable Economic Growth* and, on relative strengths and weaknesses in the economic model, Huang, *Capitalism with Chinese Characteristics*.
21. The division between the private and the public economy is not along a straight line. Public enterprises can be state owned or locally owned. There is much mixed economy, with private interests involved in the state sector and much state ownership being partial. My fifty-fifty division of the economy between public and private is, as most economic statistics for China, an approximation, but a good enough approximation.
22. By 2007 by a ratio of 5 to 1, according to Knight and Ding, *China's Remarkable Economic Growth*.

that was deregulated was that of housing, which then skyrocketed. Chinese savers have put much of their savings into housing, and households that got into the market early have benefitted hugely from soaring prices.

Behind the official banks, which are state owned, is a murky sector of quasi-private shadow banking, much of it technically illegal, which offers investors higher returns than they can get in banks and borrowers credit which they might otherwise not find. These are non-bank market-driven financial 'vehicles' (which may, however, be run by or in association with the banks that are owned by the state that forbids non-bank finance as a way of protecting those self-same state banks) that operate trusts, wealth management products, and foreign-currency borrowings, and cater to credit-hungry businesses and local authorities in an unregulated sector of high-risk finance. This sector now accounts for a third or more of all credit in the economy and has been growing ferociously in recent years, at an estimated annual rate in turnover of some 30 percent. Even rural-agricultural credit co-operatives, whose operations by law are limited to members, have extended into high-risk shadow banking.

State controls operate, firstly, through public ownership and through preferential treatment of public enterprises in credit, resources, raw materials, energy, and terms of competition. The remaining half of the economy is in central and local government ownership, fully or partially. That includes the 120 or so big state conglomerates, state banks, innumerable town and village enterprises, most 'strategic sector' firms (the 'strategic sectors' being defence, energy, petroleum and petrochemicals, telecoms, coal, civil aviation, and rail and waterway transport), and many 'pillar industry' firms (the 'pillar industries' being machinery, automobiles, information technology, construction, steel, base metals, and chemicals). All land is in public ownership, urban land state owned, and agricultural land owned by co-operatives. According to the state constitution, land cannot be bought or sold, but 'the right to the use of land can be transferred'. The big banks are state owned although with some minority non-state or foreign holdings, including the big four: the Bank of China, the Industrial and Commercial Bank of China (the world's biggest bank measured by assets), the Agricultural Bank of China, and the China Construction Bank. There are some small non-state banks which are more accessible than the state banks to private businesses, but these make up a minor sector. The penetration of foreign banks into banking proper is miniscule. Credit remains the main way of raising capital, as opposed to shares and bonds. The Chinese economy is commonly described as 'credit intensive'. It runs on debt, no less in the local government sector than in the enterprise and household sectors. Through its control of banking, the state holds ultimate control over structural trends in most of the economy. Shadow banking notwithstanding, the authorities have the power to decide which industries and areas are to advance and which are to be held back, a power that is used extensively. Public enterprises to some degree compete with each other but are also protected from outside competition.

Although there is much private capitalism in China, capital, both physical and fiscal, is overwhelmingly in state ownership or under state control. When David Cameron went to China in 2013 to beg for Chinese investments into British nuclear energy and high-speed rail, it was to the Chinese state he went begging, and when the answer came back that investments would be forthcoming, it was the Chinese state that answered, in the person of Premier Li Keqiang on his return visit in 2014. So, not Chinese interests but the Chinese *state*, the one that protects its own energy and rail transport as 'strategic sectors', will become a co-owner in Britain's strategic infrastructure.

Important prices continue to be set administratively, and at a good distance from potential market prices, including the price of bank credit and bank interest rates, of privatised land use, and of, for example, wheat, rice, pharmaceutics, petroleum, gas, and electricity. Furthermore, state controls operate through interventions into the private sector, including both direct administrative interventions, such as administrative approval, reporting, inspection, and closure, and industrial interventions and directives by various central and local government agencies, often at odds with each other.

A further heavy-handed state intervention is in a high level of corporate taxation. Businesses that obey the law pay heavy social contributions on top of wages. That includes obligatory employers' contributions to the various forms of social insurance, to housing provident funds, to the Disabled Persons' Federation and, on a different note, to the official trade unions. These fees are variable across localities but represent a burden of at least 40 percent of the payroll, and often more.

On top of state controls in business operations, and importantly, the controlling hand of the party-state operates through the presence of party organs in economic enterprises. The private economy is not in any real meaning independent but is in various ways under party-state control and integrated into the overarching control system. There is a symbiosis between the public and the private. It is the state that allows private business, and entrepreneurs know that such opportunity as they have is by the grace of the state.[23] Such opposition as there is to the party-state model does not come from the business community.

Although the stated policy is further marketisation, some observers have seen a recent 're-advance' of the state into the economy. The government's 2008 stimulus package was effectively a handout in cash and credit to state enterprises. This was repeated in late 2014 in response to dwindling growth, if on a lesser scale—and again with the stock market crash of 2015 which triggered another injection of public money into the investment machine, at least for a while. Call it quantitative easing with Chinese characteristics. In the early 1990s, prices were deregulated in the airline industry, but when that led to a weakening of the position of the three big

23. In an amendment to the state constitution in 1988, 'the state permits the private sector of the economy to exist and develop . . . as a compliment to the socialist public economy'.

state-owned carriers in what is officially a 'strategic sector', prices were re-regulated in the late 1990s, enabling the big three to regain their dominance (the big three being Air China, China Eastern, and China Southern). The housing price boom that followed from the commodification of housing and the resulting unavailability of affordable housing forced the government to revive a policy of public housing from about 2010. In early 2014, plans were announced to consolidate much of the country's iron-ore mining into a large state-controlled conglomerate. Around the capital, a 'tri-city' province of Beijing, Tianjin, and Hebei is being created (with 130 million inhabitants), in a project that involves the closure or relocation of thousands of firms and public agencies, and the affiliated inadequacy of infrastructure and services, and that represents an astonishing display of top-down command economy thinking and capacity.

Far from the economy being hived off from the polity, the Chinese economy remains firmly integrated into the polity. During the period of rapid economic growth, the state sector, rather than withering has grown more rapidly than has the GDP. The economy is investment driven and investment is debt driven. This investment machine is run by the state, through state enterprises, state capital, state land transactions, state banks, and state credit. A favourite real estate tycoon, Wang Jianlin, who has risen from the ranks of state officials to become the richest person in Asia, says that his conglomerate, the Wanda Group, has prospered by delivering what ambitious party officials crave: choice real estate developments that propel economic growth and bolster their careers. In return, he says, the officials give him the right to develop land at prices far below what his competitors pay. It has no doubt also helped that 'relatives of some of the nation's most powerful politicians and their business associates own significant stakes in his company'.[24]

China is a command economy, a socialist market economy with a heavy line under socialist and a light touch of market. Foreign visitors gaze in amazement at the lights and glitter of Shanghai and see there China's new capitalism before their eyes—but mostly without knowing that Shanghai has an exceptionally small private sector (the Shanghai economy is about 80 percent in public ownership, measured in production) and that what they are admiring is the face of state capitalism rather than private capitalism. There is a great deal of private enterprise in those sky-scrapers, but the capital is in state hands.

True, space has been cleared outside of the public sector for private entrepreneurship into which both Chinese and foreigners have crowded with relish—a great deal of space. There are about 10 million private businesses, most of them small- and medium-sized family enterprises, and a few large ones. Why not? This is a regime that rules by spreading rewards. Private enterprise contributes to growth and jobs, which is to the benefit of the state. It opens up for economic opportunity, which is also to the

24. *New York Times*, 28 April 2015.

benefit of the state. It enables foreign investment, which brings in foreign capital. But private business remains subservient to the public economy as the second sector. Even straight private firms are not free from the controlling hand of the party-state. Private entrepreneurs have massively, and for strategic reasons, joined the Communist Party, and most private firms, certainly those of some size, have encouraged the establishment of party committees and divisions of the All-China Federation of Trade Unions and are organised in the All-China Federation of Industry and Commerce, another of the organs of the party-state.[25]

The economy is open to foreign capital and has in recent years attracted more foreign direct investment than to any other country except the United States. But at the same time it remains a notoriously difficult economy for foreign enterprises to get into. As powerful an operator as Rupert Murdoch's News Corporation tried to establish itself in the Chinese media market but was denied access (however much it growled and flattered the Chinese leaders). JPMorgan Chase, the American bank, like others, found the going hard and turned to hiring junior princelings and friends of the influential and found business doors opening that had previously been shut (a policy which, however, brought it into investigation at home for the use of corrupt procedures, which is illegal under US law). In November 2012, Caterpillar, one of America's biggest companies and with more international reach and experience than most, found that it had bought a virtually defunct mining machinery company, thereby lining the pockets of national and international investors, partly because it was careless out of excessive eagerness to get a foothold in the Chinese mining industry and partly because it was led by the nose and deceived about the company's business and finances. In mid-2013, the British mega-retailer Tesco announced that it was giving up its attempt to establish itself under its own brand and would instead be joining a Chinese retailer as a junior partner trading under its name. The Chinese stock market has been effectively closed for direct participation by foreign investors although a backdoor opening known as 'the Shanghai-Hong Kong Connect Link' was created in late 2014, in a scheme of co-operation between the Hong Kong and Shanghai exchanges to give non-Chinese investors some, if limited and complicated, access to the Shanghai exchange through the Hong Kong exchange (and Chinese investors easier access to the Hong Kong exchange). As part of ongoing economic reforms, the central bank in October 2014 announced plans to allow Chinese citizens to invest in overseas stocks and property as well as to let the nation's companies sell *yuan*-denominated shares abroad. (Well, in Beijing there are always 'plans', and we who try to follow events from outside never really know what or how much follows through, if anything, or when.)

25. On state-business relations, see Dickson and Chen, *Allies of the State* and Tsai, *Capitalism without Democracy*.

In this peculiar economy, which is impressive looking but lumbering, there is a long remaining road to travel towards modernisation. The economy runs on 800 to 900 million jobs. About a third of these are in low-productivity agriculture in which tenant peasants work collectively own land on time-limited contracts, mostly of forty years. The peasantry makes up a big share of the workforce, but these are people we hear very little about in the standard accounts of China's massive development.

The next third is made up of migrant or otherwise irregular workers, who by state regulations are held down in second-class citizenship. That leaves only a final third of the workforce in regular employment or business in the modern sector, about a third of which again consists of public sector workers. This economy, all considered, is far removed from the façade of modernity in the big eastern cities and is one in which partial development sits on an underbelly of deprivation and backwardness.

There is no single labour market but effectively three separate markets with limited mobility between them. This division is regulated by the household registration system. Every Chinese has a registration which establishes his or her official geographical belonging, known as the *hukou*. By and large your registration is to the place you were born or grew up, and that will continue to be your registration through life. If you are registered in a rural area, you have rural citizenship and entitlements. If you have an urban *hukou*, you have entirely different entitlements. This maintains the urban-rural division which has been and remains a feature of the People's Republic. It is not impossible to move your *hukou* but only under strict and limiting conditions. Under the government's present urbanisation plan, 100 million people are supposed to be urbanised and obtain an urban *hukou*, which, however, does not mean that they will be able to settle in any city of their choice.

The household registration system, like everything else in today's culture of administrative reform, is under constant review. In 2014 it was announced that the 'agricultural' and 'non-agricultural' designations are to be removed, something that appears to be implemented incrementally in parts of the land. This caused some commentators to trumpet 'the end of the *hukou*' but it was no such thing. It was a symbolic, if not unimportant measure, since the official designation of a person as 'agricultural' has been seen as derogatory. Individuals may no longer carry these labels, but everyone will still have a designated geographical belonging. If that is to a rural community it will continue to come with rural entitlements. If you live and work in a city but your *hukou* is rural, your entitlements are still those of your rural community.

The maintenance of a registration system that assumes people live their lives where they happen to be born in an economy of mobility might seem irrational. In fact, however, it is part and parcel of the Chinese model. China's economic growth has come off the backs of an army of cheap migrant labour. It is the *hukou* system that has created migrant labour with Chinese characteristics and that assures its continuation.

Centres of development want continued access to cheap labour and do not want the costs that would come with allowing the migrants urban entitlements. Big cities want to control the level and quality of in-migration, something they can do thanks to the *hukou*. Migrants cannot move freely to urban areas but have to apply for a resident permit. That may not be enforced in all areas but is enforced with reasonable effectiveness in the big cities to control the numbers and select migrants by education and wealth, sometimes with the help of a points system similar to that used in some countries to control immigration.

The household registration is also integral to the state's control capacity. It splits the population into subcategories, divides the working population, and prevents both urban-rural and broad working-class solidarities. It includes all Chinese in a register, defines their rights and duties, and enables the state to require them to carry an identity card with detailed personal information. The *hukou* is not an eccentric add-on to the Chinese model; it is a part of what makes the model work, both economically and politically.

That model is entirely of its own kind. Nowhere else is agriculture ultra-socialist, in the meaning under collectively owned and managed land. Nowhere else does the state run an investment machine through its own banks and enterprises to spread highways, railroads, airports, mega-ports, sky-scrapers, malls, and plazas over the territory, and then to let private enterprise loose to put further growth-inducing life into that infrastructure. Nowhere else do economic actors, both public and private, operate under both the regulating hand of the state and the controlling hand of the party. Nowhere else is the labour market segregated by an all-intrusive bureaucratic instrument such as the *hukou*. As the party-state is like no other state, the socialist market economy is like no other economy. China is *different*, not only politically but also economically.

Nevertheless, state–economy relations have changed a great deal during the recent decades of reform, market openings giving non-state actors more space. It was expected that reform in this meaning—marketisation—would intensify under the muscular post-2012 leadership, but it is not clear even to the most knowledgeable observers whether or how this is happening. Market reforms imply a relaxation of state controls, but that may be a difficult pill to swallow for a leadership whose control genes are the dominant ones. This difficulty came to view when the Chinese stock market crashed in June and July 2015. During three weeks from mid-June, the markets lost a third of their value, following more than a doubling of value the preceding year. They continued to fall later on, in spite of energetic attempts by the government to stabilise prices. The boom had been encouraged by the government and cheered on by official media, in part to facilitate the selling of share ownerships in state enterprises. People responded, and by the time of the crash possibly a majority of urban households held stock investments, directly or indirectly through 'wealth management products'. Investors who got in early did well, but millions of often small savers, or borrowers, who went in late lost massively.

The stock market does not have the importance in China's credit-intensive economy that it has in 'normal' capitalist economies. Arguably, the crash did not matter much in macro-economic terms, but it mattered very much for perceptions. Boom and bust is something that just should not happen in the socialist market economy. The sudden slump therefore raised big questions about its inner logic and solidity. The government reacted ineptly by first trying to halt the slide, then giving that up and instead trying to stimulate demand by its usual trick of releasing more credit, for thereby to stimulate more borrowing which was part of the problem in the first instance. It all looked like panic and incompetence.

One effect may have been to halt or derail further market reforms. Another was to shatter confidence, both nationally and internationally, in stock market investments, and economic confidence more generally. Consumers overnight became more cautious with their money. Economic growth was already on a downwards trajectory, and this shock opened people's eyes to weaknesses in the Chinese economy, and its management, where many had long seen mainly strengths. Probably also shaken was the leadership's confidence in its ability to combine market reforms and command economy controls and to distribute rewards through markets under its own control. Possibly also shaken would be the confidence of middle-class people in the party's ability to do for them. If these are the people who have trusted the regime because they have trusted it to manage the economy well, trust may be the final casualty. The crash was a stark reminder that China's debt-dependent economy has less strength than had been suggested by inflated GDP statistics and that the balance of markets and controls is far from stable.

Economic Growth

There is no question that the Chinese economy has grown rapidly in a period, but that has been in the early and easy take-off. In an economy that restarts from destruction, there will be growth unless it is prevented by new destructions. This has been all the more so for the Chinese economy, which so far has had the winds of supporting demographics in its back with a pool of cheap labour to draw on.

But we do not know how strongly the economy has grown or to what size. The official statistics are not reliable, partly because local authorities falsify the statistics to their advantage. The official GDP of the provinces adds up to about 10 percent more than the GDP of the nation. The statistics from different government agencies and provinces are not in accordance with each other. There are two official sets of national GDP numbers, which differ somewhat, one measured by 'the production method' and one by 'the expenditure method'. China may have grown to the world's second biggest economy, but even if the official statistics were true, that still amounts to only about 10 percent of global GDP for 20 percent of global population. In per capita terms, China's national income is at best a sixth of that of the United States, the economy it is supposedly overtaking.

Mega-growth is now over and is starting to be seen, correctly, as a relatively short period of recovery. Growth is slowing and will continue to slow. The population is no longer growing other than by increasing longevity. The national birth rate is 1.6 or 1.7 children per woman, in cities below 1 and in large cities down to 0.7 or less. In the next fifteen years the share of the population that is sixty or older will increase from 14 to 25 percent. Just as the economy needs to make itself human-capital dependent, the pool of human capital is starting to shrink.

Measuring China's economy is obviously not easy and there are many reasons, not necessarily conspiratorial, why the statistics might be wobbly. Although official data on the economy's size and growth are often accepted, for example by international agencies, and reproduced uncritically in the international press and by admirers of the Chinese model, economists are aware that they are no more than suggestive.[26]

Attempts to 'correct' the official numbers have produced diverse results. An international consultancy, the Rhodium Group, in a report published in 2015, have suggested an upwards adjustment of the official 2013 GDP numbers, to the effect that the economy would be 13 to 16 percent bigger than officially measured.[27] This is a methodological numbers exercise of applying revised principles in the System of National Accounts to the Chinese case, apparently in a more friendly application than that adopted by the state statisticians. It assumes that the economy as officially measured is one of sound production and consumption and that the problem is how to value its different components. The biggest contribution to the upwards restatement is a higher estimate for imputed rent (what homeowners 'pay' themselves), followed by higher estimates for industry, construction, and service activity and for the value of research and development. This notches the gross figures upwards, not because anything new is happening in the economy but because what is happening is accounted differently. The exercise has little or no influence on the estimates of growth. When the National Bureau of Statistics issued its own revisions in December 2014, it similarly adjusted one of its two figures upwards by about 3 percent, with the effect of bringing its two GDP figures into closer harmony with each other.

Adjustments of this kind say more about national accounting than about real economics. Most observers probably suspect that the official statistics overstate rather than understate the strength of the economy. The more critical 'correction' is to adjust the official numbers downwards. No one knows what China's GDP was after Mao's

26. In a survey of American economists by the *Wall Street Journal* (11 September 2015), the overwhelming majority said they do not believe the official estimates accurately reflect the state of the economy.

27. Rosen and Bao, *A Better Abacus for China*.

adventurism. It was damaged but possibly not as much as has been thought. If subsequent statistics started from too low a base, growth will have been overstated, at least initially. Nor is there certainty about the rate of inflation. If national accounts do not adjust enough for inflation, growth will again be overstated. Nor is the huge volume of debt known or again whether national accounts adjust adequately. For example if, as has been widespread, new housing estates are built and never used, that pushes up the GDP numbers but represents no real economic value, all the more if they are funded from debt that the projects cannot service. Nor are the underlying data robust. The National Bureau of Statistics does not have sector-by-sector prices and for some purposes has to use more or less rough proxy estimates. The central statisticians work from provincial and local data that have to be aligned for consistency. The pressure for 'good' GDP statistics has been obvious, in particular locally, and it would be superhuman to expect there to be no tendency to adjust favourably. Even tiny biases upwards in individual adjustments can add up to very noticeable overstatements in the final measures.

An important reason why measured growth has been unrealistically high is that some of that growth has been driven by heavy debt-financed investments with a higher level of debt than the investments can reward. The government has stimulated economic activity by pouring in cheap credit and by directing its own enterprises to turn that credit into a stream of investment, some of it sound and some of it bad. The GDP statistics record all of the economic activity but do not adjust realistically for the burden of debt and for bad investments. Simply, the System of National Accounts is not geared to dealing realistically with an economy that relies on excessive debt-investment in the way the Chinese one has.

A recent study for another international consultancy, the Conference Board, finds actual annual growth in years with official rates of about 10 percent to have been typically about 7 to 7.5 percent.[28] Taking the best growth periods for China and other East Asian countries, the study finds China's growth to fall slightly short of that of South Korea, Taiwan, and Japan. By 2012, it estimates China's real growth rate to have been 4.1 percent, as compared to the official rate of 7.7 percent. Two other consultancies, Capital Economics and Lombard Street, estimate a sharper downwards slide in the pace of growth than the trend in the official statistics shows, bringing GDP growth by 2014–15 down to 4.3 and 3.7 percent respectively, as compared to the official estimate of 7 percent.[29] Estimates by researchers at the Chinese National Development and Reform Commission suggest that almost half of the total investment in the Chinese economy in the years 2009 to 2013 (the period of post-2008-recession stimulus) was 'ineffective'.[30] Their research also found that investment efficiency has fallen

28. Wu, *Re-estimating Chinese Growth.*

29. *New York Times*, 26 August 2015.

30. *Financial Times*, 27 November 2014.

sharply in recent years, which means that the economy gets steadily less additional economic growth for every unit of additional investment, to the effect that annual growth in the relevant period corrected for ineffective investment would be 2 to 3 percentage points lower than in the official statistics. These quantifications are questionable, but economists agree that there is much inefficient investment in the Chinese economy and that efficiency has declined. It is not unexpected in a growing economy that investment efficiency declines, but the decline in China is more than expected and resulting from a great deal of wasted investment.

The accumulated effect of these downgradings is that the economy is probably about a third smaller than it is made out to be officially. Rather than up there with the United States, it is a second-tier economy, more like Japan or Germany, and in per capita terms only a middle-income one. While growth is slowing in China, it is picking up in its Asian competitor, India. In the International Monetary Fund's (IMF) predictions, India will overtake China in the pace of economy growth by 2016. Another effect is that economic inequality, although grotesque even by official statistics, has probably been underestimated, since the share of wealth held by the very rich has been estimated relative to an inflated total.

These exercises are of a different kind from that of the Rhodium Group. Here it is not only the valuation of the various economic components that is reassessed but also the substance of some of those components, which is to say not just how the System of National Accounts is applied but also what it is applied to. If you dig holes in the ground and fill them up again, that is economic activity without anything being produced. If you borrow money to build highways that are never used or apartments that are never lived in, that is investment but not investment that creates real capital that is converted again into real consumption or further production.

It works like this: If an unnecessary airport it built, that is economic activity. It creates demand for steel, concrete, glass, and the like, and jobs are generated. This shows up as GDP in the statistics. But once the airport is there with little traffic, it becomes a drain on the economy. It has to be kept up and maintained and kept in service for little or no business. During the growth period, China has had a steady flow of such ineffective investments. That has notched up the GDP numbers to artificial levels. The numbers have not always been 'incorrect' but nor have they realistically reflected real economic strength. Part of the reason why measured economic growth has recently been falling is that the burden of ineffective investment has been accumulating and, so to speak, caught up with the real economy and come to weigh more heavily in the balance. The new figures are lower partly because real growth is down but partly also because the previous exaggerated figures are no longer statistically maintained.

False economies are not exclusive to China, but one of the ways in which the Chinese state-investment-driven economy is different is that it has more and bigger false economies than usual. The more realistic way of reassessing the economy is to ask what real strength it has rather than just how the numbers add up. That way of approaching it unavoidably leads to a downwards adjustment.[31]

It is difficult to get away from the obsession with GDP size although in the end it is not a very meaningful issue. If you string a border around 1.4 billion people, you have a big economy no matter what the circumstances. The US economy is not strong because it is 300 million people big but because it generates a high per capita income for 300 million people. As so often, China gets overestimated because of its bigness.

Corruption

In China's control-obsessive bureaucratic state, cheating and dishonesty is endemic. Officials and services cheat on their clients; colleagues cheat on each other; lower-level agencies cheat on their duties and misuse allocated funds; local governments falsify data that go into official statistics; police officers, judges, doctors, schoolteachers, and administrators are massively dishonest in the exercise of service. Of course, not everyone and every service is dishonest, but cheating is rampant.

And then there is corruption! Corruption is a problem for many governments; in the Chinese case it goes to the heart of the state and is on a monumental scale. It is a problem with vast consequences. When the state itself is corrupt, it is impossible to maintain a culture of honesty in business or a culture of service in public administration.

Xi Jinping has launched a hard campaign against corruption to which we will return later. Before that, we need to try to get a grip on the nature and scale of the problem. Corruption is criminal activity and is by the nature of things as much as possible hidden from public view—although there has until recently been little restraint in the flaunting of obviously corrupt wealth. We know that there is corruption of massive proportions, but we do not know with precision how much or exactly how it works. No honest student of the Chinese system would be able to say that he or she really knows what it is about, and any effort to describe it is unavoidably to some degree speculative.[32]

---

31. Additionally, standard GDP measurement does not account adequately for some social costs, such as pollution and environmental depletion. These costs have been exceptionally high in China during the period of rapid growth. Had they been brought fully into the accounts, that would further have reduced the growth estimates, more so for China than for other economies in the same period.

32. There is no comprehensive and up-to-date analysis of Chinese corruption that I am aware of (but see Rose-Ackerman and Lagunes, *Greed, Corruption, and the Modern State*). In much of the scholarly literature, economic in particular, corruption gets little or no mention. Everyone knows of it, but its economic and political penetration is often not dealt with adequately. My interpretation here is based on a range of sources, including interviews in China and journalistic reporting.

There are different kinds of corruption, and we need to pick it apart.[33] Starting at the bottom of the system, there is low-level corruption in the form of workday officials taking payments from clients for services, permissions, stamps of approval, and certificates, in everything from business permits via schooling, medical treatment, social assistance, and policing, to birth certificates. All can be granted, delayed, or denied, and all can elicit payment. Again, not every official is corrupt. A colleague who knows China well has reminded me that 'there are still officials who live in 6th floor walk-ups, ride their bikes to the office, and don't have kids living it up in the West'. But we know from surveys, for example by the Pew Research Center, that corruption on this level is a fact of life to a greater or lesser degree for most citizens and something that intrudes into their lives in a way they resent strongly.

Further up is within-bureaucracy corruption in the form of selling and buying of posts and promotions. In a state that boasts practising meritocratic recruitment, posts and positions are often sold to the highest bidder. This is true in the party, in the state bureaucracy, and in the armed forces. It also includes the buying of memberships in the people's congresses, the people's political consultative conferences, and other official committees on both central and local levels. It involves kickbacks upwards in the system for the allocation of funds downwards to local agencies. A former party secretary of the Hunan Poverty Alleviation Authority went on trial for having accepted more than 11 million *yuan* in bribes between 1992 and 2013 in exchange for funds for anti-poverty programmes.[34] No one knows exactly how widespread these practices are, but the buying and selling of promotions is sufficiently prevalent in the armed forces, for example, that most observers consider it to be factor in giving these forces less capacity than their size would suggest. Two former vice-chairmen of the Central Military Commission, who both served until 2012, have been put under prosecution for corruption. The first one, General Xu Caihou, was charged in June 2014 and confessed to taking huge bribes, some through family members, in return for appointments and promotions (he died in March 2015 before he could be put on trial). The second one, General Guo Boxiong, was arrested on 10 April 2015. A former PLA deputy logistics chief, Gu Junshan, has been charged with accepting bribes to promote hundreds of officers, taking in tens of millions of *yuan*.

A recent report that somehow got distributed by Xinhua, the official news agency, gave a rare insight into this surreal world of corruption. That was clearly a mistake, and the report was quickly removed from the Xinhua and other sites in China, but not before it was picked up outside of the country. 'The main sellers are senior officials, particularly the top official in a region or a unit who has power over personnel

33. But specific cases are often mixed and do not fall neatly into any category. Reuters (28 April 2015) reports a case of a head of hospital who 'used his position to seek bribes related to construction projects, medical procurement and doctor positions', adding up to takings worth more than US$18 million.

34. *South China Moring Post*, 1 November 2014.

matters. The number 2, and sometimes the third- and even fourth-in-command, take bribes to help people get promoted. Some borrowed from banks, while others sought sponsorship from businessmen who would reap the benefits after the official was promoted. Some used money obtained through bribes or other corruption. Buyers could also pay through instalments, just like a homeowner might pay their mortgage. Recent cases have indicated the size of payments involved. Luo Yinguo, former party chief of Maoming city in Guangdong, was sentenced to death last year for receiving more than 100 million *yuan* in bribes from 64 officials seeking promotions. Luo set posts with specific price tags: 200,000 *yuan* for a technology posting; two million *yuan* for department-level one; 10 million *yuan* for a deputy mayor position.'[35]

On top of this again is high-level embezzlement from the state. Here the term 'corruption' is not adequate; it is too kind. This is organised crime and is probably the practice which is the murkiest and on which there is the least publically available hard evidence. It is also new, not good old-fashioned bribery related to the Chinese tradition of gift giving, but a practice born out of the recent investment boom. What is often admired as the restructuring of the sector of state-owned enterprises over the last twenty years or so has consisted in part in the shutting down of poorly performing entities, which were sometimes merged with better-performing ones or otherwise sold, given away, or abandoned. This created a bonanza for entrepreneurial operators to take over faltering firms at bargain prices, or at no price at all, be it for continued activity on new terms or asset stripping. China's brand of economic growth created a further bonanza in the form of contract trading and land leasing. That bonanza was fuelled on by the post-2008 stimulus injection of cash and easy credit into the state sector.

Every infrastructural investment project, large or small, is a potential vehicle for the robbery of state funds. Someone has to dig out the coal and minerals. Someone has to run the cement factories, smelters, and steelworks. Someone has to construct the dams, energy plants, and electricity grids. Someone has to build the highways, railroads, airports, and sky-scrapers, and someone the new schools, hospitals, and universities, and further on the new museums, cinemas, city parks, and playgrounds. And someone has had to make the land available for these investments. These operators and someones, and their subsidiaries, partners, and subcontractors, may be private businesses or state or local government enterprises. All this restructuring and investment booming has been and is state driven. It is the state that has shut down enterprises and that decided what is to be done with them; it is the state that grants mining and development contracts; it is the state that grants business permits; it is the state that allocates land, which is to say that there are officials, high and low, who are in charge of it all. Those officials may be selling contracts, permits, or land leases, or they may themselves be participating entrepreneurs in disguise who are giving

35. *South China Morning Post*, 30 November 2014.

themselves or family members or friends or connections contracts or permits or land. The contracts that are successful will not be the best ones but the ones that pay the best, which is to say the ones that best embezzle the state. The delivery on contracts will tend to be substandard, enabling further embezzlement as works go on, since the oversight is in the hands of officials who are already involved or on the take.

Officials on all levels, up to the very top, down to the local level, and into the fringes of the vast public sector—such as, for example, Beijing Zoo, where procurement graft in part explains the deplorable conditions animals are held in—make themselves rich, and family and friends are able to use connections to enrich themselves. This kind of corruption has been not only widespread but by all accounts also monumental, really beyond what is comprehensible to the normal mind, cases of millions, hundreds of millions, billions being looted from the public purse. In December 2014, Zhou Yongkang, until 2012 a member of the Standing Committee of the Party Politburo and head of domestic security, was expelled from the party and arrested on charges of taking bribes and helping family members and connections to plunder the state. He was formally charged in April 2015 and sentenced in June, in a secret trial, to life in prison, the deprivation of all political rights, and the confiscation of all property. He was found guilty of bribery, abuse of power, and the leaking of state secrets. The life sentence was on the bribery charge. Also in late 2014, investigators discovered more than 200 million *yuan* in cash stored away in several flats owned by a former coal official, Wei Pengyuan. The *South China Morning Post* estimated that the stash of notes would weigh more than 2.3 tonnes (since the highest Chinese denomination is the 100 *yuan* note). This was not even the case of a top official; he had only been a deputy director of the National Development and Reform Commission's coal department. A colleague of his up the line, a former deputy director of the commission, Liu Tienan, was sentenced to life in prison and the confiscation of all personal property on 10 December 2014, for having accepted bribes of 35 million *yuan* from 2002 to 2012, some through a son. In August 2015, Gu Junshan, mentioned above, was sentenced to death, with a two-year reprieve, for embezzlement, accepting bribes and bribery, misuse of state funds, and abuse of power. The reprieve meant that the death sentence was unlikely to be carried out, and he was for good measure deprived of all political rights, stripped of his rank as lieutenant general, and had all personal assets confiscated. In a different case, one operator was reported to have paid one of his backers a bribe in the form of a Mercedes-Benz with 100 kg of gold in the boot. *China Economic Weekly* (24 November 2014) reports an estimate that public officials took 1 trillion *yuan* in stolen money overseas in the years 2000–2011. A consultancy, the Emerging Advisors Group, has estimated that the equivalent of US$1 trillion was embezzled during the post-2008 stimulus, which may amount to as much as 5 percent of GDP annually, and a Washington-based advocacy group, Global Financial Integrity, estimated that the mainland lost US$1.25 trillion between 2003 and 2012 to illicit outflows including tax evasion, crime, and corruption. A report in early 2015 by the International Consortium of Investigative Journalists on the offshore holdings of China's élite suggests that between US$1 and 4 trillion in untraced assets have left the country since 2000. Figures like these, although necessarily speculative, are not flights of fancy and give a good indication of the scale.

The driving force in this conglomerate of theft is the high-level organised crime. That is where the big action is, that is what makes public posts valuable enough down the line to be bought and sold for big money and makes it worth buying the protection of a membership of a people's congress, and it is the criminality up the line that creates the culture of low-level corruption. When workday officials see that those higher up enrich themselves, they will feel entitled to do likewise. At this level, the effect is to inflate the corruption value of public services. Where previously the expected gift was a watch, now it is a car. The Chinese are accustomed to paying for services with gifts, but gift expectations have notched up to painful and demoralising levels.

Corruption on this scale and in this breadth has manifold consequences. Income is 'redistributed' from ordinary citizens to boosting the wealth of the rich. The state is robbed of funds and deprived of capacity, leaking efficiency through corruption. Too many officials are too concerned with their own manoeuvrings and entrepreneurship and distracted from their job duties. Too many officers not only have little military competence but are also preoccupied with entrepreneurship at the expense of military planning and work.

But the consequences go further and deeper. At the top of the pyramid of corruption has emerged an oligarchic class of high officials and business operators which is parasitic on the state and not in its service or under its control. For the party-state, that is not just an economic problem but also a power problem. All governments want their officials to be beholden to them for their pay, which is how they secure their loyalty. The oligarchic officials, however, are not beholden to their formal employer. Their employment is their base for entrepreneurship, which is from where they have their real income. The state is dependent on contractors and operators for the execution of development projects but cannot control the works they deliver or the price they charge, since the operators have co-opted the controllers into criminality or the controllers have turned operators. The control-obsessed party-state that is supposed to have a monopoly of controlling power is dependent on an oligarchic class which operates a competing source of power. Around the country there are economic fiefdoms that are laws unto themselves and states within the state. The pre-2012 leadership tolerated the rot as a necessary price to pay for 'stability'. It now seems that a new kind of leadership is in place. It has pledged to wage war on corruption. That war has a double agenda. One aim is to purge political opponents within the party-state, always necessary for any Chinese leadership. A second aim is to crush the competing power of oligarchic clusters so as to concentrate not only political but also economic power in the hands of the party-state leadership. There are observers who think that the only serious aim is to purge political opponents, but that is probably too simple. More likely, what we are seeing is a leadership on the warpath both for control within the party-state and for the party-state's control in society.

The Standard

The economist Amartya Sen has recently compared China favourably to India in governance and delivery. Not only is the 'hope that India might overtake China one day in economic growth' a distant one, but also 'China has done far more than India to raise life expectancy, expand general education and secure health care for its people'.[36] That may be a pertinent comparison to highlight India's underperformance (although India is now in fact overtaking China in economic growth) but does not have much to say for or about China. It is no doubt true that China in many ways has been outperforming India, but the ambition of China's leaders is not to outperform the underperformers; it is to be up there with the best. The provision of public services has without question improved in recent decades, but then those provisions had been totally destroyed during the Maoist disasters. China may be improving in securing health care and social security for its people, but Britain, for example, introduced the National Health Service in 1948, from the start miles ahead of contemporary Chinese health care coverage, when the country was run down by war, poorer than China is today, and still had rationing in the provision of food and other necessities, and Sweden and Norway introduced their 'people's pensions' in the 1950s and 1960s, from the start miles ahead of contemporary Chinese social security, when they were not much, if at all, ahead in economic capacity to where China is now. Indeed, the political secret of the excellence of welfare services—such as in Scandinavia to take the well-known example, or Costa Rica to take a less well-known one, or for that matter China's neighbour South Korea—is that social provisions are introduced *early* in the development process, really before the country by narrow economic analysis can afford them. The reason is that it is in the early stages of development, when the risk of poverty is widespread, that there is a potentially broad political coalition in favour of effective anti-poverty measures. If the country waits until economic growth has made social provision 'affordable' it will be too late: The majority will have moved out of the poverty-risk zone, and anti-poverty policies will have been reduced to a minority concern. China's strategy is 'growth first, equality second'. In that, the regime has made a strategic mistake: It is clear to see that the rising middle class is not making itself the driving force for a policy of social solidarity. A mistake, that is, if the building of an effective welfare state has been a regime intention.

36. In an article in the *New York Times*, 20 June 2013, to accompany the publication of *An Uncertain Glory: India and Its Contradictions*, coauthored with Jean Drèze.

The standard against which China should be measured is the one the Chinese leaders have themselves set. Their claim to excellence is not that they are doing better than they have previously, since China had pretty much collapsed after the Cultural Revolution. It is more absolute: not just better but good. Nor is their claim that they are doing better than others; it is again more absolute: They are doing as well as anyone. China is a grown-up country that does not need to be patronised as 'developing'.[37]

We should take the Chinese leaders' boast of excellence seriously. That, for example, is the standard set by the World Bank and the Development Research Center of the Chinese State Council in *China 2030: Building a Modern, Harmonious and Creative Society*. Here the comparison is with Organisation for Economic Co-operation and Development (OECD) countries more than with developing countries. The regime gives itself legitimacy by the claim to represent not just strength that should be feared but also quality that should be admired. If that is the way they want to be seen, that is the way we should see them.

A Point of Reference

It is my previous work, with colleagues, on the state in South Korea (the Republic of Korea) that has led me to China, as the obvious next step. That reference has been helpful. It puts China in perspective. South Korea's modernisation is the greatest development story ever told. China's development in some ways looks similar: rising from the ashes of destruction, strong leadership by an authoritarian state, a complex mesh of state and capitalism, rapid growth. But that comparison does not hold long. When the Chinese foreign minister, Wang Yi, said, at the World Economic Forum in Davos in January 2014, that 'the Chinese story is the greatest success story of our time', he was repeating a fantasy that has now been told so many times and in so many versions that it is becoming perceived truth. The Chinese story is one of bigness, but in greatness it is not much up against, for example, the story of South Korea, or for that matter of Taiwan.

In South Korea, in forty years, there were three monumental achievements: Poverty was turned to affluence (and to real affluence, making Korea a high-income country), dictatorship was turned to democracy, and a safety net was spread under the country so that no significant section of the population was excluded from the benefits of economic advancement and with social protections that have helped to preserve Korea as a relatively egalitarian society, in contrast to China's runaway inequality. China's reform and opening up has now been unfolding for nearly forty years but has followed South Korea in only one achievement, in economic growth. And in the time South Korea made itself a high-income country, China has made itself no more

37. The Chinese leaders sometimes do present their country as still being a developing one, but you do not have to follow their doing and thinking long to recognise that that is opportunism.

than a middle-income one. Lin Yifu, the Chinese economist and former vice-president of the World Bank, has observed that in recent times only two economies, South Korea and Taiwan, have managed to leap from low-income to high-income status, implying that China is now on the road to becoming the third one.[38] But this is a false comparison (and not only because he forgot some contending countries). China's modernisation is narrowly economic. In South Korea and Taiwan, modernisation has been comprehensive; economic yes, but also political and social.

So looking at China with the South Korean story in mind, I am not as impressed as are some whose vantage may have been, for example, sluggish economies in Europe or the United States. Nor am I all that impressed with China's growth. It is not singular; we have seen it before. It is not unprecedented, not unique, and not lasting. It has been, in its best times, pretty typical for East Asia. The economy got off to a good start after the revolution in 1949, but was then ground to a halt in a wasted generation. It picked up again as of the 1980s, but if we take the entire period of the People's Republic it has been less than it should have been by the standards of the region.

This particular putting of China in perspective has been of consequence. It opened my eyes early on to two observations that have stayed at the back of my mind while working my way through this project. First, China's achievements are big in quantity but small in quality. The numbers may be impressive, but much of the substance is shabby. Second, even in quantitative terms, what bedazzles is not growth as such, although observers often think it is, but bigness. China weighs more in the world than, for example, South Korea, not because it has outperformed South Korea, which it has not, but because it is so big.

In *The Korean State and Social Policy: How South Korea Lifted Itself from Poverty and Dictatorship to Affluence and Democracy*, my colleagues and I offered a political history of South Korea from 1945 to 2000 through the prism of social policy. This was a state-led economic development, and the state that led it was authoritarian and in periods brutally dictatorial. It was a state that used social policy actively as an instrument of economic development. In the literature, it is described as a 'developmental state' with a 'developmental welfare-state' as one of its tools.[39]

It has been assumed that what enabled the South Korean state to lead as effectively as it did was that it had autocratic strength. This is also a widespread assumption for China. However, in our study we found that although the developmental state had strength, and used it, strength was still not its defining characteristic. What made this state effective was rather an unexpectedly sophisticated *use* of strength. The authoritarian leaders in Korea had power and were uncompromisingly hard when they saw that to be necessary. But it was not by subduing its population with strength

38. The *Huffington Post*, 10 February 2014.

39. See Kwon, *Transforming the Developmental Welfare State in East Asia.*

that they pulled the country along in development. They did that by mobilising their population into a grand project of modernisation. Success came from the way the state worked *with* society.

In looking from South Korea to China, the similarity is in rapid economic growth under the stewardship of an authoritarian state. But there is authoritarianism and then there is dictatorship. The Korean state, before redemocratisation, was (for the most part) only authoritarian. The Chinese state was and is a party-state. Korea was less of a command system, and the leaders were dependent on ruling through coalitions and alliances. There was a corrupt mesh of state and business, but businesses were not state owned and rather a part of the civil society that the rulers were dependent on mobilising. Both regimes were challenged by uprisings in their populations, in Korea in 1987 and in China in 1989, but reacted differently. In Korea, the authoritarian regime tried to survive through the crisis of popular revolt but was unable to hold on to power and stepped aside to allow democratic reform. In China, the regime did not give in but reached for its ultimate power resource, the military, and crushed the revolt with weaponry. In Korea, there being no party-state, the leaders could not react similarly. They did not have a similar resource of ultimate power at their disposal and did not have the justification for the use of force that is contained in the ideological and organisational structure of a party-state. Presiding over a country that was not monolithic but built on vibrant civil society institutions which had evolved during the period of modernisation, including in business and voluntarism, the authoritarian leaders could relinquish control without fearing that their project of modernisation would collapse, indeed *had to* give in since an attempt to hold on to power with force would have destroyed the project that was their *raison d'être* and their only claim to legitimacy. In China, the leaders could not compromise because that would have meant the demise of the party-state and because there was no civil society for China to fall back on, wherefore compromise would lead to chaos. Nor did they have to compromise because they had the physical and ideological means to hold on in their hands.

The authoritarian state in South Korea, from the first military coup in 1961 to redemocratisation in 1987, managed society in ways that are best described as consistently paradoxical. It worked in different ways at the same time, combining modes of governance that would usually elsewhere be seen to be incompatible and contradictory. In *holding* power, the autocrats and dictators were brutally hard. General and later President Park was the first and greatest of the autocratic leaders and the man who carved out this contradictory mode of governance. One of his early initiatives was the creation of the Korean Central Intelligence Agency as a secret police under his personal command. The trade union movement, in particular, suffered relentless oppression. But in *using* power in governance, in contrast, the Korean autocrats were shrewd, sophisticated, and in their own way surprisingly soft. President Park was as early in starting to build the Korean welfare state as he was in building a Korean secret police. While with one hand, theirs was a state of dictatorship, with the other hand a state of collaboration, co-optation, and mobilisation. It was not one or the other, not dictatorial and therefore non-collaborative, and not collaborative and therefore non-dictatorial, but both dictatorial and collaborative. This was a state that was ruthless in holding on to power (until meeting its ultimate test) but that in governance worked more through coalitions than by brute commands.

We identified four coalitions of mobilisation. A first coalition was between political leaders and their officials and advisors. Here, the autocrats used their hard hand to purge or side-line those who were not reliable. But once that was done, they showed their soft hand to the officials and advisors with whom they could work, brought them into their realm of power, gave them authority, and created institutions for them to work through, for example, powerful advisory bodies which worked more in partnership with their political bosses than as simple lackeys. An ancient idea of impartiality in officialdom survived to some degree. The Korean economy was corrupt, but public service delivery was never plagued by the kind of endemic graft that is a characteristic of China. Civil servants and advisors were flattered into being able to think of themselves as apolitical but were in reality strongly political. They were men—almost always men, although now, in a further sign of genuine modernisation, the president is a woman, Park Geun-hye, General Park's daughter—of the world who saw themselves as modernisers in the service of their nation and who brought an ethos of modernisation into the grand political project. They looked out to the rest of the world and saw, for example, that modern nations have welfare states. Therefore, they said, we too, if we are to be modern, must have a welfare state.

A second coalition was between government and business, in particular big business. This coalition is well known, but here also we need to understand its paradoxical nature. The military coup in 1961 was in part directed against the culture of crony capitalism that had evolved in the first years after the birth of South Korea in 1948, during the reign of Syngman Rhee, the first president. But General Park, against his own instinct, soon recognised that he could not realise his ambition of industrial modernisation in any other way than through the capitalists he despised and therefore accepted a settlement of collaboration with them that must have been distasteful to him. To get them to do his bidding, he had to literally buy them. What resulted was not a pretty sight. It was a peculiar brand of state-led monopoly capitalism, steeped in pervasive two-way corruption. But it was effective. The resulting economic growth has been steady and continuous and second to none the world has ever seen.

A third coalition was with civil society and voluntary agencies. This coalition has been less recognised than the government-business coalition, but was no less important. Voluntary agencies were a US import after 1945, much of it growing out of socially oriented missionary movements. They were at work from the start and continued to be active during the authoritarian period, providing much of what was delivered of social services. The autocratic rulers did not crush this movement and nor did they nationalise it, but they 'koreanised' it and dismissed the Americans. Again, they took control and let civil society agencies know who was boss and what the design was that they were obliged to work within, but once that was clear they also gave these non-government actors space and authority. They let them survive in a deal, much as with business, in which the agencies took it upon themselves to deliver services the governors needed to get delivered but did not have the means to deliver themselves, in return for the ability to engage in the formation of associations and networks.

And a fourth coalition was with the people themselves. South Korea was an unruly nation, and those who are old enough will remember, for example, the constant street battles between students and police.[40] This unrest was important, not because, until the end, it threatened the regime, but because it contributed to never silencing the demand for democracy. But this unruliness was still on the surface. Underneath was a compliant and hard-working population. The government used various means to mobilise popular acquiescence. It extracted obedience by delivering economic growth. It bought itself legitimacy with the help of education and social security. It gave people reasons for compliance by forcing employers, at least in the big corporations, to provide occupational welfare to workers and their families and to be at least marginally better employers than they were themselves inclined to be, and by directing voluntary agencies to deliver social services. And importantly, it mobilised people across the country through a cultural revolution under the name of the *Saemaul* movement, first in the rural New Community Movement and then the urban-industrial New Factory Community Movement. These were paternalistic movements that encouraged an ethos of responsibility and self-reliance. They were extractive movements that put rural communities and industrial labourers and their families to work in development projects large and small which were run 'voluntarily' and without much of government funding. But they were also organisational movements that gave millions of Koreans the experience of being members and participants in associations, committees, councils, and the like. They were grass-roots movements that fed into, as did the network of voluntary agencies, civil society vibrancy.

Most authoritarian leaders believe that they themselves can and should run their country. The South Korean ones happened on an understanding that they needed to work *with* non-state forces. They had defined a mission of modernisation for their country to which they bound themselves and for the realisation of which they needed to stimulate and co-opt the energies of officials, advisors, businesses,

---

40. For which reason President Park moved Seoul National University from the city centre to a then distant suburb.

voluntary agencies, and rural and industrial workers and families. Usually, authoritarian regimes, such as the Soviet and East European ones, seek to eliminate non-state institutions. Exceptionally, under South Korean authoritarianism, non-state institutions were stimulated and put to work. This is what finally explains the unlikely South Korean economic, political, and social development, and the role of state leadership in it. It was *not* that the governments had authoritarian strength, but that governments with authoritarian strength governed by *mobilising* rather than just controlling.

Mobilisation is a strategy with consequences. Those who are mobilised prosper and are allowed influence. South Korea's modernisation was economic, but not only economic. It had two strands to it. The economy grew in production. Society grew in institutions. When authoritarianism collapsed, the dynamics of development proved to be sustainable because the institutions of a reasonably pluralistic economic, social, and political order were there, alive and well, and democratic government could take over where autocratic government had left off without counterrevolution, collapse, or further serious drama.

In my book *Nation of Devils: Democratic Leadership and the Problem of Obedience*, I ascribe good government to political order, and I find the core of political order to be a 'settlement' between the governors and their various others, from their civil servants to the population out there in the country. Settlement, again, comes from governors giving others what they need in order to make themselves compliant and co-operative, at least reasonably so, and others giving governors the acquiescence they need in order to lead and rule with some effectiveness. When this works, there is a virtuous circle of collaboration. Most dictatorships are not settled, wherefore dictatorial governments fall back on repression. In South Korea, the dictatorship happened to find a unique form of settlement through mobilisation. It was in many ways ugly, but it worked and in the end turned for the good. The government was harsh and the people unruly, but beneath that there was a basic, and unlikely, settlement of collaboration.

This, then, briefly, is the reference at the back of my mind as I look to China. An earlier East Asian miracle. Another authoritarian state. The dialectics of command and mobilisation. A state's ability to work *with* partners. The destiny of society, the landscape between state and citizens. Political order, after a fashion. A way of managing society. Development of quality.

Do we see a similar panorama in China? There are similarities but, again, they are superficial. The party-state dominates society, is dedicated to control, and is far from working *with* non-state actors in coalitions of mutual dependency. The civil service is an organisation of the party (so much so that the very term 'civil service' does not really apply and is rarely used). Civil society remains subdued. The business community and new middle class are pulled into a top-down symbiosis with the party-state apparatus. What is known as NGOs (non-governmental organisations) are, for the most part, more like state agencies than voluntary organisations, often referred to as GONGOs, government-organised NGOs. Associational life and networking is kept under strict control. Governance is complex but not paradoxical. It is based on strength, control, and command, is without the elegant combination of being both dictatorial and collaborative that we saw in the Korean case, and is backwards in any governance by mobilisation. The state remains dictatorial and has failed to find the secret of political order and settlement. The regime has given itself the insurance that the party-state has been kept strong and civil society weak, the insurance of fear that there would be nothing but chaos for China to fall back on if the party-state were to crumble.

Here again China is *different*, now also in social structure. The party-state is all-embracing. There are no autonomous countervailing forces—no civil service and no independent business community or civil society in any real meaning. The Chinese have many social freedoms of being able to live and behave as they want, but they have no freedom of social organisation. What there are of non-state actors and institutions are tied into a grand corporatist pact in which the party-state calls the shots and holds the controlling reins.

This book has become a critical interpretation of the Chinese model. I would expect one criticism back to be that it is China observed with Western biases. But that is a criticism I reject in advance. My perspective has been regional. In some of China's near neighbours, we have seen the magnificence of modernisation that is social and political as well as economic, and qualitative as well as quantitative. We have seen that not only dramatic growth but comprehensive modernisation is possible. We have seen that economic growth and political democratisation are compatible. China's development falls short in that comparison. It is economic and quantitative but not much more. What we should reasonably expect for China is what has been seen in the region. Except for bigness, the Chinese story is not only not the greatest success story of our times; it is not even a particularly great East Asian story.

Bigness

In territory, China is about the same as Canada or the United States but smaller than Russia. In population it is enormous, now nearing 1.4 billion people, over four times as many as the United States and ten times as many as Russia.[41] Much of the country is rough mountainous terrain and a surprisingly small part comfortably arable land. The Chinese population has grown from about 500 million in 1949, and is still growing,

41. According to the National Bureau of Statistics, the population at the end of 2014, excluding Hong Kong and Macao, was 1.358 billion, 55 percent urban and 45 percent rural.

although more slowly. It is expected to peak at between 1.5 and 1.6 billion around mid-century and then to start falling. By that time, China will probably have been overtaken by India as the world's most populous country.

Size is one reason it is difficult, and in some ways unrealistic, to treat China as a country, and certainly as a country that is governed by a small leadership in the capital. That's the theory, but in practice it does not work in that way. The leaders in Beijing may well decide on this or that policy, but there is no way they can be in anything like full control of how their policies are implemented through the country. There are about 40,000 towns, townships, and similar urban units, some as large as a small European country, and about 700,000 villages and similar units.[42] The leaders in Beijing are not in control and know that there are serious limitations in their ability to impose their will on the country. Public policy is nowhere near as orderly as one might think in a dictatorship, and the implementation of centrally decided policies is all over the place, sometimes in obedience, more or less, but often also in disobedience, distortion, subversion, or inaction.[43]

China, then, is not Beijing. The governing of China is not what is done in Beijing. The rule for the student of Chinese conditions must be to keep the country's size in mind, get beyond Beijing, under the surface, and down to observing governance as much locally as centrally.

Here are some random numbers to help us grasp the size factor (which is pretty difficult, at least for someone like me, whose outlook is often from a country of 5 million people):

- 1.4 billion people (approaching).
- The largest province, Guangdong, has a population of nearly 105 million. Five provinces have populations of more than 80 million people, each larger than the largest European country. The largest city, Shanghai, has 24 million people.
- China is urbanizing rapidly with a huge shift of population from countryside to towns and cities, but the rural population is still upwards of 600 million strong.
- Economic growth has lifted millions of people out of poverty, but there are still 250 million or more left behind in dire destitution. That is fifty times as many as the Norwegian population.
- There are 114 million people suffering from diabetes (in 2012), a number that in five years had increased by the size of the Australian population.
- An important driver of economic growth in the reform period was the emergence of township and village enterprises (TVEs). Those businesses eventually created more than 100 million jobs.

42. A village may well have a population of 100,000 or more, although many are smaller, and some places that are villages administratively are very urban indeed in appearance.

43. On centre-periphery differences and tensions, see, for example, Whyte, *One Country, Two Societies* and Eimer, *The Emperor Far Away*.

- A small minority component of private education adds up to 40 million pupils and students in 130,000 institutions, from preschool to tertiary education (not including non-accredited schools for migrant children).
- A third of the world's smokers are Chinese.
- Year on year, about 1.4 million people sit the national civil service entry examinations (not including provincial and local similar exams).
- When the National Bureau of Statistics in January 2013 reported on a demographic turning point in that the size of the working-age population had slightly decreased, that slight decrease still amounted to 3.45 million persons.
- Come New Year, the Chinese want to go home to celebrate. In 2014, this migration was carried by an estimated 3.6 billion journeys during a period of about a month, up by 200 million from the year before.

Size dazzles. The rest of the world is ultra-aware of China's economic power and stands in awe of its development, but that development is not all it is sometimes made out to be. In the UN Human Development Index 2014, China ranks 91 of 187 countries. It ranks lower in human development than should have been expected by its level of economic development. While the country has roared upwards on the GDP scale, it has remained stagnant in the middle of the human development scale with little or no improvement relative to the rest of the world. This is a constellation to stop and reflect on.

Here is the basic truth about the Chinese model in all its glory, economically, politically, and administratively: *It is effective but not efficient.* There has been growth, but only thanks to massive debt and excessive investment. There has been governance, but only thanks to massive and extractive bureaucracy. The machine delivers but is exceedingly expensive to run. It gets results, but only with monumental inputs that do not translate efficiently into outcomes.

Much of the paraphernalia that leave the occasional visitor gaping—the highways, bridges, skyscrapers, high-speed trains, airports—is developed too quickly and to poor standards, and starts to crumble the moment it is finished. In Guangzhou, the city, in the kind of development that is possible only in a command economy, has in the course of a few years created a mega-university complex on an island in the Pearl River by clearing away the peasantry that used to cultivate its land and having ten universities build new campuses one next to the other. If you drive through, you see a landscape of shiny and impressive architecture, but inside, buildings only a few years old are already worn and crumbling.

The regime has thrown money into GDP growth but not generally obtained commensurate results. Standards of living have been rising, but at less than the pace of economic growth. More people have been lifted out of poverty in China than in any other country, but the lifting per capita is less than in neighbouring East Asian countries. Nearly half of the population remains rural, far removed from life in the modern cities, much of it living off backwards agriculture and in developing country conditions. The modern economy is geared to copying what others have invented or to doing the assembly work on foreign designs, but has so far developed less in innovation capacity and does not have a single world-class brand to its name. China has done well in high-speed rail by exploiting or copying Japanese and other technologies but has been unable, for example, to develop an airliner of its own in spite of massive efforts. Its auto industry is doing well in the assembly of foreign-brand cars but has not taken off in the production and sale of own-brand ones. Education has improved but less than should have been expected given the pace of economic development. Free primary schooling was introduced only in 2008 (and is still not in reality free). The People's Liberation Army is a mighty force, but the service is politicised, divided, corrupt, and inexperienced in combat training. It has for some time been on a trajectory of 10 percent plus year-on-year increases in its budget and has stocked up on land, air, and sea hardware. But behind the façade it is less than effective in intelligence, technology, communications, logistics, and co-ordination, and is in these matters behind the US-supported systems of Japan and Taiwan. The balance of military opinion seems to be, for example, that in a non-nuclear confrontation with Japan, the Japanese Self-Defence Force would be superior in equipment, training, and the quality of the officer corps and troops and prevail over a larger but more lumbering adversary. Something of the same is visible in foreign relations, where Chinese diplomacy is unable to get away from a reliance on weight. China is now a world power but has been unable to use that power to win genuine influence or, what it desperately wants, respect.[44] It is strong but has no genuine friends.

What is giving China clout in the world is bigness more than performance. It is size and the crude magnitudes and numbers that come with it, rather than qualitative development or civilisation, that enables China to command the presence it now has in other people's minds. Now that ultra-rapid economic growth is fading, China's development no longer looks as amazing as it may have seemed in the last two or three decades.

The Project

This is an essay in interpretation. It is the interpretation of an outsider. I do not come from China studies and am not an authority on China. Where I do come from is state analysis, which I have been doing for forty years, and I have tried to bring that experience to bear on a new case.

44. In an authoritative 2105 ranking by the consultancy Portland Communications of thirty countries by 'soft power'—roughly the ability to be respected—China is ranked last.

I have of course visited China while undertaking this project. The observant visitor will see many things and many contrasts: the magnificence that has arisen in Shanghai and the brutalism of provincial cities, the display of middle-class lifestyles, the destitution that village people live in and that you will find if you look for it even on the outskirts of the most advanced centres of development, the oppressive plight of armies of migrant workers who live in urban slums and dormitories and toil to uphold others' wealth.[45] I have seen people living lives of pleasure, fun, and civility, but equally the routine of cheating, cynicism, and braggadocio of money.

I have conferred and collaborated with Chinese colleagues and officials and benefitted from their insights and guidance. I have found these encounters warm, helpful, and generous. Much of the analysis is based on Chinese sources through collaboration with Chinese colleagues, such as the analyses of the social security system in Chapter 4, of the tax system in Chapters 4 and 5, and of poverty in Chapter 5. But my visits have also made me reflect on the difficulty of direct observation in the country. It is *very difficult* to find yourself immersed in the urban landscape of banks, international luxury brands, and commercial razzmatazz in Shanghai and keep in mind that this is *state* capitalism. I have become aware that when I have met, for example, a leading academic in a leading university, he will be a party man. He will be informed, interested and interesting, and charming, and will engage in open and critical discussion, but he is not a free man. Foreign visitors often do not know, or prefer not to know, whom they are dealing with. They may negotiate with a company director or the leader of a research institute and not know that these contacts are not the real decision makers in their organisations. I have often found it more difficult to interpret what I have seen and been told in China than what I have read in my study in London. Any visitor should easily see both the magnificence and ugliness of Chinese economic growth, but I have been struck by how often visitors on some more or less official errand come home, having been flattered and entertained, without really having seen the obvious combination of progress and misery. In hindsight, I have not learned all that much from my own visits, except to have my critical instinct stimulated.

So these are the observations of an outsider. I have not considered that a disadvantage. It is easy to be blinded by the glow from China. That was the case in Mao's time, when many near observers saw what they wanted to see, and some of the sharpest observations were made from a distance, and it continues on other terms to be the case today. For example, Martin Jacques, in *When China Rules the World*, fails to keep his distance and produces a book that is embarrassingly starry-eyed, servile, and naïve. My intention has been to interpret more than to report, and detached

45. There are reportedly about a million people in Beijing, mostly young migrants, who live, literally, underground, known as 'the rat tribe'.

observation is then not a bad thing, in particular when observing a state that is edging to making itself the centre of gravity in the world. I have no axe to grind. I am not inspired in one way or other by any specific hope for China, except for the hope I have for people everywhere that they be able to live well and in freedom. I have no allegiance to China studies or to any theoretical or ideological direction within that broad church. I am not aiming to make myself a China hand and am free from any ambition of future collaboration with official China.

There are other ways than my top-down one of studying China. We could start from the other end, from below, to see how Chinese people react and adapt to what comes down upon them from up high. That would show up many things that I will not be observing closely. No doubt, the Chinese are like people elsewhere; they try to make the best out of their circumstances and mostly react with reason to the way they are ruled. The Chinese live under the pressure of a heavy state. They respond and adapt in manifold strategies: by courage, by ingenuity, by helping and protecting each other, by opposing and protesting, by organising, by subverting, by pretending, by surviving, and getting on with life—as well as by acquiescence and obedience, by collaborating in oppression, by opportunism and cowardice. The rich tapestry of the human condition is there to be seen, for the good and for the bad. Some of that we will touch on as we go along, but this is not my analysis. It is the state and the nature of its rule I am trying to understand. Nor is this a book about social life in China or about Chinese culture. It is a political analysis of the state, not a sociological analysis of China. I am seeking to explain how Chinese society is ruled but not in any detail the fabric of that society.

The non-Chinese literature on politics in China is huge, rich, and diverse. No single generalisation is possible about that literature as a body. But, as much is critical, there is also a strand in China-watching of over-respectfulness. Within that strand, the detached critical eye that is the hallmark of scholarly observation is, if not blinded, to some degree relaxed. There are two mechanisms at play. One is from an ancient Western fascination with China. Many people are enraptured by Chinese history and civilisation, by its early and continuing greatness, and by its mystique. China has had, and continues to have, an uncanny ability to attract the attention of others and to get those others in their minds to add admiration to attention. This adds up to a bit of a love affair, sometimes love-love and sometimes love-hate. There is a yearning to see the interesting and the impressive, and sometimes the good, in a state grounded in an ancient empire.

The second mechanism is more mundane: self-censorship. Any foreign observer of China is himself or herself potentially under observation. We all know that what we say or write may bring down upon us official displeasure and that displeasure may follow through to disadvantage. Contacts may become hesitant, co-operation may be interrupted, invitations may dry up. Books or articles may not be translated.

Visas may be denied. Or entry denied: In early July 2014, an American academic, Elliot Sperling of Indiana University, a friend and defender of the Uighur professor Ilham Tohti, who has subsequently been tried for 'separatism', arrived at Beijing airport with a valid visa but was detained by border officials and put back on the returning flight. In May 2013, a colleague of his from the same university had likewise been turned away with a valid visa. For my own part, in October 2014, I had the Chinese version of my *Nation of Devils* 'suspended' by the censors three weeks before it was to be released.[46] Threats and actions like these work. Those who want to study or report on China live in anxiety that they may be denied the means to do their work properly. They fear that they may not be able to visit or, for example, that they may be denied access to essential archives. Everyone who wants to play the China game knows that there are rules. You can have perfectly good, friendly, and productive exchanges within those rules, but there are limits. Reporters and researchers at their computers ask themselves if this or that observation is opportune. Says one well-known American China scholar, with unusual frankness: 'I write about China and do not want to become persona non grata.'

My angle for making sense of the state I have been observing is to look to the meeting ground of state and people. As a social analyst I am, in the technical language, a methodological individualist. For me, what a state *is* is the way it manifests itself in the lives of its people as individuals and families.

That angle matters. If you look to a state without following through to how it meets the people, you will not know it. In a big state, you might see the forest but not the trees, the masses but not the people. In a dictatorial state, you may see too much of might and not enough of ugliness. Henry Kissinger, for example, in *On China*, falls into this trap. His book is learned and informative but is still in the end biased in favour of the state itself and to the neglect of the people who live under its rule—and surprisingly romantic from someone who prides himself on being a realist. The way to think about China, he argues, is as a civilisation: 'no other country can claim so long a continuous civilization, or such an intimate link to its ancient past'. Kissinger is one of many analysts who praise China as a 'civilisation-state'. But that is a term in which, however much I try to make sense of it, I find no meaning. It sounds good, but in my ears too good for a state that, now and in the past, when pushed has cared much for itself and little for the people who stand in its way. Not my idea of civilised rule. And anyway, the long continuity is a fairy-tale.[47] China's history has seen a series of fluctuations between progress and decline, and with long periods of subjugation and non-Chinese rule.

46. By CITIC Publishers.

47. As, for example, Jonathan Fenby has underlined in his books on China.

There is no shortage of information to draw on; the problem has rather been its abundance. This includes ever more material from China itself, such as policy documents, law texts, official statistics and scholarly work, much of it easily available in English.[48] It includes research and analysis from the big international agencies of development and co-operation. It includes an avalanche of academic work from universities and think-tanks around the world. I have made much use of journalistic material. The *New York Times*, the *Financial Times*, the *Economist*, and the *South China Morning Post*, all outstanding in their China coverage, have been important sources. I have equally used, more than in any previous project, Internet sources (and in the process been able to appreciate fully the magic of this technology as a research tool). I have been corresponding daily with China experts inside China and internationally and have been able to draw on their competence and insight. As I have moved from topic to topic, I have trawled the web for reports, research, statistics, and opinions; there is now nothing you cannot find at least something about. This way of working obviously requires an alert eye on what to trust and what to discard, but not much more so than when absorbing conventionally published material. I have been cautious in using the information that has flowed past me. I have usually not trusted any single source but have been looking for consistent patterns, and it is those patterns as I have seen them that I will tell you about. I list works I have drawn on at the back of the book but that represent only one kind of information from a broader range.

There is a difference between the information that is filtered (and delayed) through scholarly publication and that which flows more directly from journalistic observation and the anarchy of the Internet. The former is cautious and measured, as scholarly work should be, certainly not uncritical but balanced and sometimes too respectful. The latter is raw, near, and in your face. That kind of non-filtered information has been invaluable. It has allowed me, I think, to look not just at the regime but inside it and to some degree to get my finger on its pulse.

In whatever you read about China in any format, there is much to distrust. I have read policy documents but do not believe all they say, to put it carefully. I have read official statistics, but they do not add up. I have consulted surveys, but they are all over the place. I have read the scholarly books, but there is bias galore. So in spite of the abundance of information, there is also an abundance in what we do not know, or at least do not know with certainty or precision.

There are masses of economic and other statistics for China, both from China itself and, for example, from international agencies, some of it good, some bad, some

48. In recent years, the government's reports on its work, on the national development plan, and on budget implementation to the National People's Congresses have been available in English on the day they were delivered. In late 2014, the State Council launched a glitzy new website—english.gov.cn—to propagate the doings of the premier, Li Keqiang, and which is packed with links to white papers, publications, statistics, laws, regulations, and the like, all in impeccable English.

fraudulent. I'm a statistically minded person and do not like it, but have for the most part stayed at arm's length of statistical data, and certainly official statistics, and pulled back to a level of precision that does not go much beyond one, some, many.[49] I do use statistics, unavoidably, but generally in the cautionary language of 'about' or 'more or less' or 'near to' or 'towards' and the like. We do not know, as we have already seen, how big the Chinese economy is, how fast it is growing, or, for example, how big the labour force is. Many urban workers are rural migrants, but we do not know how many. Educated guesses are anything between 200 and 300 million, sometimes more. In the urbanisation plan launched in 2014, which foresees 100 million more people moving to cities by 2020, it is expected that there will still be 200 million migrants working in urban areas without urban *hukou* residency. That means that migrant workers will continue to make up as much as 25 to 30 percent of the workforce even if current reform plans are carried through. It is worth reflecting on that number. The regime drives its economy forward by policies that relegate one in three or four workers to exploitation and humiliation. In China, migrants are not even foreigners who are tolerated but nationals who are deliberately, formally, by policy relegated to second class.

Nor do we know what the effect has been, if any, of the one-child policy on population growth.[50] Birth rates were falling rapidly before this draconian policy was introduced in 1979, in fact more rapidly before 1979 than after, and would have continued to fall without it. China was already then past the demography of population growth being driven by birth numbers. We know that there have been horrific life consequences in the form of abortions and sterilisations, on the order of at least 300 million abortions and about 200 million sterilisations. But coercive birth control was in use before the one-child policy was declared, and except for the first two or three years there was no noticeable increase in abortions and sterilizations above the numbers during the 1970s.[51] Since people would most likely have lived differently without the strictures of dictatorial control, we do not know if there has been any 'purpose' to all that suffering.

Another thing we do not know, about a monumental event in the nation's history, is how many people were killed on 4 June 1989, when the People's Liberation Army cleared the people out of Tiananmen Square in Beijing, whether in the hundreds

49. The *Financial Times* is excellent in its coverage of China but with a weakness of packing its reporting with over-precise statistical data, as is the nature of economic reporting. That means taking official statistics on face value, resulting in many mistakes and misinterpretations. A case in point is a long interview with the premier, Li Keqiang, on 16 April 2015, in which his many statistics were reproduced with no probing and much bravura. Official statistics in China are propagandistic and should be treated with scepticism. A failure to do so is, however inadvertently, to plough the regime's furrow.

50. On the one-child policy, see Greenhalgh, *Just One Child*.

51. See Whyte et al., 'Challenging myths about China's one-child policy'.

or in the thousands, nor how many of those who died were participants and how many bystanders, nor how many were killed elsewhere in Beijing and elsewhere in the country.

There is much we do not know, and much of false information and propaganda swirling around. The observer's guide must be scepticism, always scepticism.

Chapter 2
What They Say

All human activity is guided by ideas that make sense of choices and actions. We create ideas to give ourselves meaning and reassurance, and once ideas take hold they work back on us to shape our thinkings and doings. In collective activities, such as in governance, shared ideas, often referred to as 'political culture', condition collaborative action. The force of ideas is strong. 'Both when they are right and when they are wrong,' said the economist John Maynard Keynes, 'ideas are more powerful than is commonly understood. Indeed the world is ruled by little less.'[1] When we ask of what kind a state is, the first step towards an answer is to explore the ideas that inform its governance.

Governing ideas are signposts or commands. Signpost ideas are indications for public policy. The authoritarian leaders in South Korea had 'modernisation' as their guiding idea. Their country was going to be a fully fledged member of the family of modern nations. That justified their rule and steered the direction of their policies.

Commanding ideas define more strongly than signposts the purpose of governance and separate right from wrong policies with force and authority. In China under Mao, permanent revolution was the commanding idea, and whatever advanced it was right and whatever stood in its way wrong.

Ideas take on commanding strength when they are belief systems. Belief systems are hierarchies of ideas that are organised in more or less logical coherence, derived from what are seen to be absolute truths. Belief systems can be religious or secular. Secular belief systems are ideologies. If Keynes was right that ideas are powerful, then ideologies are ultra-powerful and ultra-dangerous.[2]

Ideologies take command, as can be seen in the devastations and misery that committed regimes have brought down upon peoples, countries, and civilisations under ideological banners. They explain history and destiny, destiny above all, in a way that seems truthful to all who are entrapped in them. They make people, both rulers and

1. Keynes, *General Theory*, final page.
2. In my view that ideas matter powerfully and that ideologies are dangerous, and that these powers and dangers are often overlooked or underestimated, a strong inspiration is from the works of Isaiah Berlin, such as, for example, in a collection of essays under the title *The Crooked Timber of Humanity*.

the ruled, or many of them, *believers*. They inspire believers and justify the regimes that present themselves as their custodians. They deceive people into disregarding truth, facts, and morality. Beliefs take hold. Followers really *believe* the ideological story. They subjugate themselves to and become followers of a mission. Their ideology gives them certainty and frees them from doubt. It does that with a force that makes them accept, for example, that ends justify means and that effective means do good even when they inflict harm. Leaders spread, fortify, and propagate the official ideology but then become prisoners themselves of the beliefs they foster and re-create. When you allow ideology to reign, you become its tool as much as it is yours.

A system of ideas is ideology when it has this force of belief. It is not enough that it is an opportune story that political leaders pay lip service to. A political ideology is derived from a notion of destiny or utopia. That notion serves as the ultimate purpose and justification of rule. The Chinese leaders pay lip service to Marxism-Leninism and Mao Zedong Thought, but that is not to say that these are principles they believe in in an ideological meaning. On the other hand, if they have turned their back on the Maoist ideological legacy, that is not necessarily to say that there is nothing they believe in and that they have not absorbed other ideas to justify themselves, ideas which in turn may be taking on ideological strength. All regimes use narratives to present themselves to their people and to the world, but narrative is not ideology. A narrative becomes ideology when it is sophisticated, durable, contains a story of historical mission, and attracts the force of belief.[3]

The Chinese leaders are reticent and circumspect in explaining themselves. They are clearly ambitious but often cautious with clear language. We know that they think they are special—their institutions have 'Chinese characteristics'—but you are unlikely to get a Chinese leader to stare you in the eye and say with any precision, 'this, A, B, and C, is what we aim to make'.

But we have hints to go on about how they themselves think. We do not know their minds, but we can reasonably formulate some hypotheses about what they are in business for as they themselves understand the purpose of governing. The signals they send out about the purpose of their rule are not consistent and have been changing over time. A watershed came with the turning to reform and opening up after the Mao era. That might seem to have represented a shift from ideological fanaticism to reformist pragmatism. But it may also be that the shift was more in state practices than in state ideas, at least in the longer run.

Much of what the post-Mao leaders have said and done suggest an end of ideology, and that is a plausible hypothesis. However, the party-state is a structure that craves ideology. The state has its justification from the party, but the party needs its own justification and has nowhere else to turn for it than from the realm of ideas. The party

3. For a perspective on the Chinese regime and its need for a narrative, see Zhang, *The China Horizon*.

demands obedience, but if that is to make sense, it must be working for a purpose that legitimises its claim on obedience. Since the party-state claims much—an absolute right to lead and an absolute duty on others to follow—it would seem to need a purpose that is grand and imposing.

Along the continuum from the death of ideology to the revival of ideology, three hypotheses present themselves, which I call 'the triviality hypothesis', 'the welfare hypothesis', and 'the power hypothesis'.

The Triviality Hypothesis

Some facts are given. The Chinese state is constituted as a party-state. It is dedicated to two absolute priorities: the perpetuation of the regime itself and the protection of the country's territorial integrity.

The question then is: What more is there to it? My first hypothesis is that there is nothing more. The Chinese state is strong but does not possess any purpose beyond itself for the use of its strength. There is no ideology, no socialism, no vision for the well-being of the Chinese people, no idea about quality or glory. Everything else is subservient: economic growth, modernisation, poverty alleviation, power in the world, the delivery of public services, economic and social reform, stability—everything. The leaders always speak about 'stability', and this hypothesis says that that is all they finally have in mind.

I call this hypothesis trivial not because it would make the Chinese state insignificant or unimpressive. It is and will be a powerful state. But it would be trivial in the sense that it would have nothing to its name but force and nothing to present itself to others with than bigness. It would be a state with nothing to it that could be seen as worthy.

This is not a far-fetched hypothesis. Most dictatorships are self-serving and about strength itself or the use of strength for the benefit of the rulers themselves or their class. In today's Chinese state capitalism, where leaders and their families and friends have enriched themselves in a big way, some see a new kleptocracy or a mafia state. Under Mao, the Chinese state was a state with an ideological purpose. Mao went to extreme lengths to pursue that purpose, even so as to destroy the party apparatus itself when he thought it might be deviating from its true mission. There is still said to be socialism, although of a different kind—with Chinese characteristics, which is to say whatever the leaders of the day say it is—but that may be no more than posturing and propaganda. There is still socialism in fact in the meaning of Leninist party control, but that falls under the category of self-preservation. The rulers hold up the perpetuation of the regime as a purpose in its own right with no hesitation or embarrassment. In a debate in official media in 2013 over the force of the constitution, stimulated by perceived reformist signals from the new leaders, the official line quickly turned to warning against 'constitutionalism' as alien to the Chinese system, in part because it would undermine the stability that is guaranteed by the supremacy of the party above the law. Political leadership after Deng has been collective and in the hands of relatively colourless bureaucrats, and it may be beyond the capacity of a cabal of technocrats to imagine a vision for themselves and to articulate any sense of moral purpose. No observer will find any difficulty in reconciling much of what can be seen in action from the regime with a theory that its business is the preservation of itself and little more.

The triviality hypothesis is consistent with the state being a party-state. Applied to China, this hypothesis says that a state constituted as a party-state has turned away from ideology and made self-preservation its purpose. That state would then retain, and not shed, the party-state structure since that structure gives it an unequalled apparatus of control.

A trivial state is not the same as a weak state. Military dictatorships, as were once widespread in Latin America, or, for example, as until recently in Myanmar, can be as ruthless as they come and use force without mercy, but they are still trivial. A state that is dedicated to its own promotion makes itself as strong as it can be. Pursuing strength is not evidence that the state is not trivial. If the Chinese state is trivial, it is trivial in strength.

Nor is a trivial state necessarily a passive state, or even likely to be passive. A primitive state may put all its trust in force and repression, but a sophisticated state will be activist. It will shore itself up with the purchase of legitimacy in addition to the use of control. The Chinese state now is, in this meaning, a sophisticated one. Indeed, it may be argued that the transition in state practices that has followed from reform and opening up is rather in more sophistication than in less dictatorship. This Chinese state is clearly activist. It is pursuing economic growth in a big way. This is why observers are ultrasensitive to any sign of weaker growth. A decline in the official growth rate from, say, 8 to 7 percent is no big deal economically but is significant in China because it goes to the core of the state's claim on legitimacy. The headless pursuit of GDP-growthism is consistent with a theory that this is a state whose leaders understand growth but have no idea what growth is for.

The sophisticated state is likely to be activist across the board in public policy. It wants order and stability, and it will want to be seen to be effective. It is likely to display as impressive a range of policies as its resources allow in everything from defence to social security. These policies will, however, be limited in content in the sense of being self-servingly for the state as such and for its legitimacy.

The trivial state is non-ideological. The state is not an instrument for any higher purpose or idea; it is for itself and stability and nothing else. That does not mean that state leaders may not speak ideological language when that is useful or, for example, cloak themselves in a fancy national narrative, but state policy will not be committed to the advancement of any ideology. The Chinese leaders do indeed speak ideological language—they are 'socialist' in all their doings—but does that now contain any reality to which they are bound and committed, or is it just window dressing for reasons of tradition and expediency?

For the people, a trivial state is not necessarily a bad thing. It will not be repressive for ideological reasons but only for reasons of prudence, which is likely to mean only moderately repressive. A trivial dictatorship is likely to strike a deal with the people that they can get on with life much as they want, as long as they do not make serious trouble.

However, a trivial state has an unavoidable problem with its self-image. It is for itself but not genuinely for anything else. It has an intellectual emptiness which makes it vulnerable to criticism and prone to uncertainty and doubt about itself. The leaders of this state live in fear because they know that they are without legitimacy beyond what they can buy with posturing, rewards, and public policy bribery. They will be at risk of using repression more than is prudently necessary and to be unpredictable in the use of repression. They may trap themselves in a vicious circle where repression stimulates resistance and resistance calls for yet more repression.

Internationally, a trivial state is likely to be unpredictable. If it is prudent, it will avoid adventurism that might strike back as trouble for itself, which would be good news for neighbours and others. But it also brings with it into its dealings with others its lack of solid grounding at home which might make it an anxious and paranoid actor on the world stage. States that are not sure about themselves at home may seek to improve their standing by finding enemies abroad.

Strength without purpose can be a threatening constellation. A state that has no other strings to play on than strength has no other way of pursuing its interests than with weight, bullying, and force. The Chinese state *is* a bullying state. Perhaps it has no other capacity because it has no other vision of itself than being bigger than others? Perhaps the leaders who make it known that they expect respect from others have no idea in their own minds about what they should be respected for and therefore no way of attracting respect except by spreading fear. China's threatening behaviour towards neighbours is a mystery. If the Chinese leaders were safe and confident in their model, why should they not be magnanimous and get small disputes settled by sprinkling a bit of gold dust in the form of generosity on their lesser neighbours and in return reap genuine respect in the world? Since one way of shoring itself up at home is to be forceful outside, a state that is trivial at home is exposed to making itself aggressive abroad.

A state that relies on hard power only will be an exposed state, however big it be, and may for that reason again be dangerous. At home, it will remain despised, if feared. It will lack any authority of purpose and will know that its population may be subservient but not a partner. Worse, it will have to hold that population under control with repression since it will be unable to make its people followers by volition. Abroad, it may find other states fearful of its strength but not respectful of its qualities. It may be able to advance its interests, but it cannot aspire to genuine leadership because there is nothing in it that will attract admiration from others and inclination to follow.

All states pursue their interests and use whatever strength they have, but not all states define their interests narrowly, and not all states are limited to relying on force to advance their cause. Some states define themselves by some purpose or mission that in some meaning goes beyond self-interest. My triviality hypothesis says that in the Chinese case the state is its own purpose and that there is nothing more or less to it. That may be the case for other states as well, but there are also states that are inspired by a sense of purpose. An obvious example is China's nemesis, the United States. This state and its policies are, say the leaders, dedicated to the protection and promotion of a set of values such as freedom and democracy. The American state presents itself to the world as a strong state and as willing to exercise its strength, but not only that. It is also a state that stands for certain principles which are promoted as being of broad virtue. This is sometimes a source of criticism of the American state as an imperialistic one. It is seen to be zealous in pushing its values on to others. But when others look to the United States, they do see a state that stands for *something*. They may like or dislike it, but there is something there: principles, values, ideas, and purpose.

Another example would be from the Scandinavian countries. Here, the state embodies a 'model' which combines high productivity in the economy with a social system of solidarity, fairness, and equality. What gives the Scandinavian regimes identity in the world is not that they are protecting their interests—all states do that—but that they represent principles which they and others think merit respect, and do so with success.

In both the American and Scandinavian cases, there are benefits to the states of shrouding themselves in a frock of ideas. The United States is a world power by force of both strength that generates fear and cultural ideas that generate admiration and sometimes envy. The Scandinavian states have more clout internationally than they should by force of power, because they are admired, or at least noticed, and because their model serves as a moral reference in global discourse on the management of modern capitalism.

The trouble with the triviality hypothesis in the Chinese case is that, although a trivial party-state is not an impossibility, party-statism has its own logic in which the absence of ideology would seem to represent a troubling void. The party that claims supremacy needs justification. It must make it credible that there are reasons why it should be in control and why its rule should continue. Stability for the sake of stability is not much of a story to go out to the people with, or for the regime to boost its own self-confidence, certainly when it is aligned with the burdens of dictatorship. Stability on earth for a heavenly purpose, on the other hand, is something to fall back on and to make the demands on obedience from a forceful structure of control meaningful.

The Welfare Hypothesis

In a book published in 1941, *Citizen and Churchman*, William Temple, Archbishop of Canterbury from 1942, made a distinction between two kinds of states, which he called 'welfare states' and 'power states' (and in the process inaugurated the concept of 'welfare state'). Welfare states were then the democratic ones and power states the communist and fascist ones. In welfare states, the purpose of rule is to advance and protect the well-being of citizens. In power states, the purpose is to perpetuate the might and glory of the nation and its destiny, while citizens are subordinate in a duty to serve the state. The difference is in their ideas of state–society relations, whether the state serves society or society is made to serve the state, whether or not, to return to George Orwell, rule is for 'the cause of the common people'. In welfare states, the common people are cause and the state an instrument for their good. In power states, the state is cause and the common people reduced to instruments for its perpetuation.

My second hypothesis is that the Chinese leaders are forging a welfare state of their own making out of reform and opening up. Even if China is not on a path to democracy, it might be turning into a more benevolent autocracy with a strong component of social protection to its public policy. This hypothesis is supported by the building in recent years of, in many ways, an impressive social state. In *Providing Public Goods in Transitional China*, Tony Saich considers recent developments in social security and health care up against established welfare-state theories and sees much in China that is recognisable through a welfare-state lens. Within China, regime insiders who are social reformers interpret their country as being on a welfare-state path. For example, Zheng Gongcheng, who is professor of social security studies at Renmin University and a member of the Standing Committee of the National People's Congress, in his book *China's Social Security during Thirty Years*, sees the social state that is now taking form as a building block to realize in China a 'welfare society' by the centenary of the revolution in 2049.

This hypothesis says that there is more to the Chinese state than self-preservation and that the leaders are seeking to realize an idea of purpose. That idea is in the nature of being a moderate signpost rather than a system of ideological force. It is a benevolent idea, and since it lacks the force of ideological command, it represents the Chinese regime as a pragmatic autocracy.

China is modernising economically. Non-market socialism is a thing of the past. Now the order of the day is competition and inequality, but also social security—the standard paraphernalia of welfare capitalism. Any idea of a communist route to socialism is abandoned. The party still labels itself 'communist', but that's just historical language.[4]

However, although modernising, China is modernising in a way that is different from other paths before it. Just what that means is not entirely clear, but there is no lack of assertiveness in the leaders' claim that they have their own model. They are doing what others have done before—growing—but they are doing it in a way they say is special. They are dismissive of 'Western' capitalism, which they see as fickle and unstable, and are inventing, they say, a new experience of more solid and durable development.

China is an old state, and the current regime continues in an old tradition. China has seen itself as 'the middle kingdom', the centre of the world, with others around on a lesser scale. The Chinese regime today is again expecting something of that old deference. But the old claim to being better than others is now grounded in the regime's custodianship of a new model. What makes that model not only different but also better is that it is *socialist*. Everything the regime does is socialist. Their market economy is socialist, their democracy is socialist, their laws are socialist. In 2006, in response to concerns over urban-rural disparities in the wake of rapid economic growth, the leaders launched a programme of rural reform under the slogan of building 'a new socialist countryside'.

The welfare hypothesis is to be taken seriously. There is a strong link between socialist theory and of welfare-state theory. There are two theoretical versions of socialism, the communist one of revolution and the social democratic one of gradual reform.The link between socialist theory and welfare-state theory is that an ambitious system of social protection is thought of as an instrument in the gradual and social democratic transformation of society towards a socialist order. Since communism is abandoned, since public policies are manifestly reformist, and since current socialist thinking is about gradual transition, what may remain of socialist ideas in the Chinese model might be a version of the social democratic version of socialist theory. Professor Zheng, for example, promotes a theory that might well be described as social democracy with Chinese characteristics.

This thinking has recently been prominent in the state leadership. In 2006 and 2007, the party enshrined the principles of 'scientific outlook on development' in order to build a 'harmonious society'. That could represent a shift in the state's self-presentation from an ideological to a pragmatic mode. A Chinese welfare state would still be a dictatorial state. It is possible that its leaders have genuinely believed that the stability that is grounded in dictatorial control is necessary for growth and for the state to translate growth into adequate social security and public services for the

4. The party officially stopped calling itself 'revolutionary' in 2002.

population. The idea of the Chinese party-state as a welfare state is therefore not necessarily a fantasy.

The adoption of these signals was the work of then Party Secretary Hu Jintao and Premier Wen Jiabao. They had become concerned about the deep divisions of inequality that had emerged during the reform period, about the grievances these divisions created in the population, and about the threat that these schisms might represent to the stability of development and ultimately to the regime itself. 'Scientific outlook' was code language for more political control over market forces, in particular to carry the half of the population living in the countryside along in progress. The 'harmonious society' is obviously a society without disruptive differences, one in which all the people are served by the state's policies and by the growth that these policies have unleashed. Here, the leaders were reaching back to classical socialist theory. In all socialist thinking, there is a pre-utopian interim that has to be traversed and in which policies can be unattractive, for example, by wages being held down because of the need to reach a certain level of capital accumulation. That is seen as necessary for the realisation of socialism in the next stage. In this narrative, China is still in its interim. The ground is being cleared for the coming of socialism, and socialism is defined in terms of 'harmony'. The then leaders even committed themselves to a date. They looked fifteen years ahead and proclaimed that 'the harmonious society' was to be built by 2020. By then China should be out of its interim and well into the specialness which would establish their model as the superior one not only in economic efficiency but also in social quality.

It was Hu and Wen who made 'harmonious society' official party terminology. But the concept and idea sits deeper in the Chinese tradition. At the beginning of the revolutionary period, Mao articulated a vague goal of the 'great harmony,' which he again drew from Confucian ideas. The socialist tradition came into it in Mao's view that harmony would be the eventual outcome of a painful interim. The specifically Chinese tradition comes into it from the Confucian idea that it is the state—then the emperor, now the party—that is to be the giver of harmony to all living things. The new leadership as of 2012–13 is possibly lifting the People's Republic into a new phase of development. It could be that this new phase is dedicated to the realisation of what has been prepared during the preceding interim.

This, then, is a powerful narrative. There is Chinese continuity in it. It conforms to socialist theory, to the idea that something better is to come out of the interim, and that that betterment is for the people and not just for the strength of the state. It is supported by theorists and has its own articulation in official thinking. We do not need a precise definition of 'harmony' to know that the Chinese society today is not a harmonious one and that the absence of harmony neatly captures the strains of Chinese life and the challenges to the regime. But this does not negate the theory. Socialism means harmony at the outcome of the interim, not harmony during the process.

Welfare states are likely to be non-ideological. There is a superstructure of ideas that are guiding in public policy but that do not have the force of command. They *can* be ideological. The Swedish state in the period of social democratic dominance was an ideological welfare state that was committed to classical social democratic theory and the peaceful transformation of society into socialism. As usual when states subvert to ideology, this one was led astray into utterly impractical, if ideologically logical, policies. Starting in 1983, it launched itself into the 'third stage' of its democratic transition to socialism by starting to socialise the control over production capital. It did that in so-called 'wage earners' funds. The ownership of capital was to shift into 'funds' which in theory were to be under democratic wage earner control. That experiment, however, failed spectacularly, both economically and politically, and was abandoned in 1990. The experience changed Swedish social democracy into a non-ideological movement. Sweden has continued to be a welfare state, but is now, like most others, whether under social democratic or other rule, a welfare state on pragmatic terms, guided by a vision of promoting the security and well-being of its population without commitment to any more overarching ideology or grand utopian vision. There is something of a contradiction between ideology and welfare, since an ideological state is the custodian of some absolute truth that may easily relegate the well-being of citizens to a second-order concern.

Welfare states are obviously activist in domestic public policy. What makes a state a welfare state is practical administration. In this respect, a welfare state and a trivial state may look much the same. But while they may not differ in being activist, they differ in why and how they are activist. One is activist for its citizens, the other one for itself. They are therefore likely to differ in policy designs. In the trivial state, public policies, however activist, are geared to the generation of legitimacy for the regime. In the welfare state, they are designed for the purpose of giving citizens protection, justice, support, and opportunity.

A welfare state is likely to be a confident state that knows what it is about and is safe in the knowledge that its mission is worthy, and one that is therefore predictable and not prone to adventurism either at home or abroad. This was Nelson Mandela's vision for the new South Africa as a 'rainbow nation, at peace with itself and therefore with the world'. Welfare states *can*, however, be aggressive in international relations. They may succumb to self-righteousness and to promoting themselves with a degree of zealotry. Norway and Sweden, for example, do not have the power to make themselves imperialist nations, but both have used a vision of virtue to promote themselves aggressively for maximum influence on the world stage, Norway as a peacemaker and Sweden for its model as one of unique excellence. A welfare state with power behind it is not necessarily a pretty sight internationally (and the world may well be relieved that Norway and Sweden do not have more power to play with). If China were transforming itself into a welfare state domestically, that would not necessarily make it an unaggressive state internationally.

The difficulty with the welfare hypothesis, akin to that of the triviality hypothesis, is that ideas of welfare may not be enough to sustain the party-state. A welfare state does not need to be a party-state. If the Chinese leaders were to define their state as a welfare state, they would be building a state in which the party has no theoretically justified rationale. It may be there as a historical fact but is not needed. Welfare ideas offer no ideological justification for party-state control.

The Power Hypothesis

Power states are strong states in which the state and its strength are for a higher purpose. They are different from strong trivial states where the state is its own purpose and there is nothing more to it. They are also different from welfare states in that their purpose is different. Welfare states make it their purpose to work for the good of citizens. In power states the purpose is given by an official ideology, and citizens are subordinate to the advancement of the ideologically defined purpose.

Power states (disregarding brute dictatorships which in my schema are trivial) are ideological states and party-states. The state serves a higher purpose, that purpose is defined by an official ideology, the party is the embodiment of that ideology, and the party-state machinery serves as its guardian. The party is the instrument of the official ideology and as such the supreme authority. The state is the instrument of the party, and state institutions have a duty to serve the party by force of the ideology that is embodied in it, and citizens by the same logic have a duty of obedience and service to state and party. This is what generates and justifies the ruthlessness which is endemic in power states: when ideology rules any action that is ideologically correct or productive is justified. It is not strength alone that makes a state a power state but the way strength is constituted and used.

Power states are obviously dictatorial. They are likely to be activist in public policy domestically and may in this respect be similar to trivial states and to welfare states. While trivial and welfare states may or may not be aggressive in international relations, power states are likely to be aggressive.

China has the institutional build-up of a power state. It was previously, during the Maoist period, an ideological state. The question now is whether reform and opening up represents a departure whereby China has disestablished itself as a power state and made itself either a trivial state dedicated to its own survival or a welfare state dedicated to the betterment of its people—or whether it is still a power state in a new guise.

Many observers believe that reform and opening up represent a radical departure from the Maoist past and that China is now reformist, liberalising, moving in a pluralistic civil society direction, and so on. That is possibly the case; hence, my two first hypotheses. But, although much is changing in China and in the lives of the Chinese, various observations still stand against this optimistic view:

- Once a state is constituted as a party-state there are facts on the ground that shape its character. There is the double system of control. This is a system that needs and attracts ideology and lends itself to harsh dictatorship rather than benevolent autocracy. State control is justified by obedience to the party. The party would seem to need a set of principles that explain and make sense of why and how it should control the state and society. The idea of a pragmatic, non-ideological, and benevolent party-state is something of a contradiction in terms.
- The party is still the Communist Party and the leaders speak the language of continuity and of socialism as the hallmark of their model. Those who believe that the party-state has been transformed into a pragmatic one tend to dismiss ideological posturing by the leadership as mere rituals and symbolics. Perhaps they are right, but it could also be that the leaders say what they mean and mean what they say. It is usually unwise to dismiss what leaders say about their aims and intentions and outlooks as only tittle-tattle.
- The term 'opening up' is a bit of a misnomer. Politically, what followed was a re-consolidation of controls. As a result of Mao's excesses, state control had broken down. Deng's reforms did not liberalise China from state control; they re-established a system of control that had been destroyed.
- The consolidation of party-state control has continued under the post-Deng leaderships, and there has in this respect rather been a further tightening than subsequent liberalisation. The change in leadership in 2012–13 has brought with it yet further consolidation of party-state control.
- The new leadership has strengthened the bonds between the political apparatus and the military and consolidated further the alliance between the party and the People's Liberation Army.
- This leadership has notched up nationalism, militarism, and aggression in language and behaviour, both in its propaganda and in its dealings with neighbouring countries and more broadly.

So the trappings of a power state are still there. The final question is about ideology. Is the strong Chinese state now pragmatic, or is it still, or again, in addition to being dictatorial also ideological? A strong state could still be benevolent—that is not impossible—but a strong state that is also ideological is another matter. All historical experience is that strong ideological states are repressive, ruthless, and dangerous.

It could still be prudent and sophisticated in the way it uses strength, but when the chips are down ideology rules and everything else, such as the common people and their needs, is secondary.

The regime was without question ideological under Mao, and the ruling ideology was then revolution. That ideology was discredited and has not been restored. Deng presented himself as the consummate pragmatist, but that was in economic affairs and was in political terms window dressing. He restored the system of party-state control, used it with ruthlessness when necessary, and was the power behind the decision in 1989 to turn the state's guns on the people. His reign was low key in ideology, but did it represent the end of ideology in China in favour of a post-communist regime that is pragmatic as long as it is able to stay in control?

Perhaps not. The leaders continue to claim the right to dictatorial control and do so under ideological authority. The two (long and tedious) constitutions, of the state and of the party, are steeped in ideological language: Marxism-Leninism, Mao Zedong Thought, Deng Xiaoping Theory, the important thought of Three Represents, and so on. The party's constitution enshrines the Four Cardinal Principles, the ones Deng appealed to as guidelines for reform and opening up and which include 'the upholding of the people's democratic dictatorship'. It is not easy for a party-state to give up on ideology, because if it does, it has no justification for its awesome apparatus of control. The leaders continue to speak in ideological language, however vaguely, and it might, again, be unwise to not think that they mean what they say.

If we take the leaders seriously in what they say, as I for one think we should, we have about the following possible storyline: Deng re-established political control, redesigned the rules of economic behaviour, and spoke the language of pragmatism. For a while, the rebuilding of state and economy after years of destruction was purpose enough and there was not much need for further ideological rhetoric. But there is an inherent urge in the party-state to cultivate or invent some system of ideas to serve as justification of and giving meaning to dictatorship. Deng's successors inherited a restored and dictatorial party-state but also an ideological vacuum. His mission of salvaging the regime from destruction was accomplished, but he had not articulated a new narrative of purpose beyond growth and prosperity. The new leaders, as custodians of dictatorship in more normal circumstances, again felt the need to justify themselves in more than managerial terms. A party-state without an acknowledged higher purpose has a problem with its identity, and once Deng's reconstitution was done, that problem became acute. When economic growth on its own ceased to be justification enough, the leaders again took to ideas, possibly to ideology, to fill the regime's vacuum of identity and purpose.

A first attempt was to justify the party-state in a vision of a 'harmonious society'. That attempt, however, failed. The idea of a welfare state was too distant from Chinese reality. It failed to take hold in popular imagination. It failed to square with the reality of economic ruthlessness and widening inequalities. It lacked the ideological force to provide rationalisation of party-state control. The leaders failed to reconcile the ideas they spoke of with the realities of their policies. One reason why many observers are sceptical when Chinese leaders rehearse any kind of ideological vision may be that this first attempt at ideological restructuring proved to be pretty much empty talk.

Then came the change of leadership in 2012–13. The new leader, Xi Jinping, initially concentrated on getting a grip on the reins of power, something he achieved with impressive determination and speed. He then turned to reform on a broad agenda and to speaking about the direction and purpose of his rule in high language. He praised the People's Liberation Army as the bastion of state power. He spoke out about the need for better discipline within the party-state and for the fortification of the order of state control. He launched initiatives to streamline and legalise the administrative apparatus of the state. He lectured officials high and low to lead by example and to shun bad and extravagant behaviour. He clamped down on corruption within the system. And he dressed up his initiatives, administrative manoeuvres, and repressions in a new super-message under a new slogan, that of the China Dream.[5]

One interpretation of 'China Dream' is to see it as a second attempt at ideological renewal, after the failings of 'harmonious society'. The party-state is there, it is as controlling as ever, or more so, it needs justification. China has been advancing economically for a long time. There is a need to explain what it is advancing for. It is entering a period of more normal economic development and will no longer be able to rely as strongly as it has on economic growth for legitimacy. The regime is asserting itself internationally and needs a storyline to explain itself. There is a need to justify the continuation of dictatorship. That justification needs to be found in a narrative that is attractive to Chinese people and reasonably aligned with historical traditions and current state practices. In the China Dream, then, the party-state is finding, or trying to find, a narrative of ideas to justify its rule.

If this interpretation is valid, two further questions present themselves. Is the China Dream enough of a belief system to establish itself as ideology? And if so, what kind of ideology is it? But these questions I leave hanging for now, to be returned to towards the end of the book.

Testing

We have three hypotheses: the triviality hypothesis (the state is for itself only), the welfare hypothesis (the state is for the good of the common people), and the power hypothesis (the state is for an ideological mission). All are plausible and none can be dismissed out of hand.

5. I prefer 'China Dream' to 'Chinese Dream', since Xi Jinping's evocation was of a dream about China, not a dream of Chinese people, a distinction to which I return in the postscript.

These hypotheses are alternatives to each other and testable. Although real cases never fit perfectly to theoretical models, a state like the Chinese one must conform, or be in the process of conforming, most closely to one of these hypotheses, and cannot conform to more than one.

The givens apply: The Chinese state, of whatever kind it is, is strong, dictatorial, and constituted as a party-state. Of whatever kind it is, it is likely to be activist in domestic public policy and may or may not be aggressive in international relations. We might think, perhaps, the welfare hypothesis to be the 'good' hypothesis, but a Chinese welfare state might well be an aggressive state.

A testing of the hypotheses up against each other would proceed in two steps. The first test is of the welfare hypothesis. If the Chinese state were confirmed as a welfare state, that would both secure the second hypothesis and dismiss the two other ones. A welfare state is neither a trivial state nor a power state. This puts the welfare hypothesis at the core of the analysis to follow. No alternative interpretation is credible unless the benevolent one has been disproved.

The welfare test rests on the structure of public policy, on the way the state gives and takes. A welfare state does not depend much on ideology. There will be an idea about security, opportunity, and better living conditions for the people, but otherwise this state stands or falls on its giving and taking. A state that is dedicated to the cause of the common people, and whose policies are in conformity with that intention, is a welfare state. That, again, will depend, as a first step—the 'narrow test'—on the structure of social protection, on whether social policies are designed for social justice or merely as instruments for the purchase of regime legitimacy. Then it depends, as a next step—the 'broad test'—on the shape of the wider state system within which social protections are embedded, on whether the state in its totality is dedicated to the good of its people. A state that subjugates the common people cannot make itself a welfare state by bribing them with social protection.

The second test is in ideology. If the welfare hypothesis were disproved, the two other hypotheses would be viable. What distinguishes these two hypotheses, in turn, is ideology. If the state is ideological, it is not trivial. It is then for something beyond its own self-preservation. By ideology, to repeat, I mean not just that leaders pay lip service to some ideological notion, such as 'socialism with Chinese characteristics' but that there is an articulated belief system which is absorbed in the party-state and which the leaders see as binding on themselves and the advancement of which they take to be their ultimate purpose and justification. If the state is in this meaning ideological, it is a power state. If it is not, and is not a welfare state, it is a trivial state. This in turn will come down to the meaning of Xi Jinping's China Dream. Is that just loose talk, or does it represent the state's ideological rejuvenation?

Chapter 3
What They Do

Today's rulers have two main strategies of self-preservation. With one hand they purchase legitimacy in the eyes of the ruled; with the other hand they keep down anything that can threaten their hold on power. The way the regime deals with society is through an intricate good-cop, bad-cop act.

The means of control are hard, brutal, and ruthless. China is a police state with omnipresent overt and secret security forces. The military is an internal as well as an external force. The judiciary is under party control. Persecution, intimidation, imprisonment (often arbitrary and often unlawful), torture, beatings—these are rampant. When the regime saw itself under threat in the uprisings in 1989, it turned to political murder as a means of control. Censorship over what is considered dangerous information or expressions of opinion is harsh, including the Great Firewall against threatening uses of the Internet. The press is under government control and as much an instrument of propaganda as of information, never mind free debate. And so, effectively, is the Internet. Propaganda and thought work are integral to governance.

The means of purchasing legitimacy are many and sophisticated. The regime maintains and cultivates an ideological identity through the branding of itself as 'socialist' and now possibly a dream factory. These are flexible brands which, however, hover over all government activity as part of a superstructure from which the regime claims its mandate, much as previous Chinese rulers claimed to rule by a mandate from heaven. It takes further legitimacy from its own strength. It liberated the country, gave it reasons for pride, has held it together, and kept external and internal threats at bay. It delivers and thereby claims the right to rule.

The claim to delivery includes the maintenance of stability and order. That is important. Until very recently, the living memory in China was of deadly disorder. That was true of 'the century of humiliation' from the Opium Wars around 1840, of the internal disorder in the nineteenth century—the Taiping and Boxer rebellions (of 1850–63 and 1899–1900 respectively, which were really civil wars)—of the warlord era into which the Republic of China disintegrated after 1916, and the civil war leading up to 1949, and of the disasters under Mao. The current rulers are without doubt right that the Chinese people want order—they know what its absence means—and can trust the people to thank them for providing it. It is true that its order is haphazard and has come at a high price, but in the eyes of the Chinese and against their historical experience, it is not surprising that some order at a price is better that no order at an even higher price. But it is also sensitive. The most recent disorder, that caused by Mao's despotism and that included the worst famine in human history when (conservatively estimated) 30 to 40 million people died, was the work of the same regime that is now providing order, and the present rulers bask both in continuing the communist rule and in leaving the communist past behind.[1]

It takes legitimacy from economic growth, from having brought population growth under control, and from having given its people economic freedoms—freedom to own, freedom to do business, freedom from poverty, freedom to consume, freedom to be rich or hope to be rich, freedom to dress, behave, and travel much as one wants. There are limits, but historically minded Chinese, or many of them, know that they have never had it so good, and the regime is able to claim, not without justification, that it is to be thanked.

The purchase of legitimacy through economic growth has come at a price. One part of that price is pollution, contaminated soil and groundwater, and material and environmental depletion, blights throughout the country that can only be described as atrocious. Equally atrocious is the blight of graft and corruption which intrudes into the daily lives of ordinary people. A further blight is rising inequality, both between urban and rural areas, and between rich and poor within urban areas in particular. China is now one of the most unequal countries in the world in the distribution of income and wealth, competing with South Africa and two or three Latin American countries for the position as *the* most unequal country, mass raw poverty at one end and extreme riches at the other.[2] We know from survey evidence that these blights—pollution, corruption, and inequality—are on the top of the list for ordinary people of what they find burdensome and objectionable in their living conditions.

For now, the regime has the strength it needs to exercise the control it wants. It is able to contain the unrest that simmers in the far reaches of the land and has the means to crack down where and when it needs to. Throughout the territory there have in recent years been about 500 'mass incidents' a day, mostly local reactions to land seizures and mistreatment of workers, and mostly easily manageable. Its Achilles' heel is legitimacy. It enjoys much less loyalty from its people than admirers are prone to thinking. The regime lacks the authority of ruling by force of consent by the ruled. That is a great weakness and is the reason it cannot make do without the brute force of dictatorial control. On the occasions when it has relaxed its controls and encouraged or allowed free debate—the 'hundred flowers' movement in 1956–57, the democracy

1. The authoritative reference on the famine of 'the great leap forward' is Yang, *Tombstone*.
2. See Li et al., *Rising Inequality in China*.

wall movement in 1979, and the liberal period that culminated in the occupation of Tiananmen Square and similar actions elsewhere in 1989—the debate turned to a demand for democracy and against the regime, and was crushed. In 2014, young people, mainly students, organised a massive manifestation in favour of democracy in Hong Kong by occupying core areas in the city's business centre. The Chinese government, which has ultimate authority over Hong Kong, wisely refrained from interfering. But there should be no doubt that the men in Beijing took note that in this part of China, where people have freedom of speech and expression, young Chinese, when provoked, took to the streets in a demand for security, say in public affairs, and democracy.

So this is, as dictatorships always are, an ugly regime. The rulers do what they can to pretty themselves up, but the combination of dictatorship and consent is an unsquarable circle, in China as elsewhere—wherefore distrust, wherefore the fall-back on controls, which erodes trust again, which enforces more controls—and so it goes on.

The Matrix of Power

The pillars of power in the Chinese system are:

- The party
- The military
- The executive
- The legislature
- The police
- The judiciary

The party, the military, and the executive are the three overpowering and nation-wide bureaucratic systems. To split these pillars apart as separate from one another is an oversimplification since in reality they are deeply intertwined, albeit with the party at the top of the power pyramid. When the government congratulated itself on its achievements in its work report to the 2014 National People's Congress, and added that they had not come easily, it expressed its thanks to, in this order, 'the correct leadership of the Party Central Committee with comrade Xi Jinping as general secretary as well as to the concerted efforts of the whole Party, the entire armed forces, and all the people of all of China's ethnic groups'. (In the 2015 report, only the Central Committee and Xi Jinping got explicit mention.)

These central organs stand on layers of local government, generally in this form:

- The country is divided into *provinces*, of which there are thirty-three, including five that are called autonomous regions (Tibet, Xinjiang, Inner Mongolia,

Guangxi, Ningxia), four directly administered municipalities (Beijing, Shanghai, Chongqing, Tianjin), and two special administrative regions (Hong Kong and Macao, both with separate political systems and, Hong Kong in particular, extensive internal self-rule). Provinces (but not directly administered municipalities and special administrative regions) are divided into prefectures and prefecture-level cities, about three hundred in all (some of which are being phased out).

- The next level is that of *counties* (sometimes called municipalities), including county-level cities and urban districts, in all about 3,000 units. The counties report upwards to provinces.
- Counties are divided into *towns*, townships, and urban subunits (districts and sub-districts), in all about 50,000 units.
- Below that level again are *villages* and somewhat similar urban units (communities, street offices, neighbourhood offices, and the like), almost 700,000 in all. These are 'administrative villages', some of which are big and distinctly urban in real economic and social structure. There are many more 'real' villages, many of which are small communities within administrative villages, towns, or cities, and many of which are vanishing under the force of urbanisation. Within villages and local urban units there are various administrative subunits and committees that extend the reach of party and government down to the micro-local level.[3]

This matrix of authorities one next to the other and the levels from central to local makes for a rather complicated grid of public management. It is big, the largest bureaucratic system ever created. At least 75 million people are in jobs paid for from the public purse (not including government-owned enterprises). It is fecund, in a document-based political culture producing a never-ending stream of papers in a formalized system in which the various central and local party and government organs issue decrees that range from 'orders' (that are to be implemented to the letter), via 'instructions' or 'decisions' (to be implemented with local discretion), and 'circulars' (for information), through to mere 'opinions' (which, however, underlings who wish to be in favour are well advised to keep in mind). It is obscure. There are organs—committees, bureaus, offices, and so on—in abundance, but the actual patterns of governance according to conventions and practices are fluid and constantly changing and cannot be read out of any organisational chart. The bureaucratic monster is made up of thousands of units, committees, and agencies that report to each other, boss each other, and control each other in ways that are rarely straight and clear. Posts

3. For a superb portrait of one version of village economics and politics, see Saich and Hu, *Chinese Village*.

and committees that are separate in authority overlap in membership. Who 'really' decides what, does what and reports to whom is always ambiguous.

One of the consequences of size and complexity is that it takes enormous energy from the top to get policies followed up and implemented down the line. The leaders are light-years away from being able to just decide and get done. They cannot get more done than they are able to put systematic and relentless pressure behind. If they want to get anything done at all, as opposed to just deciding things, they are forced to prioritise, to choose what they want done, and let other matters lie. Administration is omnipresent but policy, by necessity, selective.

One of the consequences of the radicalism of economic reform that was unleashed by Deng Xiaoping was a lack of experience and knowledge in the leadership about how to run a market economy. There was, for example, a naïve belief that social problems would melt away as economic growth rolled on, so that social protections could be removed without consequence once growth was unleashed. From the outside world, the reform process may have seemed straight enough. Inside, however, it has been convoluted, twisted, and characterised by continuous trial and error. That is still the state of affairs.

The four main levels of government are nation, province, county, and town. These form a hierarchy of command from top down. The People's Republic is a unitary state with, in principle, no division of power between national and local authorities.

Villages, however, are constitutionally autonomous and not part of the hierarchy of command. They are different from the other local authorities in that the village leadership is nominally elected by the people of the village. Direct elections at the village level have been in operation since 1998. The experience is that these elections, and certainly the selection of candidates, have mostly been controlled or manipulated by the village party (and sometimes village clans) and by town cadres from above. In a much-noticed case in 2012, a revolt in the fishing village of Wukan in Guangdong province led on to village committee elections in which the leaders of the revolt won control over the committee. But two years on, since the party does not forget or forgive, higher-level party authorities had regained control over village politics and started to reinstate party bosses who had been ousted in the 2012 elections. In towns and higher-level units, the leadership is appointed from above and hence answers upwards to their superiors. Practically, however, villages and equivalents are the lowest administrative units in the system and far less autonomous in fact than in constitutional principle. On the other hand, the higher-level local authorities, towns and up, which are constitutionally subordinate to the national government, and to higher-level local authorities, have more autonomy in fact than in constitutional principle. Although China is formally a unitary state, the provinces (and lower-level units) have powers that *de facto* make it a federal state.

This local subdivision applies to party, executive, legislature, judiciary, and security services so that roughly the same institutions are reproduced on each level. There are, for example, people's congresses at the various levels down the line, at the village level called 'assemblies'. Only the supreme security services, the People's Liberation Army and the People's Armed Police, have separate local organisations of their own. The PLA is divided into seven military regions which cut across provinces, and the PAP into forty-five divisions.[4]

The party

In the party-state, the party leads.[5] It sets the direction and principles of government policy and monitors the rest of society to get both public and private actors to follow the party line. There has over the years been much internal debate about how the party should do this and how tight a control it should hold, and a great deal of oscillation in practice—during the Cultural Revolution the very architecture of the party-state crumbled—but the remarkable thing is how the idea and practice of party leadership has persisted and survived. China is modernising, but the party continues to dominate society on distinctly unmodern Leninist principles. The theory is that the party is the custodian of an official ideology that unites the people, indeed unites the hearts of the people, that adherence to the official ideology is a universal duty and something the party itself must promote and ascertain, and that the party can thereby guide China to stability and strength.

The party is everywhere in Chinese society.[6] It is present in every government agency, central and local, in every unit of the military, in every town and village and neighbourhood, in every school, in every university and university department and every student residence, in every business, and in every officially registered social organisation.[7] The military and security services are under party control and command. It is present through party committees, party cells, party secretaries, and party representatives, and through its All-China affiliates. Even in Hong Kong, which constitutionally is not within the party-state and where the CCP officially does not exist (not having formally registered), the party maintains an extensive

4. Excellent monographs on the structure of the party-state include Lieberthal et al., *China's Political Development*; Saich, *Governance and Politics of China*; Joseph, *Politics in China*; Lieberthal, *Governing China*; and Lam, *Chinese Politics in the Era of Xi Jinping*. The organisation of the PLA is currently under revision.
5. For an authoritative analysis, see Shambaugh, *China's Communist Party*.
6. Two recent and informed and informative books, McGregor, *The Party* and Callick, *The Party Forever*, both drive the same message: The Chinese Communist Party is omnipresent.
7. 'Social organisation' is the official designation of all organisations that are not a part, directly, of the party-state apparatus.

semi-clandestine network, described by the Hong Kong politician and democracy activist Christine Loh as an 'underground front'.

Although it is correct to say that the party is everywhere, everywhere still does not mean literally everywhere. There are activities and institutions that 'should' be under direct scrutiny but that for some reason escape it. Not all representatives are competent and some are indifferent, or exercise their duties only by pretence. The party may be everywhere but not necessarily everywhere yet; it is still working on completing its representation in the private business sector (from its present penetration in about 85 percent of private enterprises). But non-scrutiny is still the rare exception. With some careful caveats, it is still correct to say that China is a country in which the party knows everything.

The business of the party's branches is to observe, collect information, report upwards, channel orders and propaganda downwards, and control. Two crucial activities of the party system are information collection and propaganda dissemination, in which the entire apparatus is involved. Information is gathered continuously, on persons and activities, and in particular on anything that looks like organising or the formation of networks. In China, 'they' know what is going on. From top down, propaganda flows ceaselessly into all corners of society. The party controls what is done in public and private organisations through its power of consent and veto. Everyone knows that wherever the party is present, it is the ultimate decider. It keeps vigil against 'instability'. There is much pressure of instability from below but not much that is unknown or unobserved. Insurrection that is manageable is not necessarily stamped down, but that which is dangerous is, in particular where insurrection threatens to form networks or to be organised.

The CCP is a vanguard organisation of élite cadres, in the tradition of 'democratic centralism', but still has more than 87 million members, up from about 20 million in fifty years, organised upwards from 3.5 million primary party units. This, about 10 percent of the adult population, is the Chinese system's organised establishment. Those who want to get on, the best and the brightest (except for the determined dissidents), crowd into the party. Only a minority of these, obviously, are party officials with executive authority, but even that select group counts in the millions. What was once a party of peasants, workers, and soldiers is now a predominantly technocratic party with members more highly educated than the population, and with higher incomes, and with an increasing inflow of professionals and business people. Being a party insider is both a way of advancing and a way of protecting your advancement, such as acquired wealth, so much so that big money is being paid for seats in even provincial people's congresses.[8] Becoming a party member normally depends on

8. The 2014 National People's Congress, according to the *Financial Times*, had 86 billionaires among its 2,900 delegates, up from 83 in 2013, and the Chinese People's Political Consultative Conference another 96 billionaires, up from 52 in 2013. The super-rich delegates are from the very top echelons of the rich list

being recommended by existing members, serving a period of probation, surviving examination, swearing loyalty, and being approved by a higher party level.

Although it is correct to say that the party leads, that also implies that someone else executes. That would be the government and its various agencies. While that, too, is correct, in the sense that the government does what the party instructs, it is also wrong in that the nominal division between party and government is a fiction. Most of the people who sit in leadership positions anywhere in the system, from top to bottom and into the fringes of state-owned enterprises and other tightly or loosely affiliated agencies and organisations, are party members.

A second necessary qualification about party leadership is that the party has never been united. As there have been fluctuations in party practices over time, there are divisions within the party, along both ideological and pragmatic lines, between factions, coalitions, and bureaucracies, and between central and local interests.[9] Internal discussion about the direction of policy, within limits, is tolerated and to some degree encouraged from above. The system has been described as 'consultative Leninist'.[10] What is suppressed is not necessarily participation or even opposition, but systemic dissent. There is managed competition over ideas. Trusted advisors and party-state think-tanks run a closed-shop debate over policies. They have connectors into the top leadership through confidential reporting and briefing. The Central Party School edits at last one non-public journal, *Internal Reference of Ideology and Theory*, which is distributed internally and to only a few dozen people. This controlled openness is to the benefit of the regime through the demonstration that its organs of power are alive and reflective and helps to ensure that the policies that get adopted have stood the test of deliberation. It helps the system to protect itself against excesses and extremism and to work by consensus and compromise. However, it makes it difficult for the leadership to be bold and decisive and puts veto power in the hands of manifold vested interests.

Leadership is centralized and from above. The top organs are the Politburo, with about twenty-five members, the Standing Committee of the Politburo, with seven members (reduced from nine in 2012), the real centre of command, and the general secretary, who is by present convention also president. If there is any supreme national leader, it is the general-secretary–president, but central governance in the era after Deng Xiaoping has been collective with no single supreme wielder of power. Mao was in that position as party chairman, a title that has subsequently gone out of use (as of 1982), as was Deng in a period, although without formally holding any top position, except that of Chairman of the Central Military Commission from 1981 to 1989. The

---

and have been getting richer faster than the average for the super-rich in the country. In 2015, according to the Shanghai-based *Hurun Report*, 203 of the 1,271 richest Chinese people it has tracked were delegates to the People's Congress and CPPCC.

9. See Callahan, *China: The Pessoptimistic Nation* and Leonard, *What Does China Think?*
10. See Tsang, 'Consultative Leninism: China's new political framework'.

present leader, Xi Jinping, was able to make himself party secretary, military chairman, and state president in one go and has established a bold style of leading from the front. Beneath the formality of collectivism, persons continue to matter enormously and the party power game runs on personal connections, clientelism, and patronage. Leaders and elders tangle with each other to get their protégés into positions of authority and then use their relations with their dependents to influence policies.

Top party officials are nominally elected by the Central Committee, which has about 370 members and meets once or twice a year. These are the important party 'plenums' from which the big decisions emerge, although not where they are made. The Central Committee is elected by the National Party Congress, which has about 2,000 delegates and meets every five years. In reality, elections are settled in advance through more or less invisible procedures, although the convention is now established to give elections a sheen of reality that a few more candidates are nominated than the number of available posts. And even the formal procedures are convoluted. For example, the Central Committee elects the Politburo and its Standing Committee, the Standing Committee nominates members for the Secretariat, and the Central Committee elects, or approves, the Secretariat.

Party administration is run by the Secretariat, four general departments, such as for organisation and propaganda affairs, and various administrative departments. The powerful Central Commission for Discipline Inspection is at the top of the list of departments and is charged with holding cadres in line. This commission has police-like and judicial authority within the party and the ability to protect party members from 'civilian' judicial scrutiny. Its powers were enhanced by decisions of the party's Third and Fourth Plenums in 2013 and 2014 so that lower-level discipline organs are now supposed to report directly to the central commission, rather than through local party organs. This has shifted the power of control from local to central authorities and has been instrumental, for example, in giving Xi Jinping's anti-corruption drive more force than previous efforts have had.

The party appoints the Central Military Commission, a committee of eleven members which is a core institution in the national leadership and whose chairman is, effectively, the commander-in-chief of the armed forces. This commission constitutionally reports both to the party and the executive but is in reality a party committee, and the armed forces is thus in the hands of the party. The Central Military Commission is the third supreme body of power in the system, next to the party's Politburo and the government's State Council.

The top leaders run the apparatus of governance by dividing functional responsibilities between themselves and by heading up small, or not so small, leading groups or commissions with party and government members in each field. The top broad portfolios are party affairs, government work, propaganda and ideology, state security, and foreign affairs, which together cover everything, and then there are more narrowly defined additional portfolios. The leading groups are of different kinds; their number is unknown and their composition often unknown. Working quietly under the radar, these groups are the party's instruments of the nitty-gritty of policymaking and control. They direct the work of rafts of bureaucratic agencies in their fields. Most of them are headed by a member of the Politburo Standing Committee, or at least of the Politburo, and Standing Committee members usually have at least a couple of such responsibilities.

The party's Third Plenum in 2013 decided to establish two new super-leadership groups, a 'national security committee' and a 'central reform leading group', both with almost unlimited remits. Two further leading groups were set up shortly afterwards, one on 'Internet security and information' and one on 'military reform', all headed by Xi Jinping. He had already taken the chairmanship of the leading group on economic policy, all of which has served to fortify his power position. These new groups are part of a pattern of political reform to strengthen central control.

Top party and government officials have personal offices with secretaries and advisors. These are the bosses' connectors into the system and together form a network of 'agents' behind the scene. They have a personal security detail which lends them a patina of physical force. The top leaders live in a secluded compound in Beijing, the *Zhongnanhai*, in comfort and security. In a country in which food is notoriously unsafe and contaminated, the top brass have their own protected food supply. In a town that is poisoned by air pollution, they live behind the safety of air filtering systems.

Various other organisations are affiliated with the party, if technically not of it. Prominent among these are the Communist Youth League, the All-China Federation of Trade Unions, the All-China Students' Federation, the All-China Women's Federation, which refers to itself as a mass movement and an NGO, or a federation of NGOs, and the All-China Federation of Industry and Commerce, which organises private enterprises. Affiliated organisations are referred to as 'mass organisations', distinguished from 'social organisations' which are nominally independent. The current line is to restrict the space of action for social organisations. During 2015, foreign organisations, broadly defined, were put under tighter legislation and regulations and will need to be vetted by the security police before being registered and able to operate in China.[11] For Chinese NGOs, the Politburo issued a decision that party groups should be set up in all social, cultural, and economic organisations. On mass organisations, the Politburo in July 2015 issued an opinion, following up on previous similar opinions earlier in the year, on 'strengthening the work of mass organisations', instructing officials and cadres on all levels to energise mass organisation work. The

11. In early 2016, final legislation on foreign NGOs was still pending.

effect of this pincer movement is a civil society that is steadily less civil and more controlled.

There are recognised non-communist 'democratic' parties, eight in all, conspicuously loyal, including a Kuomintang Party with about 50,000 members that was formed after the 1949 revolution by Kuomintang left-wingers who did not flee to Taiwan. These parties have a nominal representation in the National People's Congress and local congresses, and the People's Political Consultative Conferences, but under CCP control. The party, then, is finally bigger than itself. The broader party system amounts to a corporatist network that incorporates public and private bodies and associations, and persons, into a grand symbiosis under top-down control.

Outside observers tend to see the CCP as inscrutable and opaque. So it is, but it is not as bad as is often thought. From villages and up, the party organisation is in the hands of a secretary, with deputies (typically, for example, two or three in each village), and a party committee. There are local commissions of discipline inspection down to the town level that report up the line, ultimately to the Central Commission for Discipline Inspection. The party runs about 2,800 political and administrative schools, from the Central Party School, with its superb campus next to the Summer Palace in Beijing, and down, that offer shorter (say two or three months or less) and longer (say a year) courses that cadres with ambitions need to attend to get ahead, and are often obliged to attend at regular intervals.

The rule is that officials are appointed by the next level up, so that on any level party officials answer upwards, much as in any other bureaucratic organisation. The exception to this rule is at the bottom, at the village level, and at the top. At the village level, party members elect the party secretary, but only 'sort of' since those elected must still be approved and can be vetoed by party officials one level up. At the top, the leadership must re-elect or renew itself, and this is where things do get seriously opaque. Formally, the leaders are elected by the Central Committee of the National Party Congress, but in reality the elections are settled in advance through complicated discussions, negotiations, and manipulations between people representing party factions. This process has been simplified by (more or less fixed) term limits and age rules of retirement—a term limit of five years in most top jobs, a maximum tenure of two terms, a maximum age of sixty-seven to start a new term—but is still complicated (and term and retirement rules can be relaxed when needs be). Party elders tend to emerge from the woodworks and get involved in backroom machinations to get matters settled and manipulate their outcomes.

The party organisation is Leninist from top down so that at any level the party secretary, up to the general secretary, is the boss. But the officials work with the help of party committees, up to the National Party Congress. These are nominally recruited from below. At the village level, the party committee is elected by village party members, but again only 'sort of' since the final selection is controlled from above by the town-level party. From there up, party committees are made up of 'delegates', some of whom are selected by the party committee below and others by various stakeholders. The National Party Congress consists of delegates from the provinces and from party and government departments, state-owned enterprises, banks, army and police, and a cluster of invited delegates, mainly party elders.

Formally, the party does not decide on policies but, according to its constitution, 'provides leadership and assists administrative departments' and others. Laws are made by the People's Congress and government decisions by the State Council and ministries. But the party decides what is to be decided, appoints the main deciders, and monitors how policies are implemented. In Chinese governance, indeed in Chinese society, nothing (important) happens that the party does not want (which is not to say that what the party wants always happens).

Its first task—deciding what is to be decided—the party pursues in two ways, by commands and by signals. Commands, including appointments, are issued on paper, as resolutions, communiqués, or in other forms. For example, when the party decided to move China into the period of reform and opening up in 1978, this policy was set in stone at the Third Plenum of the 11th Central Committee, which was held in Beijing from 18 to 22 December of that year. The Central Committee did this in its 'Communiqué', adopted on 22 December, in which its decisions and conclusions were summarised. The new policy was driven through by Deng Xiaoping, who had been rehabilitated for the second time in 1977, and who was now able to get it formalised.

As it happened, however, that was not the end of the matter. Conservatives in the party continued to resist the reform direction. There was a constant jostling for leadership positions, in which Deng usually prevailed, but after the uprisings in 1989, the reform policy was in the balance. Deng, although officially retired, managed to tip the balance back in favour of reform by means of shrewd and elegant politicking in what became known as his 'southern inspection tour' in 1992, to China's most prosperous region, where he was able to put the benefits of reform, and popular support for it, on sharp display. Although the reform decision had been made fourteen years earlier, it was only now that it became irreversibly established.

The important Third Plenum in 2013 and Fourth Plenum in 2014 both concluded as usual with communiqués. These were rather bland and bewildering but were then followed up, about a week later, by summary documents labelled 'decisions', under the authority of the general secretary, which was where the leadership's ambitious reform agendas were spelled out in some more detail. In the 2014 case, this was followed up with yet another document of 'interpretations' by the general secretary.

So from the party flows a stream of commands that others are expected to comply with. But public policy co-ordination is never a matter of simply giving orders and certainly not in so big and complex a system as the Chinese one. More subtle means are also needed, in part to shore up orders by encouragements and in part as an alternative to the crude mechanism of issuing commands. The Chinese leaders are deft in the use of signal politics: Slogans, catchwords, indications, encouragements, and campaigns proliferate. When Hua Guofeng became party chairman after Mao's death in 1976, he vowed to continue to do 'whatever' Mao had said and done, and 'whateverism' became a signal of policy direction. Hu Jintao, general secretary and president until 2012, used the slogans of 'harmonious society' and 'scientific development' to try to temper China's obsession with GDP growth with more concern for social justice and regional balance. In 2007, when Hu took up at a Politburo meeting the issue of illegal land seizure by local governments, he did so by urging the resolution of 'contradictions and problems' in the countryside. That was a signal to lower-level authorities to deal with the problem practically. What was initially done at the top was only to signal. It was then for those lower down the line to do something about it, first for provincial governments to pick up the gauntlet and then for lower-level governments to move according to pressures from the provinces. Although the central government later moved to set up a bureaucracy to oversee rural land use, it is not clear what action eventually followed on the ground, or what was done where. In 2013, Xi Jinping made the China Dream his grand slogan.

The second task of the party is to monitor the follow-up to and compliance with the leadership's will. That it does, firstly, by the means of brute control that a dictatorship has at its disposal and by the presence of party committees or organs in non-party organisations of all kinds.

Furthermore, and importantly, the party controls personnel matters and appointments in all sectors and levels of the party-state, including executive agencies, the military, the police, the judiciary, government-owned enterprises, cultural institutions, media, academies, universities, institutes, and schools. It runs tight procedures of cadre management through what is known as the *nomenklatura* system, in principle lists of posts under party control and lists of candidates for those posts. Officials, from the lowest level and up, are monitored annually and their performance graded on a points scale in relation to established priorities, targets, and performance indicators, resulting in their being classified as excellent, competent, or incompetent. This is done by party officials one level up, or for junior cadres by their own leaders. Leading cadres sign performance contracts in relation to policy priorities and are held personally responsible for the attainment of those targets. Party and administrative leaders are subjected to 'democratic appraisal meetings' where they are evaluated by colleagues and representatives of 'the masses' below. Good performance is a condition of promotion and is otherwise rewarded with economic bonuses, elevation in the party hierarchy, or fancy titles (e.g., 'advanced leader' or 'model leader' or 'outstanding party secretary'). Through this system, not only does the party control appointments and promotions, but also policy priorities given from above are turned into personal incentives, officials are made to answer upwards, and promotions made dependent on satisfying those higher up the system.

Personnel management in this form is executed in astonishing detail as an effective tool of cadre control. But it is also a system wrought with defects. It is shot through with corruption and with the buying and selling of positions and promotions. Officials are made to identify with orders from above and towards indifference to the concerns and interests of the people below whom they govern, who are bereft of oversight power. If leaders translate their priorities wrongly or with poor balance into their points lists, distortions may accumulate. As always with targets, cheating and misreporting is rampant, something that cannot easily be checked when those in charge sit above and do not know except theoretically the conditions on the ground, and those below have no say. Recently, what has given the most performance points, although the details vary across the country, is economic growth, maintenance of social order, the collection of tax revenues, and the meeting of birth control targets, while the maintenance of environmental quality or social welfare has counted less.

The military

The People's Liberation Army is the armed wing of the party. It is the ultimate guarantor of party-state power, on standby to be mobilised whenever needed anywhere in the country (a capacity greatly enhanced thanks to the new network of high-speed rail). It is today a fairly straight professional military organisation. That is a recent development and has grown out of two previous incarnations. In a first period, roughly the Mao era, the PLA was a combined military and political organisation, with a strong involvement in political decision-making and public administration. In a second period, roughly the Deng era, it metamorphosed into a combined military and business organisation, while its political role was rolled back. State finances were depleted, and Deng let the military leadership know that they would have to find other sources of funding and encouraged them to go into business. That they did with relish, and the PLA engaged in entrepreneurship on a grand scale, in manufacturing, construction, pharmaceutics, foreign trade, hotels, entertainment, and more, much of it illegal and mired in corruption. This period came to an end during the 1990s, when the PLA was promised adequate funding from the reformed state budget and forced to divest from its business activity, although far from all of it, something, along with the affiliated corruption, that had worn seriously on its standing and esteem in the population.

The PLA is still very much a part of the Chinese political system. It not only controls the guns on behalf of the party but is also represented in the major state organs and exercises indirect veto power in top appointments. Almost all PLA officers are party members. Those who want to lead China must have the backing of those who lead its ultimate apparatus of physical force. When Xi Jinping won the battle for party leadership in 2012 and was able to take up the chairmanship of the Central Military Commission without delay, it was in part thanks to his connectedness inside the military system. Once in office, he returned the compliment by flattering the military for its importance to the nation and increasing its budget, cementing the intimacy of party–military unity.

It also remains an integrated part of the apparatus of governance. Measured in personnel, it is an organisation between 2 and 3 million strong.[12] In addition to national security, PLA garrisons around the country are used for internal purposes, such as to assist in emergencies, provide human resources to major construction projects (probably now to a lesser degree), and to quell civil unrest (although heavy security duties are increasingly taken over by the People's Armed Police).

The PLA is under the political control of the party through the Central Military Commission. The Ministry of Defence is mainly an administrative agency without independent command capacity. The system is infused with party control and sheltered from other civilian control. It runs a network of military industries, transport facilities, including airports and railways, hospitals, education institutions up to university level, and its own court system.

Under the Central Military Commission, there is a general staff with various administrative departments, the army, navy, and air force organisations, militia and reserve forces, and seven military regions. The People's Armed Police reports to both the Central Military Commission and the State Council.

The executive

Public administration is under the direction of the State Council, nominally the executive organ of the legislature. This is a body of some twenty-five members, headed by a premier and consisting of heads of ministries and core commissions. But this being China, one leadership body is not enough. On top of the State Council is an executive council consisting of the premier, four vice-premiers, five state councillors (super-ministers with broad briefs) and a secretary general.

Nominally, the State Council works through its ministries and their subordinate agencies down the line, but the real workings of this machinery are obscure and often different from how it is presented in organisational charts. Not only are there party secretaries and committees operating side by side with the administrators, but there is also a swath of formal and informal groups and committees across ministerial

12. In September 2015, Xi Jinping announced an intended reduction of military personnel by 300,000.

lines and with party and administrative representation that lead, control, direct, and coordinate.

Like other governments, the Chinese one is constantly scrambling to make itself more streamlined and effective. At the 2013 National People's Congress, the number of State Council Ministries was reduced from twenty-seven to twenty-five. The Ministry of Railways, a hotbed of corruption, was abolished and its functions absorbed into the Ministry of Transportation. The National Population and Family Planning Commission and the Ministry of Health were merged into a National Health and Family Planning Commission. Various other lower-level agencies were reorganised or merged. There is much experimentation, in the spirit of 'new public management', with outsourcing of public service provision to non-governmental organisations, which, however, are generally less non-governmental than we are used to thinking of NGOs in Western societies. The administration works prudently and often consultatively. In mid-2014, for example, the Guangzhou city government published a draft regulation of 'social organisations' for consultation, in which was included a provision that NGOs would be barred from receiving foreign financial support. That led to strong objections from the local NGO community on the argument that many would be unable to continue their work. When the final regulation was published, the proposed ban on foreign funds had been removed and replaced by a duty to report on the receipt of foreign support.

It is also a reform-oriented government. This reflects, no doubt, a genuine awareness that public administration must improve in delivery and effectiveness to keep up with economic and societal developments but also a need to be seen to be a responsive and dynamic government. The leadership that came in in 2012–13, not least Xi Jinping himself, spread indications around with much energy of pending reforms. Corruption was to be cleaned up, economic management modernised, capital controls relaxed, the household registration system reformed, birth control policies relaxed, the labour camp system abolished, and so on. What will come of it is uncertain, both because the road from intention to implementation is long and steep and because (in the words of one observer) 'policy pronouncements are two a penny in Beijing'. Those who might have hope that 'reform' would mean a relaxation of Leninist principles have been disappointed.

The administration is reproduced down the line of what is often referred to as 'the local state' so that most central organs, including ministries, work through 'their' local sub-organs (although not in a unified way across the country), with the complication that central sub-organs and genuinely local organs often work side by side and with overlapping responsibilities and authorities. The local executive is headed by a quasi-premier—governors of provinces, governors or mayors of counties, and heads of towns and townships.

The provinces and equivalents, counties/cities and towns/townships, are organised with mainly the same organs as the centre and with government and party organisations next to each other. At each level, the executive is responsible to the local people's congress and its standing committee at the same level, and to state organs one level up. The local people's congresses and (at the county and province levels) their standing committees have legislative power, within the limits of higher-level law.

In this orderly hierarchy, there are two irregularities. First, provinces (except directly administered municipalities and special administrative regions) are divided into prefectures. These, however, are not local governments within the chain of command but administrative units of the provinces. Second, some 'special economic zones', which also do not sit neatly in the chain of command, govern themselves and have legislative powers of their own in certain questions.

The central-local structure has been rearranged in several rounds under the People's Republic but now seems to be roughly settled. There are, however, considerable movements of authority within the general framework. One movement, of great importance, is in the division of labour between the centre and local government. During the reform period, there has been a radical decentralization of responsibility downwards to local levels. The central government increasingly works through regulatory 'mandates.' These are specific duties imposed on local governments which, more than in the previous habit of management by command, it is up to the local government to decide how to resolve, and often to fund. A second movement, at the local level, is to increase the role and authority of county-level governments, which are being cultivated as core units of local administration. And a third movement is towards rationalisation at the town level towards the merger of villages and townships into larger town units.

Decentralisation has represented a radical change in Chinese public administration. More than previously, what the state *does* is being done locally. But it has still been only a partial decentralisation. While government *expenditure* has been decentralised, the control over *revenue* has been centralised. About 80 percent of all government spending is now in local hands, up from about 50 percent thirty years ago, but upwards of 50 percent of all government revenue is under the control of the central government, up from about 15 percent thirty years ago.[13] Decentralisation, then, has been of responsibility while power has instead been centralised. To the degree that decisions by the 2013 Third Plenum are implemented, there will be further centralisations of power in the years to come. The doing will still be decentralised, but the deciding centralised so that increasingly local governments will act as agents of the central command.

13. The intention in the great fiscal reforms in the early 1990s was to raise the central share of public revenue to 60 percent, but, as with so many decisions in Beijing, this has not been achieved.

Who does what in this complicated system of public administration is not easily said. The division of labour between ministries, and between their subordinate organs down the line, is pretty straightforward although, as in most government systems, there are stronger and weaker ministries, and there is all nature of party and governmental co-ordinating organs that may well eclipse the formal authority of ministries. From a chaotic management of public finances, China is (supposedly) moving to all public revenues and expenditures, central and local, being contained in a consolidated fiscal budget. That would mean more central economic control and more clout to the Ministry of Finance.

The division of labour in the local state is, however, thoroughly intractable. There are shared, overlapping, and competing responsibilities in areas such as tax collection, education, and the provision of public services. What is done locally, and at what level, varies across the country, much depending on financial capacity, which differs enormously both between and within provinces. Affluent villages, for example, may provide a range of services for citizens and poor ones next to nothing. There are different traditions locally of obedience or resistance to central government instructions, and different cultures of governance. With some simplification, we can say that provincial-level governments form a second layer of central government in the sense that they are mainly in the business of deciding what should be done and of exercising oversight, while the doing is in the hands of lower-level authorities, which is to say that local government proper—where the state meets the people—starts at the county level. From there down, there is no straight division of labour. Tax collection and other forms of revenue raising is a major issue for everyone. All local governments are involved in the production of administration, in bloated public bureaucracies and hence in the provision of employment, importantly so in poor areas. The preservation of social order is another shared responsibility at all levels of government. Education and social security are strongly, but not exclusively, county responsibilities, and social services a town and village responsibility. But the only general rule, in the new spirit of decentralisation, seems to be that local governments at the various levels can by and large do what they can afford to do. One result of decentralisation of responsibility is that local governments are encouraged to initiative and allowed to enjoy the fruits of economic success, whereby success breeds success, affluence breeds affluence, failure breeds failure, and poverty breeds poverty.

Villages have surprisingly broad responsibilities, including public services, land management, order, birth control, social welfare, and dispute resolution. Governance is under the oversight of a village assembly, comprising all adults or heads of household, the village committee, and a village head (both elected, the village head usually being a party member), and obviously the party committee and secretaries. Villages and local urban units work through arrays of subcommittees and subunits, often interspersed with other local agencies under state control, as government tentacles, along with the omnipresent party ones, that reach down to the street and neighbourhood levels.

At the end of the line, the citizen is a pretty helpless subject, under the weight of the many party-state bureaucracies. His or her station is to grin and bear. That strain causes unrest, which is continuous, most of it in reaction to wrongdoing and power abuses by local authorities, little of it directed at systemic defects. In an ancient tradition, local people can 'petition' central authorities to rectify local wrongdoings, now even online. This, however, is mainly a safety valve that allows discontents to let off steam. It is generally ineffective and, although legal, frequently dangerous. Petitioning does not reflect well on local governments, which often have agents in provincial capitals and in Beijing looking out for petitioners from their districts and who round them up to be returned home or confined to black jails before they are able to bring their discontent to the attention of higher authorities. But in the post-2013 spirit of reform, even petitioning is to be improved, and petitioners to be given stronger legal protections.

The legislature

It's a reflection of the real hierarchy of power to deal with the legislature after the party and executive. The lawmaker is not paramount, and 'law' does not have the same meaning in the party-state as in a rule-of-law system.

The top lawmaker is the National People's Congress (NPC), a body of about 2,900 members. It is composed of deputies from the provincial-level units, state and party organs, and the armed forces, works on five-year terms, and meets annually. It makes law, amends the constitution, and appoints officials to senior state posts, including the president and vice-president, the State Council and its premier and vice-premiers, the Supreme People's Court, and the Supreme People's Procuratorate (and formally the Central Military Commission which, however, in reality has already been appointed by the party). It approves national economic plans and state budgets and has various other duties as nominally the highest organ of the state. All these duties, of course, it exercises under party leadership in the usual obscure ways. The normal route for legislation is that at least significant laws are approved by the party's Politburo ahead of being finally submitted to the legislature, which, however, in a recent development, is also directly and formally involved in the drafting of laws.

The NPC does not have a monopoly on lawmaking. On the national level, also the State Council can make law, at least law-like regulations and decrees, and locally so can local peoples' congresses and administrative and party organs. Party rules as well are formally laws. The Supreme Court and the Supreme Procuratorate both publish judicial interpretations, and various ministries and similar agencies judicial regulations, all spelling out the specifics of laws passed by the people's congresses. The Supreme Court regularly issues instructions to lower courts (which are often not published and hence 'law' although not necessarily known by those it applies to), which may contradict formal law but still have overriding status.

China is no longer a society without laws, as it pretty much was under Mao's rule. The state constitution is a big and in many ways admirable code which prescribes the rules and limitations of governance in detail, the current one adopted in 1982 with amendments in 1988, 1993, and 1999. It enshrines various social rights, including the right to assistance from the state, the right to education, women's rights, and the rights of elderly people, of children, and of people with disabilities. Various workers' rights are included in the Labour Law of 1994 and later revisions. A Law on the Protection of Senior Citizens' Rights came into force in 1996. In 1989, in the Administrative Litigation Law, and further in the Administrative Reconsideration Law (1999), Chinese citizens gained the right to sue government agencies, mainly local, a right that has subsequently been used quite extensively although not without risk of retaliation by the relevant or superior agencies. In the reforms announced in the 2014 Fourth Plenum, this right is supposed to be extended to the important matter of land management. Party organs cannot be sued, and the availability of suit against more central state organs and quasi-state organisations, such as universities, is ambiguous. In 2007, the People's Congress passed a Law on the Protection of Disabled Persons and a resolution on The Rights of Disabled Persons, and in 2010 a Law on Social Insurance.

The prevailing legal theory remains that law is in the service of socialism, which means that the party can both make law-like rules by its own actions and override legal decisions that are 'wrong'. Exactly what 'the law' is is never clear. It is now less unclear than it has been previously under the People's Republic, but given the precarious state of law earlier, that is not saying much. Nevertheless, the direction of movement has been towards better regularisation of governance in law. The Fourth Plenum in 2014 represented an energetic continuation of that movement.

The National People's Congress elects a Standing Committee of about two hundred members that has legislative power when the NPC is not in session and meets about every two months for about a week at a time. In addition, there are nine subcommittees, for areas such as finance and economics, law, and agriculture. These committees have a staff of their own and work continuously. They are involved in the drafting of legislation and have certain powers of supervision in their respective fields of authority. The Standing Committee is the nearest in China to a parliament or national assembly as that would be understood elsewhere. The National People's Congress is not where major policy decisions are made and is often described as a 'rubber stamp' legislature, but that characterisation still underestimates its real functions as it has evolved in recent years.

The Chinese People's Political Consultative Conference (CPPCC) is a consultative body (although it had more substantive functions in the early years of the People's Republic) and a forum for not insignificant debate. It has about 2,000 delegates and meets annually, at the same time as the plenary session of the National People's Congress, and, like the NPC, has a standing committee that meets more frequently. Effectively, the People's Congress meetings bring together a national élite of some 5,000 delegates for about a week each year. The 2014 CPPCC included a delegation of thirty-five expatriate Chinese from twenty-one countries, all with foreign nationalities. There are also local consultative conferences.

The police

China is a police state with a huge security apparatus, within which society is poorly policed. Lawlessness is rampant in business and government, and resort to police protection hard to come by. Police forces are poorly trained, and in much of the country in short supply for the provision of law and order in daily life. Officers in leadership positions generally have some formal police training, while patrol officers often have little or no training other than on the job. Police behaviour is abusive, thuggish, and corrupt, in poorly equipped and low-morale services. The use of torture in interrogations is widespread although illegal.[14] There have been gradual improvements in law as to the regulation of police activity and the protection of the individual, but the police still have wide discretionary powers within the law, including of detention, and legal limitations on policing are routinely flaunted.

The very concept of 'police' is ambiguous. There are various police forces, on all government levels. Non-police forces and authorities engage in policing and have police-like powers, including the army, party organs, and administrative agencies. The investigation of crime by party and government officials is not usually handled by the police but by the party's Discipline and Inspection Commission. Police officials often operate in civilian dress and appear out of thin air at, for example, threatening gatherings or manifestations. Civilian thugs engaged in stability management, easily visible to even the cursory visitor, are often contract workers with no formal police authority or position. On critical occasions, such as the meeting of the National Party Congress or National People's Congress, more or less well-known more or less oppositional activists may be visited at home by 'someone' who orders them out of town for the critical period, on unknown authority but with the threat that if they do not go of their own, they will be removed and possibly locked up. The extent of secret policing is obviously unknown but is by any reckoning extensive. The security forces

14. On the use of torture and mistreatment in pre-trial detention, see Human Rights Watch, *Tiger Chairs and Cell Bosses*, May 2015.

include networks of spies and informers, including 'security volunteers' and 'security informants' who are paid by the piece of information they deliver.

The prime business of the security apparatus is stability management and state security. That business is under tight central control, as one of the main party-government leadership portfolios. Stability is a core administrative responsibility for party and government authorities on all administrative levels, down to the lowest local level. Security organs on all levels are under the dual control of their territorial party committee and of the security organs one level up.

There are two security ministries, the Ministry of Public Security and the Ministry of State Security. The Ministry of Public Security heads up the police service proper, a force about 800,000 strong, the paramilitary People's Armed Police (which, however, also reports to the Central Military Commission), and manages affiliated affairs such as the household registration and identification card systems. The police force works through Public Security Bureaus down the administrative line, the Public Security Stations the end-line organs. Police officers now more usually than previously carry arms. The People's Armed Police forms a national force of its own, perhaps a million and a half or more strong, organised in forty-five divisions, with responsibility for internal security, border control, the guarding of government buildings, and various specialised services (including executions in capital punishment cases). In recent years, the internal security system has been growing relentlessly. The security apparatus is one of several 'states within the state' and is, as usual in dictatorships, difficult to control. From the 2011 budget, allocations for domestic security, central and local, have outstripped even the large and growing military budget.[15]

The Ministry of State Security heads the People's Republic of China's domestic and external intelligence services, including espionage, counter-espionage, and counter-revolutionary surveillance.

The Ministry of Justice is in charge of legal affairs, including the court and prison systems.[16] Other ministries and agencies, such as rail, transport, and aviation, have security organisations of their own with policing powers.

Although some previous police powers of detention have been removed, such as the 'shelter and investigation' provision which allowed the police to hold detainees indefinitely, others remain. Citizens can be detained in various forms of extrajudicial 'black jails' under police control or held in, for example, 'residential surveillance', either at home or in 'a designated place' (which, for example, were the circumstances of the artist Ai Weiwei's eighty-one days of secret detention in 2011).

---

15. Although it is not known how much was actually spent or whether the military budget might subsequently have caught up.
16. But not, for example, the Qincheng prison north of Beijing, which confines many of China's fallen élite, in better conditions than most prisoners, and which is run by the Ministry of Public Security.

Since its inception, the People's Republic has maintained a network of 're-education through labour' camps, an administrative provision that was used widely and with detention in principle for up to three years but in practice often longer. The sanction was decided by local committees of approval and management and executed by the police without further judicial control. The detained were not considered criminals and their confinement not considered imprisonment, wherefore judicial controls under normal criminal law did not apply. The re-education through labour provision is supposed to be phased out, following decisions by the 2013 Third Plenum, but what that means is not clear. It is not known if the labour camps will be closed down, renamed, or modified, nor what may come in their place. The security services can hold persons in 'criminal detention' for extended periods, certainly up to two years, in extra-legal detention centres, such as for prostitutes and drug addicts, in 'legal education classes', or 'detention for education', in 'work-study detention for juveniles', in all of which cases detention again is or may be by administrative decisions much as in previous labour camps. They also run secret ('black') prisons and 'chastisement centres'. An obscure authority is that of the para-police *chengguan*, a local government agency to enforce rules on street trade, parking, and the like, but which in some cities has taken on policing powers and police paraphernalia and been deployed to, for example, round up, fine, and evict migrant workers and vagrants, often with thuggish and violent means.

The judiciary

The judiciary is under the management of the Ministry of Justice, the Commission for Legal Affairs, the Supreme People's Court, and the Supreme People's Procuratorate. The exercise of law is overseen by a system of courts and related organs. To some degree the courts function as neutral mediators of conflict, but the court system is underdeveloped in capacity and expertise and, in important matters, under political control and command. The system is also widely corrupt. Judges do not enjoy high social esteem in Chinese society and are not well paid. Indeed, the whole legal profession is held in low public regard. Professional legal services are often provided by non-lawyers. Lawyers need a state licence to practise and undergo annual performance evaluations, the outcome of which influences decisions about maintaining or removing the licence.

The court system builds hierarchically downwards from the supreme court and includes high courts on the provincial level, intermediate-level courts, and basic courts at the county level. Courts are under double political control and pressure, from local and central authorities. The centre may want to clean the court system of local political control, but that is easier said than done. Local courts are funded locally and hence under local political control. In a reform push from 2006 to

2008, the Politburo decided to take the funding of courts out of the hands of local governments and put them under central funding so as to give the courts more independence, but this turned out to be another decision that was never implemented.

Each court is divided into civil, criminal, and administrative chambers, and sometimes has additional specialist chambers. About 80 percent of cases are handled in the basic courts. There are special jurisdiction courts for military, railway, transport, and maritime cases. The military court system is vast, headed by the PLA Supreme Military Court, under the Central Military Commission, and with sub-courts in the military regions and services and in the People's Armed Police. It has both civil and military jurisdiction in cases that involve military institutions or personnel. Basic courts operate local subdivisions, known as People's Tribunals, which hear simple civil and criminal cases. Tribunals mediate in local disputes and assist in the local implementation of government policy, such as tax collection, birth control, and the like.

Courts consist of a president and vice-presidents, who are elected by the people's congress at the corresponding level, and of judges, who are nominated by the court president and approved by the standing committee of the relevant people's congress. None of these officials have security of tenure. Most cases are heard by a panel of three judges, under the supervision of the court presidents. The quality of the judiciary is low and inconsistent, judges poorly trained, if legally trained at all, competent lawyers generally preferring more lucrative private practice to underpaid court service. It continues to be dangerous for lawyers to take on 'sensitive' cases, and the authorities have strictures they can apply to 'difficult' attorneys. Access to court procedure is cumbersome, in administrative cases, for example, because of tight statutes of limitation, and because the courts have extensive discretionary authority to reject submissions. Courts have low authority, administrative courts, for example, often being unable to even summon the parties complained against. In civil cases, there is a low ability to get verdicts enforced. Even in successful administrative cases, little tends to be awarded in compensation for wrongs suffered.

The procuratorate system down the levels of government is in charge of criminal investigations, therein directing the police, and of prosecutions. It is also charged, along with the supreme court, with supervising the execution of law and with seeing to it that that the law is applied as politically intended. It can initiate the overruling of verdicts in the courts that go in a 'wrong' direction. In theory, there is a division of authority. In criminal cases, for example, the procuratorate decides on prosecution, the security services investigate, and the courts rule on dues, guilt, and punishment. But practice is more 'flexible'. The procuratorate is not supposed to decide on guilt and punishment, but in reality it often can and does. Criminal cases that are brought to court generally result in convictions, often through brief and summary proceedings.

Punishable offenses are political as well as criminal, the first category including, for example, the spreading of rumours, the disturbance of public order, and transgressions against public security or state secrets. A frequently used charge is 'picking quarrels and causing trouble'. Independent social organisations, such as think tanks, find themselves unable to register as non-profit organisations and instead register as private businesses. This makes them vulnerable to being charged for 'illegal business', a charge which is often used to disrupt uncontrolled action.

The most severe reaction in criminal law is the death penalty. The number of executions has been going down steadily for many years, to about 2,400 in 2013. That is still three times as many as in the rest of the world combined. Prison conditions vary but are generally primitive and harsh. The prison population is not excessively large and is, for example, smaller relative to the population than in the United States or Russia.

The present reform-minded leaders are, they say, determined to strengthen the standing of the law and of the judiciary. Among the many reforms adopted by the 2013 Third Plenum were measures to improve the judicial system, in principle towards greater judicial autonomy.

The Fourth Plenum in late 2014 dealt specifically with the rule of law. As usual, a raft of policies and reforms were announced, as usual leaving observers in confusion about what might be intended and unfolding. The co-existence of two legal systems was ratified, the state system and the party system, the *shuanggui*. The law is the party's servant rather than the party being the law's servant, and the supremacy of the party above the law was confirmed. So were the 'three supremes' according to which legal duty, including of judges, is to the party, the people, and the law, in that order. The concept of human rights is mentioned in the decision from the plenum, but human rights lawyers are not given reason to hope for much or any improvement in their working conditions or in the resort to law by their clients. Rule of law means and will continue to mean 'socialist rule of law with Chinese characteristics'. The plenum did not suggest any substantial institutional redesigns or improvements of the judicial system and is best seen as a continuation of efforts towards more controlled procedures of political management.

To the degree that pronouncements are followed up, not only the judiciary but also public administration and the military will be, step by careful step, increasingly regulated by a more effective body of law. That is not nothing, but nor is it rule of law in a non-Chinese understanding. It is rather what an authority on Chinese law, Jerome A. Cohen, has called 'legalist Leninism'. Legal theory has not changed much since Mao pronounced on it in 1958: 'We can't do without this law stuff, but we have our own way. Civil law and criminal law has so many provisions—who can remember them all? I participated in drafting the constitution but even I don't remember what it says. We basically don't rely on these things to maintain order.' Practice remains that the law does not bind party and state authorities when those authorities choose not to be bound by it.

The party still holds ultimate power over the interpretation of the nation's constitution.[17] To the degree that the party is bound by constitutional constraints, it is bound by its own constitution, which is different from the state constitution. While the leaders in the Great Hall of the People were praising 'the rule of law', their *shuanggui* officials in the anti-corruption campaign were pursuing real and imagined malfeasants in entirely extra-legal procedures. This campaign is in the hands of party organs and shielded from 'civilian' judicial control. Those under investigation are at risk of mistreatment and torture. They are without adequate defence in the process and once handed over to the judicial system for trial without effective rights to offer evidence and call witnesses. In the tradition of Chinese justice, almost all of those who have been brought to trial have been convicted.

State Capacity

A constant concern among China watchers is the capacity of the state machinery to deliver the governance that is needed in so big and changing a society as the Chinese one. Warnings are often sounded that the combination of capitalism in the economy and Leninism in the polity is unsustainable. Many have over the years predicted the system's demise because of its in-built contradictions.

This concern is, however, misplaced. The good-cop, bad-cop act is fine-tuned and effective. That fine-tuning gets adjusted as conditions change, 'stability' the outcome.

It is true that there is much waste and inefficiency in public administration and that much that is decided politically does not get implemented administratively, or implemented in full. It is also true that it is difficult to know just what is going on. The regime is eager to inform about decisions, plans, and intentions, but information about what follows through, and where and how, is more difficult to come by. Judgments are therefore often made from interpretations of policy pronouncements and of what *might* happen, with less of facts on the table about what actually *does* happen. But for all that, there is no shortage of public policy. Reading the premier's reports on the work of the government to the National People's Congress is dizzying. In one way, they read like the report of any ambitious government – a Scandinavian social democrat would take delight in language in the 2014 report: 'to achieve the goal of ensuring housing for all, we will . . .' Policies are rolling forward in virtually all areas of economic, social and cultural life. The 2015 report singles out small businesses which it notes 'can accomplish great things', wherefore 'we need to give them a leg

17. Constitutionally, that authority sits with the Standing Committee of the National People's Congress, but that committee is without ability to exercise this authority.

up to get them going'. The endless list of 'we will . . .' is obviously self-promotion but not a pack of lies. This is a government that is *doing* and that has its finger in every national pie.

Chinese governance is anything but static and is in continuous movement and revision. The rules and procedures of administration are in constant, perpetual, and energetic development. In 1994, in what might be described as the mother-of-all administrative restructurings short of revolution, the whole system of public finance and taxation was redesigned in one big bang, bringing with it a realignment of power and functions between central and local authorities and fortifying the fiscal basis of the state. When Premier Zhu Rongji got capital markets operating, sold off poorly performing state-owned enterprises, saw 24 million state workers laid off, and guided China into the World Trade Organisation (in 2001), he was not presiding over a sclerotic political economy.

The current leadership is determined to continue shaking up their systems. Reform is everywhere and is the leadership's message wherever they look. Officials are admonished to change their ways and improve their methods. The 2013 Third Plenum, which we have visited several times, laid out a broad agenda for the new leadership, touching on almost all areas of governance (down to a decision to scale back the entertainment corps of the People's Liberation Army—in which the singer Peng Liyuan, the glamorous wife of Xi Jinping, was a general until the title was reformed out of the corps in 2013). Reforms were announced across the board, almost two hundred specific reforms in all, including both the content of policy—economic management, marketisation, birth control, penal policy—and the making of policy—central-local realignment, fiscal management, judicial management. The agenda indeed looks bold on economic reform, notably in further marketisation. If it looks less bold politically, that may be because some observers were looking for the wrong things. There was obviously no movement towards democratic opening up, but much was put in motion on policymaking and administration.[18] The Fourth Plenum a year later was equally hawkish on legal reform. All this was in line with the leadership's tightening of its grip on its own system.

Administrative capacity

The capacity of the Chinese state is visible in two arenas, in the generation of public policy and in the use of administrative force for social control.

On the first account, so far, the evidence is that the system is up to delivering what is needed for the maintenance of the regime. There are many shortcomings in public policy, and often setbacks, but if we keep in mind what it's about—

18. On the meaning of 'reform' in the Chinese system, see Fewsmith, *The Logic and Limits of Political Reform*. See also Pei, *China's Trapped Transition*.

self-perpetuation—what has been needed has been done. When Mao left the stage, the regime was in various ways bankrupt. It was bereft of moral authority, and state finances were depleted. The turnaround that was then imposed from above was monumental. No less than a new economic model was invented and implemented. The sector of state-owned enterprises was completely redesigned, as was public administration. The state was salvaged from bankruptcy. The People's Liberation Army had (some of) its rotten business cleaned up and was professionalised.

In recent years there has been much concern over 'fiscal imbalances', such as uncontrollable shadow banking, unsustainable debt, including in local government and state-owned enterprises, and housing and investment bubbles. Probably, no one truly understands Chinese finances, and certainly not Chinese banking, and something could blow up any day. In mid-2015, something did blow up in a stock market crash that took both political bosses and economic investors by surprise and showed up the limitations in the state's control of the economy. Shadow banking on a massive and out-of-control scale is a new irregularity with as yet unknown consequences, sometimes said to be a Ponzi scheme on a gigantic scale. Still, so far, 'contradictions' have been managed. For example, in the late 1990s, even before debt had become a critical concern, the government set up four 'bad banks', known as 'asset management companies' (under the names of Huarong, Orient, Great Wall, and Cinda) to help deal with non-performing debt in the banking system by taking some of the bad loans off the books of banks and credit vehicles. They have in turn been able to mobilise additional non-state and non-Chinese capital and bail out failing products, such as, for example, one known as 'China Credit Equals Gold #1' which had lured investors with extraordinary interests rates and been sold through one of the big state banks, the Industrial and Commercial Bank of China.[19] In October 2014, the Great Wall Corporation came to the rescue of a company known as Shanghai Chaori Solar Energy Science and Technology that was about to default in China's onshore bond market. The 2015 crash in the stock market that the government had itself hyped reignited old fears of fundamental imbalances. But, although many people lost a great deal of money, when the dust settled it again appeared that contradictions had been managed, or swept under the carpet, and that reasonable market participation and confidence seemed to have survived. Business observers may be annoyed with China for not making itself a 'proper' capitalist system, but normal capitalism is not the aspiration of the Chinese state. The economy is for the state; it is not the other way around.

The current leadership, and very much Xi Jinping personally, are determined not only to improve administrative capacity but to clean up state and party operations and to repair their tarnished reputations in the eyes of the citizens. They have done that in much-publicised campaigns against extravagance and corruption. It took

19. *Financial Times*, 31 August 2014.

the commentariat some time to grasp that these campaigns were serious. The initial instinct, in the light of previous similar campaigns, was to see it as propagandistic window dressing. But there are good reasons to think that this time it is different.

The anti-extravagance campaign has been to rein in bad habits in lavish meals and banquets and other perks. That campaign works, not so as to wipe out hospitality, which was never the intention, but to impose some sobriety. I know from my own experience as a recent guest of universities that Chinese generosity is alive and well, but now within limits and regulations. University administrators who do not follow up are at risk of being punished or demoted and take care to regulate matters on their own turf in a way that is visible to potential inspectors. The campaign has dampened excesses enough for the effects to be noticeable as less demand flowing to the restaurant and wine trades.

The anti-corruption campaign is on another level of drama. There have been campaigns against corruption under previous leaderships, but not as aggressive, deep, or lasting as the present one. It now appears to be the main concern of the party's discipline and inspection bureaucracy, which has been given enhanced powers and designated sub-agencies for the purpose. Its head, Wang Qishan, a member of the standing committee of the politburo and apparently Xi Jinping's closest ally, has by all accounts long believed that the party must, in self-interest, clean itself up in a serious way. The campaign has been running for a good time and does not seem to be being phased out. It is aimed at 'tigers' (high officials) as well as 'flies' (low officials), and more recently also 'spiders' (who sit at the centre of economic fiefdoms), and 'foxes' (corrupt officials who have taken their loot and themselves abroad). In a break with previous policy, in the 2014 G20 meeting of world leaders China signed up to international anti-corruption collaborations. Other governments, including the US one, are collaborating in fox hunting. Both low-level and high-level officials, both central and local, both serving and retired have been caught in the dragnet.

This campaign, like the anti-extravagance one, works. It has been put in the hands of central authorities whereby local authorities are less able to protect local officials. It has become more of a risk on all levels to engage in corruption. That probably means less corruption. Anecdotal evidence is forthcoming of people reporting normal access to services where they would previously have expected to pay. Writes one contact: 'One of our local village officials was hauled off a few weeks ago, the kind of corrupt thug I spent years fruitlessly battling. People like him once seemed bullet proof.' The gambling business in Macao has seen a sharp decline in activity, something the casinos ascribe in part to the anti-corruption drive in mainland China, be there less corruption money flowing or more caution with its display.

Corruption is as old as is history in China and has been a constant feature of governance under the People's Republic. So what is the campaign about and what is going on? Is it aimed to free China of public corruption, and could that be done?

Neither is likely. Xi's campaign may be more energetic than previous ones but is still, as previous ones, at least on low-level corruption, more about bad behaviour than about bad systems. The anti-corruption bureaucracy is being strengthened and improved and is spreading more fear, but the larger system is not being redesigned to become more corruption-proof.

The Chinese bureaucracy is as made for corruption. Always there are authorities controlling authorities. Officials answer upwards in systems that lack mechanisms of information on malfunctions or malpractices downwards. Higher officials have the power to punish or reward lower ones. Most activities, economic or social, depend on permission or authorisation from some agency or official, usually several.[20] Central regulations are often general and leave a good deal of discretion to local authorities. Favourable interpretations may come to those who return the favour and show their appreciation. It would be to expect superhuman virtue to think that a bureaucracy made for corruption does not breed corruption.

China in the era of economic opening up is a money culture in which money has become the measure of all value. In this culture it would seem unlikely that officials who have favours to distribute or withhold would not expect to be rewarded. Indeed, it is unthinkable that they, and probably also their clients, would not feel that they have a right to be rewarded if they give or do for others what is to their benefit. This is stimulated by an ancient tradition of gift giving: It is right and expected to bring gifts to those who help you or can help you. Corruption is not always a crude matter of payment being demanded. It can be subtle: a mutual understanding that a service today will be followed by a gift tomorrow, or a gift today by services tomorrow, in such a way that neither giver nor getter is embarrassed. If you know that you will be dependent on an official's beneficence next year, it may be prudent to clear the ground with a touch of generosity now.

Corruption comes about through individual action: The official lets the client know that appreciation is expected. It is a matter of misbehaviour by persons who break the rules. High-level embezzlement is straightforward crime, but in the Chinese case some low-level graft is in some ways different. It is systemic and institutionalised. It has become a regular feature of public administration. Rewards through corruption have come to be seen widely as a normal compensation for public work. It is a mechanism inside the system through which public officials get access to what they have come to experience as their fair share of rewards from the country's economic progress. It has been tacitly condoned officially. The removal of access to graft in a

20. A report on administrative reform written by a city mayor, Wang Tianqi of Suqian in Jiangsu province, identifies 569 types of licence, permit, and vocational qualification that city and district governments in his area are responsible for granting. In addition to being a source of graft (not the issue in the report), government departments generate huge revenues in fees from the required paperwork (*South China Morning Post*, 12 May 2015).

system that has become infused with and dependent on the distribution of corruption rewards would amount to a massive punishment on the purse of the public servants on whose service the leadership depends. That is simply something the leaders cannot afford to do. It is probably a reasonable interpretation of the campaign that it is not about ending low-level corruption but about getting it back to manageable proportions. Anti-corruption action is for obvious reasons popular and is a way, in a Chinese tradition, for the leadership to let people see that however they are abused locally there are at least honest and concerned leaders in Beijing.

Dictatorships do not have loyal servants. They only get service by giving their servants reasons to be loyal. In his *History of Government*, S. E. Finer explained a cardinal feature of any polity in what he called the problem of baron-management: 'The king can give effect to his orders only through them, the barons, who must therefore be induced to enthusiastic support (the best outcome) or acceptance (the next best) and discouraged from foot-dragging or, at the very worst, open resistance.' The Chinese kings have millions of barons, high and low, on whom they depend for effect to their orders. Enthusiastic support is beyond their reach, but also they are sufficiently in control that open resistance is unlikely. Their problem is to get acceptance and avoid foot-dragging. For some time now, the regime that has turned to ruling by rewards has allowed rewards to filter down to its servants through systemic graft and has in return had reasonable collaboration of acceptance back from those servants. If these rewards are removed and not compensated by other rewards or inducements, a slide from acceptance to foot-dragging is unavoidable. That may be happening. Anecdotal evidence suggests a tendency that officials revert to paralysis because they feel persecuted and are fearful of doing anything that may meet with displeasure from above.[21]

When there is corruption everywhere, enemies can be taken down for being corrupt and therefore with a sheen of legality, and anti-corruption becomes a sharp tool in internal machinations. The high officials who have been purged so far have systematically been from outside of Xi Jinping's camp and outside of the protected circle of princelings (except for Bo Xilai).

But the campaign clearly goes beyond internal power struggle and is a part of Xi and Co.'s determination to win real control over the system that is made up of the party-state and the socialist market economy. To achieve that, they must have control of their political machine, hence the purging of internal enemies. But they must also have control of their economic machine. That depends on crushing the power of the oligarchic class that has emerged through high-level corruption. When

21. At a state council conference on clean government in February 2015, the premier, Li Keqiang, complained about a combination of corruption and dereliction of duty in local government, saying that 'some officials are taking a wait and see attitude, being reluctant to implement major policies of the central government, and not caring to take their share of responsibility'. He announced an initiative to make local officials sign a written pledge to carry out policies faithfully (*China Daily*, 10 February 2015).

former security czar Zhou Yongkang was put under investigation in early 2014 and arrested near the end of the year, this was not just about a single man who had been misbehaving but about an oligarchic complex of officials, business cronies, and collaborating family, many of whom had already been taken down. When the vice-president of the Supreme People's Court in Beijing, Xi Xiaoming, was put under investigation in July 2015, it was allegedly for involvement in shady affairs in a coal company in a different part of the country.

What has emerged through high-level corruption is a kind of economic warlordism (not too strong a characterisation) in which essential powers are wrenched away from state authorities so that they lose real control of the realm. Central and local complexes of officials and business operators are outside of the reach of the state and able to plunder it with impunity, amassing both private wealth and economic power. Their crime is economic, and on a monumental scale, but also political. The party-state boasts being in control. But under the veneer of order and stability, a criminal class has been able to operate freely and challenge the party's supremacy of power. The anti-corruption campaign is no doubt about coming to grips with excesses in low-level corruption and the trading of public posts, but the final target is high-level organised crime. The present leadership takes the party-state-socialist-market-economy model seriously and intends to eliminate competing powers. For a Chinese leadership that takes itself seriously, 'control' is explanation enough. It wants control because anything it does not control, be it oppositional activities or economic operations, represents a threat against its determination to self-preserve. Previous leaders have allowed organised crime free rein out of fear that they might otherwise damage economic growth (and also taken the opportunity to dip their hands in the till themselves). The present leaders have reversed priorities and now set political control above economic growth.

The anti-corruption campaign is a display of administrative top-down capacity. The leadership is able to mobilise and reorganise its bureaucracy in pursuit of its political priorities. It is not just a campaign of words but of action which is felt high and low. It is not only determined but also ruthless. People kill themselves out of fear that they are next—several cases have been reported within the armed forces. But it is also a campaign *for* capacity and to make the model work as it should with some efficiency.

Much is at stake. The leaders are waging war against their own people and against enemies of the state within the state. Perhaps the party-state will come out of this a more efficient machine, but that is far from certain. It could pull itself apart. The party-state has done well in the reform period by restraining itself. The price has been progress with many blemishes, but progress nevertheless. When the party-state was dedicated to perfection, under Mao, things went terribly wrong for it. Perhaps it is the 'weak' leaders of the last decades who were the wiser in renouncing on perfection.

Their bureaucracies did the job of delivering the governance they needed to keep the wheels running. Now the leaders seem no longer content with that trade-off. If the new men again demand perfection, they may instead of progress with blemishes get new blemishes without progress, and demise rather than self-perpetuation.

They are in a bind. They cannot claim legitimacy for a state that is systematically dishonest and abusive. Growth is slowing, and they can no longer afford waste on a massive scale. They cannot let oligarchic economic cliques make a mockery of their own rule. But nor can they alienate the servants they depend on to do their work for them. They may have the capacity to clean some of the corruption out of their system, but they are at risk of doing that in a way that destroys their capacity to get work done through that very same system. The test for the regime is whether the leaders are able to get the balance right between pursuing high-level crime with a hard hand and cleaning up low-level graft with a soft hand. The danger is that they may fail in the first and turn on the small wrongdoers with a harshness that paralyses their own apparatus. They may think that they get what they want, but the risk is that oligarchs from outside and bureaucrats from inside take revenge by turning from acceptance to foot-dragging, and possibly to outright resistance.

Control capacity

If public administration is reasonably up to the job, it is, however, when we turn to social control that we see the state with its true and awesome capacity. In a population of close to 1.4 billion people spread out over the vast territory, its apparatus of control is everywhere, including through 'thought work' into the minds of Chinese women and men. The new leadership as of 2012–13 raised hopes of some liberalisation but soon turned instead to more intensive and systematic controls and crackdowns against and detentions of activists and refusenicks. We outside of China would mostly think, by instinct, that as China grows more affluent and confident, political controls would be relaxed. In fact, the trend is the other way. China may be opening up economically, but politically it is being shut down. Foreign journalists, foreign or foreign-supported NGOs, human rights lawyers, and university academics have experienced increasingly difficult working conditions and tighter controls. Both legislation and practice in these areas are being consistently tightened, for example, in expansively restrictive legislation on foreign NGOs as of 2015. Gradually, more people in such areas of work have become affected by political pressure, including moderates who had not previously expected that they would be of much interest to the authorities of control. The present leadership appears to be genuinely fearful of 'Western' ideas and influences. Activism and reasonably free expression of opinion in academia is not supressed in any blanket way, but the space for autonomy has been narrowed and become more enclosed. The Chinese leaders continue to abide by the wisdom ascribed to Lenin that trust is good but control better.

Here, summarising dispersed observations so far, is what this tight ship apparatus looks like and how it works.

(1) A constant duty of all party and state organs, in particular party organs in localities, businesses, and organisations, is information gathering. This even reaches beyond state borders. Chinese students in foreign universities, like other expatriates, are observed, as are their China scholarship teachers. Anything that is or might become dangerous is likely to be known of. The Chinese know this. When a brave mainland student in Hong Kong after much agony wrote an open letter in support of the 2014 revolt there, she did so under a pseudonym, since otherwise her future life and career in China would be in ruins.

(2) The security services are on hand to strike down on anyone anywhere who is in any way engaged in activities that are seen to be politically threatening. What is officially called 'stability maintenance'—*weiwen*—works. By and large citizens look after themselves. The controls are such that active opposition is not only difficult and dangerous but also futile.

It remains dangerous in present-day China to engage in political activity, manifestations, and social organisation. It is getting more dangerous. The organisation Chinese Human Rights Defenders documented 955 rights activists detained in 2014, almost as many as in the two previous years combined.[22] In coordinated raids in most of the country's provinces in early July 2015, more than two hundred human rights lawyers and activists were detained, on various vague charges such as 'colluding with petitioners', 'inciting subversion', and 'provoking trouble'.[23] According to the *People's Daily,* the Ministry of Public Security launched the operation to 'smash a major criminal gang that had used a Beijing law firm as a platform to draw attention to sensitive cases, seriously disturbing social order.'[24] In early September 2015, again in a coordinated action, five human rights lawyers were prevented from travelling to Hong Kong, two at Beijing airport, one at Wuhan airport, and two at the border at Shenzhen, on the grounds that they 'threatened national security'.

It is not necessary for the activism to be directed against the system for it to be seen as dangerous. It is official policy to combat corruption, but anti-corruption activism is still dangerous. It is official policy to protect children and the rights of women,

---

22. *New York Times*, 17 March 2015.
23. As of 20 July 2015, at least 132 lawyers and 104 law firm staff and activists had been caught in the dragnet, 14 criminally detained or under residential surveillance, 6 disappeared, and 216 temporarily detained (China Human Rights Lawyers Concern Group). 'This is the biggest crackdown on lawyers in China since the legal system was re-established in 1980 after the Cultural Revolution.' Teng Biao, *Washington Post*, 19 July 2015.
24. *South China Morning Post*, 13 July 2015.

but activism for children's or women's rights is still dangerous.[25] It is official policy to cure the ill, but AIDS activism is still dangerous, at least outside of quasi-official settings, such as the Family Planning Association. There are government-orchestrated anti-prostitution campaigns, but private activism for the same cause is still dangerous. And, of course, activism for democracy, human rights, religious freedom, and the like—be it in the form of defending, organising, manifestations, or the spreading of information or opinions—is personally dangerous for anyone involved. Known activists are watched. The academic Ilham Tohti, whose case we will visit below, was continuously followed by security agents before he was detained permanently. His university classes were videoed, and such video recordings turned up as evidence in his trial.

The regime is pursuing a difficult balance on social organisations. It is encouraging NGOs to take on the management of outsourced social services but also limiting them to social work. Groups that are seen to be activist have had their spaces of action limited in a systematic campaign of control during the last two or three years. They have come under more careful and direct scrutiny by security officials, have had more activities denied, such as the publication of reports or the holding of seminars or discussions, and have found it more difficult to receive funding from abroad.[26] Some organisations have been shut down or forced out of business, and some activists detained. We are not seeing an end to grass-roots activism, but social organisation is increasingly squeezed by both brute and subtle means of tighter control.

Anyone who engages in opposition, even moderately, must count on the risk of being persecuted, denied work or education, fired from jobs, being thrown out of his or her home, and on being detained, and on the risk that he or she is putting family and friends in danger. The academic and human rights lawyer Teng Biao, who has been in exile in Hong Kong and the United States since 2013, and who is probably unable to return to China, was three times suspended from teaching as a lecturer at the China University of Politics and Law (and formally dismissed in 2014), in 2008 stripped of his lawyer's licence, and in 2011 detained in solitary confinement for seventy days. In July 2014, Zhang Shaojie, a Christian pastor, forty-nine years old, who had been detained with twenty other church members in late 2013, was convicted for 'creating a public disturbance' and on a trumped-up charge of 'fraud' to twelve years in prison and a substantial fine. His appeal was dismissed six weeks later.

25. In early 2015, there was a burst of clampdowns on feminist activists in Beijing and other cities. At least five were arrested in three cities, on the eve of International Women's Day, 8 March, while planning awareness campaigns about sexual harassment in public transport. They were released on bail after thirty-seven days in detention. A warning had been put out.

26. In April 2015, a well-known Beijing think-tank, the Transition Institute, was charged with 'illegal business activity' for publishing reports and periodicals. In the case documents, the police named some foreign NGOs that were said to have helped to finance the institute. This is not illegal, and the foreign NGOs were not charged. But a warning was put out.

The court ruled to confiscate his home to pay the fine, resulting in an eviction order to his eighty-year-old father, seventy-eight-year-old mother, and disabled wife to leave the home. The eviction was resisted by his mother threatening to self-immolate and may not have been carried out. One daughter and her husband and son escaped to the Unites States with the help of ChinaAid ten days after the trial. In February 2009, the human rights lawyer Gao Zhisheng had his licence revoked, his Beijing law firm shut down, and was arrested and subsequently convicted of 'inciting subversion of state powers'. He had defended some of China's most vulnerable people, such as underground Christians, and had called in an open letter to the Chinese leaders for an end to the persecution of Falun Gong. He has accused the authorities of torture in prison. His immediate family has fled to the United States. At the Chinese New Year 2014, more than a year had passed since family members had last been allowed to contact him in jail. He was released in August 2014 but kept under round-the-clock surveillance at the home of in-laws. He was emaciated and ill, having suffered malnutrition and psychological abuse in prison. China's oldest dissident, as far as is known, is Zhou Youguang, who turned 109 in January 2015, a revered linguist known as 'the father of Pinyin', the system for transliterating Chinese characters into the Roman alphabet. In an interview on his birthday he said that 'China needs to take the path of democracy. I have always believed that.' He continues to be active and to write, and his works continue to be censored.

The human rights activist Hu Jia, a winner of the European Parliament's Andrei Sakharov Prize for Freedom of Thought, spent three and a half years in prison from 2008 to 2011 for inciting state subversion. After his release, he lived under varying degrees of surveillance and house arrest in his apartment in Beijing. His wife, Zeng Jinyan, who has moved to Hong Kong with their daughter, writes among other things the following in an essay about that experience:

> He has been threatened, violently harassed, put under house arrest, abducted, and followed. At the end of May 2014, secret police showed up at the home of Hu Jia's parents and told them that their son would soon be detained, and when his 76-year-old mother begged to see him in order to give him rice dumplings for the Dragon Boat Festival, they refused, saying, 'Arrangements have already been made, and it's too late to visit him.' Right now he lives an agonizing existence, which I can only compare to being roasted on a spit—the conditions are in some ways harsher than jail. Every day he must fight for the right to leave his house. Sometimes the struggle pays off, and he's able to walk around outside while accompanied by plainclothes police. But the greater direct danger comes from the public: bystanders who are powerless to help, idle onlookers who act as accomplices, or crazy people. On July 16 near the Caofang subway station in Beijing's Chaoyang District, two anonymous assailants attacked Hu Jia. And this came on the heels of numerous death threats. He has reported to the police five different telephone numbers from which he has received threatening messages, but while state security personnel may subject him to draconian restrictions, they

> don't lift a finger when someone spills red paint all over his car, when an ill-wisher leaves a dagger embedded in a rag doll on Hu Jia's parents' doorstep, when strangers take pictures of his house and send him death threats saying they're digging his grave. Even my parents have received threatening phone calls in the middle of the night. I have no idea how these strangers get hold of our phone numbers, and why messages sent to us from different social media accounts all say exactly the same thing, as if they had been coordinated. Strangers have sent paper garlands, a paper iPhone, a paper coffin, and even a message, delivered into the hands of Hu Jia, that our daughter would be 'the first to die'.[27]

The security services have the power to take people away and lock them up for relatively long durations, with or without court procedure. On 14 March 2014, the human rights activist Cao Shunli, who had been detained in September 2013, died in a military hospital to which she had been transferred after having fallen into a coma in prison. The human rights lawyer Pu Zhiqiang was arrested in June 2014. The legal investigation period expired in September but with no change in detention status. On 15 May 2015, he was formally indicted on charges of 'inciting ethnic hatred' and 'picking quarrels and provoking trouble,' with a prospect of up to eight years in jail. In November 2014, the rights activists Yang Maodong (also known by his pen name Guo Feixiong) and Sun Desheng went on trial in Guangzhou on a charge of 'assembling a crowd to disrupt public order'.[28] They had been advocating for officials to be obliged to disclose their wealth and for a relaxation of censorship and the repression of dissent. In an eloquent defence statement at his trial, which the court tried to prevent him from making by interruptions and other obstructions, Yang told of torture and sadistic interrogations in prison and harassment of his wife and children (who subsequently escaped to the United States) and compared today's China 'blow by blow' to the nightmare state of George Orwell's *1984*. At the verdict session in 2015, he again tried to speak in his defence but was interrupted and dragged out of the courtroom. He had already been imprisoned from 2007 to 2011, after having helped villagers near Guangzhou to organise protests against corruption and land seizures and for having defended Cai Zhuohua, a prominent Beijing church leader, who in 2005 was sentenced to three years in jail (also after torture in prison) on charges of 'illegal business practices' and fined 150,000 *yuan*. The illegal business practice was the printing of Bibles; the pastor's printing business did not have a licence to print religious material. Detainees are mistreated and tortured. Family and relations are persecuted and punished. Intimidation is routine. When Liu Xia was able to visit her

27. Chinafile.com, 19 September 2014.
28. Their trial took place more than a year after they were detained, and it was yet another year before the court delivered their verdicts, in November 2015. Yang was sentenced to six years in prison and Sun to two and a half years. In a separate case, the activist Liu Yuandong was sentenced to three years in prison for 'gathering a crowd to disrupt order in a public space', having waited twenty-two months since his trial for the verdict. According to a statement by Amnesty International on 27 November 2015, all three had suffered torture during detention.

husband, Liu Xiaobo, the Nobel Peace Prize winner, in jail for the Chinese New Year in 2014, she was denied sharing a celebratory meal with him. Liu Xia herself is under house arrest in her home in Beijing, and other family members have been detained. Medical problems are disregarded and medication ignored or refused. In July 2015, Tenzin Delek Rinpoche, a Tibetan monk who had been imprisoned since 2002, died in prison at age sixty-five, in poor health with a serious heart condition for which he allegedly had received no treatment.[29] Against the requests of the family to have his body released for funeral rites in the Tibetan Buddhist tradition, it was hastily cremated in the remote prison.

The trend is not in the direction of liberalisation. Rather, during 2013 and 2014, repression increased and it became more dangerous to be an activist. A report published on 22 June 2014 by the US-based website ChinaChange.org gives a list of examples:

> June 4th has passed, but the arrests continue, and every day brings bad news from China. While scholar Xu Youyu, artist Chen Guang and others have been released 'on probation', many are still being held and others have been formally arrested, including Jia Lingmin and two others in Zhengzhou, Henan, and lawyer Pu Zhiqiang in Beijing. On June 20 in Guangzhou, lawyer Tang Jingling and activists Wang Qingying and Yuan Xinting were formally arrested on subversion charges. Earlier this week, three New Citizens Movement participants Liu Ping, Wei Zhongping and Li Sihua were harshly sentenced for fictitious 'crimes'. This wave of large scale repression of civil society started last year with the arrest of the 'Beijing Xidan Four'. On March 31, 2013, Yuan Zhong, Zhang Baocheng, and two others gave a speech at Beijing Xidan in which they called on government officials to make public their property holdings. They were arrested on the spot. This was the official prelude to the authorities' repression of the New Citizens Movement and the civil society. Within a year, throughout China no fewer than two hundred human rights activists were arrested and incarcerated. These included: Xu Zhiyong, Wang Gongquan, Guo Feixiong, Li Huaping, Chen Baocheng, Zhang Lin, Ding Jiaxi, Liu Ping, Yuan Fengchu, Ilham Tothi, and others. Among these human rights activists, the authorities tortured to death the noted activist Cao Shunli. Suppression has increased markedly not only against human rights activists but also against dissidents, underground churches, Falun Gong adherents, petitioners, activist netizens, and liberal scholars. Meanwhile we have been witnessing a marked tightening of information dissemination and ideological control.

Security officials often try to deal softly with troublemakers. They visit them, or invite them for a conversation over a cup of tea. They reason with them and try to get them back on to the straight and narrow. They warn, and always there is a threat of retribution in the air. When necessary, retribution moves from threat to reality. Ahead of the 25th anniversary of the 4 June Tiananmen Square massacre in 2014,

29. Radio Free Asia, 13 July 2015.

the rounding-up of activists started in early May. In a sign of how well the authorities know what people are doing, a planned commemoration by a handful of participants to be held in a private home was disrupted when some participants were detained on their way to the gathering and the host arrested.

They *really* do know. In early July 2014, the Tibetan writer and activist Tsering Woeser, who lives in Beijing, received an invitation to the American embassy by a call to her mobile phone while she was outside of Beijing. The day before the meeting was to happen, security officers arrived at her home and confined her to house arrest until after the time of the meeting. On 26 November 2014, a young legal activist, Liu Jianshu, twenty-eight years old, was detained by police in Beijing. He holds a law degree from Oxford and was setting up a legal aid organisation. His sin, however, was not activism, which was only moderately subversive, but organising, or not even that, just loose networking. His detention was one in a sweep in which at least five other activists—in magazines, think tanks, and educational organisations—were also detained. What had enabled the police to roll up this network was that an associate had copies made in a photocopy shop of materials that touched on the Occupy Central movement in Hong Kong and received a receipt in the name of one of the organisations in the network. Like many photocopy shops in Beijing, this one was linked by computer to the police, who identified the content of the materials copied and moved on a group of idealistic activists.[30] In the early morning of 29 April 2015, in the eastern city of Suzhou, ahead of a ceremony to mark the anniversary of the execution of Lin Zhao, a young Christian woman and critic of Maoism who was executed in prison in 1968 and who rests in a cemetery in the city, a huge police force busted homes and guesthouses and detained dozens of people who had gathered in the city for a mourning at her graveside.[31] During the Occupy Central movement in Hong Kong in 2014, parents of mainland students in Hong Kong would be visited by security officials and warned to caution their children not to get involved.

Three features are recurrent in stories of political persecution. One is that it is often, perhaps usually, unclear who the persecutors are. The agents tend to be in civilian dress. The second one is that people who are detained disappear, sometimes for a short time and sometimes for long durations, and that family, friends, and lawyers cannot contact them or even know where they are. The third is that victims suffer beatings. Troublemakers, women and men alike, at home, on the streets, or in custody, get beaten up. People are physically hauled out of their homes by hired bullies in official land-grab schemes. The persecution of activists is, systematically, in the hands of thugs with unknown authority and who use beatings as their habitual method of retribution.

30. *New York Times*, 10 December 2014.

31. Radio Free Asia (29 April 2015) reported that a force of 'thousands' of riot police was deployed to round up 'dozens' of activists.

Although activism is dangerous, it is not impossible, and some activists are able to get on with it without too much trouble. There is a heroic and not insignificant underground, more or less officially accepted, with various activities, from the publication of non-authorised journals to help for (prospective) mothers who evade the birth control strictures, that are able to operate although unlikely to be unknown. The Chinese dictatorship rules by fear. The technique of arbitrary force—sometimes being meted out when there is little cause and sometimes held back when it should be expected—is cultivated to perfection.

(3) The courts are under political control. The dispensation of such punishments, including incarceration, as is politically desired is in the will of the authorities, as is the administration of the law as wanted politically. As always, there are exceptions and sometimes courts rule independently and awkwardly, but generally, in political cases, they do as expected. Political authorities have the power to get those punished whom they need to get punished, including locked up. The criminal law allows for convictions for broad and vaguely defined political and civil offences. Punishable crimes include, for example, 'spreading rumours', 'causing trouble', 'creating a disturbance', 'gathering a crowd', and 'damaging the nation's image', a new charge that appeared in 2014. In addition to the deprivation of freedom, convicts may under the law be deprived of civil or political rights after completing a prison term, possibly for life, such as the right to leave the country.

In early 2014, in a closely observed case, the legal scholar and rights activist Xu Zhiyong, the leading initiator of the 2012 New Citizens' Movement (NCM), was sentenced to four years of detention for 'gathering a crowd to disrupt order in a public place' and other vaguely specified crimes, in a process that independent judicial observers characterised as making a mockery of the pledge to move towards the rule of law. At least four other NCM activists were detained in the same case (as was a former policeman who had protested outside of Xu's trial).

At about the same time, the prominent Uighur academic Ilham Tohti, a professor of economics at Minzu (Nationalities) University in Beijing, was detained a final time and now permanently, when he was prevented from boarding a plane in Beijing for the United States, where he was to take up a temporary visiting post. He was transferred to Xinjiang and had his computers, personal papers, and bank cards confiscated. Seven students said to have been collaborating with him were taken into custody at the same time and transferred to custody in Xinjiang. A consistently moderate voice for better conditions and recognition for China's mainly Muslim Uighur minority, Professor Ilham was charged with promoting separatism and organising and leading a separatist group, in a case that took on huge symbolic importance in respect to the scope for even moderate oppositional activity. The case went to trial in September in Urumqi in Xinjiang province. After two days of proceedings, he was sentenced to life in prison, then the harshest court punishment of a dissident in many years and according to Amnesty International an 'affront to justice'. The court also ordered the confiscation of all his assets, including his life savings, leaving his wife and their two young children, then five and eight, destitute. Ilham denied and refuted all charges against him. During his eight months of pre-trial detention, his family, including his wife, who was herself put under house arrest, were forbidden from seeing him. According to his lawyer, he was chained with leg irons and denied adequate food and warm clothing. The court proceedings were closed, and the court denied the defence's request to summon some dozen witnesses. His household registration was in Beijing, wherefore his case should by law have been heard there and not in Xinjiang. His grown daughter, Jewher Ilham, with whom he should have travelled to the United States when he was detained, and who has remained there, has said of her father that he 'has used only one weapon in his struggle for the basic rights of Uighur of Xinjiang: words, spoken, written, distributed and posted. This is all that he has ever had at his disposal, and all he has ever needed. And this is what China finds so threatening.' In November, the Xinjiang court refused his appeal. Shortly afterwards, the seven students who had been detained emerged from confinement, were put on trial on charges of being members of a separatist group, and all sentenced to three to eight years in prison.

As the Fourth Plenum on rule of law was packing up, it became known that a documentary film maker, Shen Yongping, was about to go on trial for 'illegal business operations', having been held in confinement for several months. His crime was to have produced and shown a video history of 'constitutionalism' over the last century. Possibly to avoid the embarrassment of timing, the trial was postponed to an unspecified future date. In late November, a veteran journalist, Gao Yu, then seventy years old, who had been in confinement since 24 April in the round-up ahead of the 25th anniversary of the Tiananmen Square massacre in 1989, went on trial in Beijing on a charge of having leaked state secrets to a foreign news agency and on the strength of an orchestrated confession, and was subsequently (on 17 April 2015) sentenced to seven years in jail, the third time in her career that she was jailed. The secret she was supposed to have leaked was an internal party document, known as Document 9 (on which more below), which had warned party cadres against 'seven Western perils' to be avoided and combatted. A year on, in November 2015, her sentence was reduced from seven to five years, after a confession, and she was released on medical grounds to serve the rest of her sentence outside of prison. Also in November 2014, a Mongolian political prisoner, Hada, fifty-nine years old (known by his single name), was released from prison. His case is outlined in a report by the Southern Mongolian Human Rights Information Center, issued in New York on 10 December 2014. He had then spent nineteen years in prison, the first fifteen years on a sentence of 'separatism', and then on his 'release' in 2010 another four years in extrajudicial detention. On his re-release, he was not allowed home but taken to a guarded apartment to house arrest. It was to be another three weeks before he was allowed to meet his wife and other family members, who were themselves under close surveillance, in his new confinement. In November 2015, he was still under constant surveillance by security agents on guard at his home and following him when out. He and his grown son were denied passports to enable him to travel abroad for medical treatment. At one point, his son was taken into detention for 'obstructing official business'.[32]

(4) The administrative apparatus is organised in two lines, one of government organs and one of party organs. Both form unbroken chains from the centre down to the micro-local level, and at all levels both control each other. Any form of governance, at any level, is always under the oversight of someone in addition to the executor. Down to the micro-local level, local government organs, local organs of the state, and party organs, side by side and overlapping, are all charged with duties of stability management. In addition, there are networks of secret police and informers. Potential dissidents and troublemakers are identified and targeted for surveillance. In Tibet, for example, a residual population strand is officially classified as 'those who do not accept re-education and do not have faith in the motherland and the party', and those thus classified are kept an eye on.

(5) Public and party officials, from top to bottom, are assessed for performance, and these assessments are part of the basis for promotion, non-promotion, or (occasionally) demotion. The criteria they are assessed against may vary somewhat across the country, but always a high priority criterion is the maintenance of order. This assures that it is in the urgent personal interest of every single one of the millions of officials anywhere the system, high or low, to do whatever he or she can to exercise control in his or her area of responsibility. The promotion system also uses, in an ancient Chinese tradition, formal competence testing. There is hence a combination of control selection and meritocratic selection. The top leaders no doubt want the most able administrators to rise through the ranks, but for control-obsessed leaders political loyalty is crucial to perceived ability.[33]

(6) In a population of 1.4 billion, every person is registered in the household registration system. The *hukou* is a core instrument of rule. It splits the population into subgroups with different kinds of citizenship and creates a divide-and-rule social structure with built-in protections against broadly based or class-based solidarities.

(7) Adult Chinese are obliged to have and carry a photo identity card which gives the name, date of birth, gender, ethnicity, domicile, and identification number of the holder, and to produce it on demand. ID cards are issued by a state agency through the local public security bureaus. They are needed for various activities and leave an information trail on people's doings. For example, participants at a farewell ceremony

32. Radio Free Asia, 26 November 2015.

33. In *The China Model*, Bell interprets meritocracy to be a core feature of the unique Chinese system.

in honour of the former reformist and ousted party secretary general Zhao Ziyang on 28 January 2005, had to register under police watch with their ID cards.

(8) Personal files, the *dang'an*, are held on Chinese citizens. There are supposed to be four kinds, probably overlapping, on cadres, students, employees, and military personnel. Copies are supposed to be held by the local Public Security Bureau and by the person's employer or supervisory organisation. Files are built up locally from the time of (secondary) school entry and accumulate over the years with entries from teachers, officials, and employers. They contain educational, professional, political, criminal, health, and other information. The file, or a copy, follows the citizen as he or she moves along, for example, into university or professional life. The information in the file regulates the ability of the person to change jobs, be promoted, join the party, relocate, and the like. Every employee has a personal file with his or her education and employment history. This may include information on qualifications, applications, posts held, promotions, training, and the like, as well as assessments, references, investigations, troubles, medical records, and so on. The party holds personal files on party members and public workers as part of the *nomenklatura* system.

These files contain varied and detailed information, most of it not accessible by the person. That may for female workers include gynaecological information from health checks. Information once included in a file is not supposed to be removed. Any black stain on a person, professionally or politically, such as having voiced discontent with public services, is likely to follow that person for life.

Although the person is not allowed to see his or her file, it is in his or her interest that it is maintained. It may, for example, be by resort to the file that the person can prove his or her work history. It is the responsibility of the person that the file is taken care of. An employee may for that reason (have to) get it deposited with a quasi-public agency that is charged with the storage of files, for which he or she will have to pay a fee.

With the emergence of private business and the dissolution of the work unit system in the reform period, the keeping and maintenance of personal files may have become more difficult and the system may have fallen into some mess. For young people who leave education before university, their file is likely to lapse. But the party-state does not give up a useful tool of control. The whole cabal is now being computerised into an ambitious 'social credit network' which aims to cover all citizens and to contain more detailed and up-to-date information than has been possible in the original paper-based system, the ultimate purpose of which is to strengthen 'the sincerity consciousness of the members of society'.[34]

(9) The ultra-dictatorial 'one-child policy' was introduced in 1979, as a temporary measure, to restrict urban couples to having only one child, but with lesser or

34. State Council Notice, 14 June 2014.

no restrictions in rural and ethnic minority populations: Ethnic minorities were not subjected to the one-child rule, and rural couples were allowed a second child if the first one was a girl or had a disability. Recently, restrictions have been gradually eased first by allowing urban couples who are themselves single children to have a second child and then by removing the one-child rule completely and allowing all couples to have a second child. This decision was taken by the party in October 2015 and is expected to be implemented gradually by local authorities. It was hyped by the party as a big turnaround and in the international press as 'the end of the one-child policy' but was little more than a codification of what was becoming practice and did not represent the end of birth control.[35] The policy is run from the National Health and Family Planning Commission and enforced through lower-level commissions down the bureaucratic line, ultimately by local family planning officials and centres. The means are information and propaganda, detailed oversight of women in childbearing age, heavy fines for unauthorised births, and sterilisations and abortions, when necessary enforced abortions, sometimes as late as towards the end of the pregnancy.

The policy—officially known as 'family planning', but which I refer to, more correctly, as 'birth control'—assumes that children are born to married couples and prescribes a limit to the number of children a family can have. Parents who break the rules on child numbers or otherwise must, at the least, pay a fine—officially a 'social compensation fee'—generally at four times their annual salary and progressive. Children born outside of wedlock are technically illegal and may be left to live in limbo as non-citizens without normal rights, for example, if parents are unable to pay the fine.

Couples who are expecting a child must first apply for a 'birth permit', which is required for the baby to be born legally and for a birth certificate to be issued once the baby is born. The application is to the local family planning office. It requires a marriage certificate, the approval of the respective parents' employers, or university for students, or their local residents' committee, presumably to confirm that the applicants are who they claim to be and that they qualify. In case of migrants, the application also needs the approval of their home family planning office. Once these matters are in order, the permit will normally be issued. Practically it is (at least in

35. My explanation of the policy change, in response to a question from Bloomberg News, was this: 'There never was a one-child policy. There was/is a birth control policy: couples who wish to have a child must first obtain permission from the state to have that child. What has been decided now is to modify the rules within the policy. There will be little or no consequence demographically. The experience during the gradual relaxation of the rules is that very few couples have taken up the opportunity to have a second child. The reasons are difficulties of family-work balance and that it is now very expensive to raise a child (an unintended consequence of the restrictive policy). The new decision is mainly a bureaucratic matter. A huge birth control bureaucracy has been built up with now vested interests in maintaining birth control. On the other hand, the leadership is under pressure from economic and demographic experts who want policy changed because it has been and is very costly, both economically and socially. So the leaders are doing a bit but not much, only enough for it to be seen as a step in the right direction.'

Beijing) a red booklet, about the size of a small paperback, with about ten pages with space for the requisite stamps of the participating agencies.

The application will normally be filed once the pregnancy has commenced. Under the new two-child policy, however, the assumption is that the application for the second child is filed ahead of the pregnancy, for example, to impose a required birth interval or to disqualify parents who are too old. It can be turned down, and if so the assumption is that the pregnancy is aborted. Reasons for an application to be turned down are that the couple do not qualify, that there is missing documentation, or that there are age or health impairments, such as certain communicable or mental diseases.

Mothers may not get their children officially registered if they are not married or the father does not participate in the registration process. Prospective mothers without a partner are presumed to abort. Those who refuse may not be issued a birth permit and are liable to a fine to get the child registered, akin to the fine for children beyond the birth quota.

In local communities, workplaces, universities, and the like, women of childbearing age are monitored by birth-control authorities, down to menstrual cycles and contraceptive practices, to prevent unauthorised pregnancies and to terminate pregnancies that should not have happened. Responsibility for birth control may be collectivised so that, for example, workplaces that have workers who transgress may be punished collectively in budgets or pay rises. The substitution of the new two-child rule for the one-child rule may lighten the burden for some prospective parents, but birth control is not being abolished. The family planning bureaucracy is in place to monitor prospective parents as previously and, as previously, prospective parents must apply for permission.[36] The social meaning of the policy is, finally, a manifestation by the state into the intimacy of every family of its will, ability, and ruthless determination to control their lives according to its own dictate. In this meaning, the policy persists. It is a stark reminder to the people that they have no other rights than those it is in the pleasure of the state to grant them.

(10) The policies listed so far are about controlling behaviour, keeping people in line, and preventing dangerously subversive activism. However, the politics of social control goes beyond the restriction of behaviour and includes also 'thought work' to control mindsets. This is done, firstly, by censoring what people outside of the inner circle know and have information about. Everything is censored: press, the web, literature, film distribution, museums. Dangerous information is censored out of foreign books in translation.[37] This is effective. For example, Hu Yaobang, who was

36. The birth control bureaucracy is made up of an apparatus of administrative and professional staff, somewhere between 500,000 and 1 million in all, backed up by perhaps a million local party cadres with 'family planning' as a dedicated responsibility and about 100 million members of the official Family Planning Association.

37. For example, in the 2014 Chinese translation of Paul Auster's novel *Sunset Park*, which contains passages about the imprisoned dissident Liu Xiaobo and his wife, the objectionable sections were either deleted or cut, without the author's approval.

purged as party leader in 1987, has subsequently hardly so much as been mentioned in the state press and is today officially near to being an unknown non-person. Each year, the anniversary of the 1989 massacre in Tiananmen Square passes without mention or discussion in Chinese media. This monumental upheaval in the nation's history is effectively being managed into being forgotten in China itself. There is no indication that censorship is being relaxed. According to the International Federation of Journalists (in their annual report entitled *Back to a Maoist Future*), 2013 was a regressive year for press freedom in China. China is ranked 175th of 180 countries in the 2014 press freedom index compiled by Reporters Without Borders. According to the Committee to Protect Journalists (in a report published in December 2014), there were forty-four journalists in prison in 2014, up from thirty-two in 2013.

The media are not censored directly by censors with red pencils in editorial offices but indirectly through edits issued by the State Council Information Office and similar offices lower down in the administrative hierarchy. Or they are *mostly* not censored directly: When *Southern Weekend*, a weekly published in Guangzhou, intended to run a New Year editorial in 2013 in favour of 'constitutionalism', it found it rewritten by provincial propaganda authorities before publication. Bad stories that are repeated get killed and disappear from further reporting. During the unrest in Hong Kong in 2014, CNN news broadcasts, which can be seen in China, would routinely black out at the point of reporting from Hong Kong. (I cannot help thinking that somewhere a little man sits in a back office with his finger on the switch, which he flicks when a bad story is about to start, and screens go blank all over the country—but the controllers probably have more sophisticated tools.) In early 2014, the State Administration of Press, Publication, Radio, Film and Television introduced a censorship-first rule whereby online companies would have to obtain pre-broadcasting approval for the streaming of video content. Disagreeable video content, such as targeted popular American TV series, gets removed. Book publishers are required to have pre-publication approval of new titles, as are film distributors before films can be shown—even museums prior to new exhibitions.[38]

But in large measure, press censorship is through instructions for self-censorship, in writing or by phone messages, day in and day out, and in great detail as to what is to be reported and what not, what is to be emphasised and what deleted, how to make reporting positive and how to avoid negativism, how stories should be angled and how not, what photos to include and suppress. The word 'monopoly' is banned

38. The best form of censorship is providers self-censoring out of awareness that they might be censored. 'In a 2013 script for the movie *Pixels*, intergalactic aliens blast a hole in one of China's national treasures—the Great Wall. That scene is gone from the final version of the sci-fi comedy, starring Adam Sandler and released by Sony Pictures Entertainment this week in the United States. The aliens strike iconic sites elsewhere, smashing the Taj Mahal in India, the Washington Monument and parts of Manhattan. Sony executives spared the Great Wall because they were anxious to get the movie approved for release in China, a review of internal Sony Pictures emails shows' (Reuters, 24 July 2015).

from press coverage of state enterprises. It has been forbidden, or at least not the done thing, to portray top political leaders in cartoons, but in March 2014 an official website, Qianlong.com, to great surprise, carried a friendly cartoon strip rendition of Xi Jinping, and others have subsequently followed, for example, in a video late in 2014 of a ballad celebrating the model love between daddy Xi and mamma Peng. The relentless flow of edits, and the detail, is mindboggling. It gives all editors an instinctive feel for what is accepted and expected and what to avoid. When Chancellor Angela Merkel gave Xi Jinping a historical map of China on his official visit to Germany on 28 March 2014, which showed 'China proper' without Tibet, Xinjiang, Mongolia, Taiwan, and even Hainan, Chinese media either did not describe the map or replaced it in their coverage with another one that included all the 'missing territories' in the Merkel map, all apparently without any censorship instruction having to be issued.

Here are some examples of what state media instructions look like (observed and translated by China Digital Times, a project at the University of California, Berkeley):

- 'All news websites, including interactive platforms, are asked to immediately carry out the following tasks: 1. Delete reports related to the court case concerning Li Tianyi taking turns having sex. 2. Delete all contents related to the riot in Hotan, Xinjiang (including text, images, and video), and report to the State Council Information Office within half an hour' (1 July 2013).
- 'Please ensure that you strictly comply with the related reporting requests distributed earlier. Maintain positive coverage. Do not produce negative material' (on the commemoration of the fifth anniversary of the heavy earthquakes in 2008).
- 'Report on the new provincial budget tomorrow, but do not feature it on the front page, make no comparisons to earlier budgets, list no links, and say nothing that might raise questions.'
- 'Find and remove the foreign media report "China's Secret Offshore Tax Havens".'
- 'Downplay stories on Kim Jong-un's facelift.'
- 'Allow stories on Deputy Mayor Zhang's embezzlement but omit the comment boxes.'
- For sensitive topics on which central media have already said something, the instructions may say 'reprint Xinhua but nothing more'.
- For topics that cannot be avoided because they are already being widely discussed, there are such options as 'mention without hyping', 'publish but only under small headlines', 'put only on back pages', 'close the comment boxes', and 'downplay as time passes'.

- 'Media that report on the knife attack incident that occurred 1 March at the Kunming Railway Station must strictly adhere to Xinhua News Agency wire copy or information provided by local authorities. Do not treat the story with large headlines; do not publish grisly photos. Please respond to confirm that you have received this message. Thank you.' (1 March 2014)
- On a day in mid-February 2014, for example, these instructions went out: For Obama's meeting with the Dalai Lama, 'only Xinhua and national media copy may be used'. All websites were advised to delete a Tencent article about tensions in Hong Kong–Mainland relations. Also unacceptable was a story about Zhejiang secretary and 'Western hostile forces'. Finally, an article about the financial services firm UBS setting up an offshore company for the wife and daughter of the disgraced former Ministry of Railways official, Zhang Shuguang, was ordered removed.
- 'Effective immediately, find and delete all news related to the 6/22 Hong Kong referendum, thoroughly clean up related comments, and promptly send a work report [on your progress]. Forcibly cancel blogs and microblog posts reprinting harmful information. Ensure that no information related to the referendum appears online. Guangdong Province is to cut signal on all programs from Hong Kong television stations, especially.'
- 'Hyping the following articles is forbidden. Cease from highlighting these stories and allow focus to naturally die down. 1) Accidental Explosion at Hengyang Military Armory Kills 17. 2) Thugs in Yechang, Xinjiang Crash Into Police Headquarters; 13 Shot Dead.'
- 'All major websites please prominently display the article "Over 70 Mainland Tourists Detained at Hong Kong Airport With No Food or Drink for 16 Hours" in the headline section of both homepages [that of the portal itself and of the news centre].'

On 28 September 2014, when serious unrest was breaking out in Hong Kong, the following instruction went out from central censorship authorities in Beijing: 'All websites must immediately clear away information about Hong Kong students violently assaulting the government and about "Occupy Central". Promptly report any issues. Strictly manage interactive channels, and resolutely delete harmful information. This [directive] must be followed precisely.' Without delay, where stories and images from the unrest had started to appear, they were taken off, leaving only a few officially controlled comments in official media. This followed through to the usual cat and mouse game where bloggers tried to get Hong Kong–related messages around the firewall of censorship, for example, posting photos of Xi Jinping with an umbrella, the umbrella having become a symbol of the protest movement in Hong Kong, or of themselves with heads shaved. In the main, however, and again as usual, the cat ruled and mostly had the mice hiding in corners. According to Amnesty International, by 1 October at least twenty people had been detained in mainland China for showing support for the protesters (on the web) or planning to travel to Hong Kong to participate, and another sixty had been called in for questioning. On 2 October, about ten people were detained at or on their way to a poetry recital in an artists' enclave outside of Beijing, including a Chinese assistant employed by the German newspaper *Die Zeit*, who spent nine months in detention before being released in July 2015 without charge. Many, or some, mainland students in Hong Kong joined the protest action. On the mainland, some parents of students in Hong Kong were visited by security agents and advised to discourage their offspring from participating. A Shanghai professor was interviewed on a morning radio programme in London and asked if he knew what was happening in Hong Kong and could follow events there. He knew of it, he said, having accessed some information through the BBC.

(11) Internet control is a high-priority matter for the government, under the charge of the State Internet Information Office, whose director, Lu Wei, is also the secretary to the Internet security leading group headed by Xi Jinping. Censorship is exercised by the blocking of search terms and sites, such as, for example, those of the *New York Times*, Bloomberg, Reuters, and the *Economist*. Non-Chinese media apps, such as Instagram, Facebook, and Twitter, are inaccessible and Chinese alternatives tightly controlled. It appears that during 2014, Internet censorship was extended from the blocking of objectionable sites to so-called 'mirror sites' which may not themselves be objectionable (they may, for example, be business portals) but through which users may be able to access blocked sites, such as YouTube, which means that they are blocking not just sites but possible gateways to sites. In January 2015, an attempt was made to block VPNs, through which sophisticated users had been able to access foreign sites not available in China, possibly as a technical experiment, possibly with different effects in different parts of the country. Domestic websites are monitored and scanned before or as material is posted, by a team of more than 2 million 'Internet opinion analysts', and can be shut down.[39] China watchers report the experience of websites disappearing from the screens as they are reading them. Those that are not shut down may have their content controlled, and with astonishing efficiency. In an incident in Beijing on 28 October 2013, a car crashed into the barrier in front of the gate into the Forbidden City at Tiananmen Square and burst into flames, in an apparent terrorist attack, possibly by Uighur activists. By the next day, postings about the event on the domestic Internet were low key and photos of it, except distant and convoluted ones, had as good as disappeared. When anti-Chinese demonstrations in Vietnam in May 2014 resulted in flurry of microblogging comments in China,

39. The actual number of Internet monitors is unknown, but the number of about 2 million is assumed by sources such as the BBC and Index of Censorship.

many of the comments were deleted as soon as they appeared and prevented from spreading, the pattern being that anti-Vietnamese comments were left and allowed to spread. A contact in China posted a photo of the cover of the book *The Barefoot Lawyer* by Chen Guangcheng on his Weibo site, only the cover with no text or comment. Within ten minutes the photo was deleted.[40] In June–July 2015, as the government was pumping money into the stock market and in other ways trying to stem the crash, media outlets and commentators were instructed to write in support of the government's efforts, in which they by and large obliged. The terms 'panic' and 'stock market crash' were cleansed out of the Internet.

In addition to being controlled, websites are directed actively. Official agents write online stories, content, and messages, often under the guise of being private citizens. When a story reflects well on the party, web editors may receive instructions to place it prominently on the home page or recirculate it without delay. The authorities use the web actively for their own purposes, both openly and clandestinely. Information, comments, and opinion that appears to be from and between ordinary people, and that appears to be spontaneous, may well be put there by official agents.

Internet censorship is delicately sophisticated. The web is open and functions and full of material that is critical of governance, in particular local governance. It offers people an arena to express views and let off steam. But what is seen to be dangerous is prevented. In early 2014, it was announced through Xinhua, the state news agency, that the government was launching an intensified training programme for civil servants in all aspects of government—police, judiciary, academia, even press officers in state-owned enterprises—on Internet control and supervision.

Through 2013, described by the Network of Chinese Human Rights Defenders as a 'nightmarish year', under the inspiration of the new leadership, a relentless campaign of crackdowns imposed new controls on the distribution of information and opinion, including arrests of journalists and bloggers, the shutting down of websites, reinforced online content control, and restrictions on foreign media. China, says Reporters Without Borders, is 'a model of censorship and repression'. The new leading group on national security (not the Internet security leading group), which started operation at the beginning of 2014, has included 'unconventional security' as part of its remit, a term that includes defensive action against cultural and ideological influences from 'Western' value systems.

In a separate initiative, schools of journalism were instructed to improve their ideological education and to glean journalistic education away from 'freedom ideology' and towards 'Marxist news outlook'. Top journalism schools were to come under the charge of the party's propaganda department and directors and deans to be recruited from the ranks of provincial party officials. By mid-2014, at least nineteen universities

40. This was in May 2015. The photo had been taken in a bookshop at Hong Kong's airport. Weibo Sina is the Chinese equivalent of Facebook. *The Barefoot Lawyer* is obviously banned in China.

had announced that they had started or were starting to restructure their journalism schools in co-operation with local propaganda departments or official media outlets. Serving journalists are to sit a national political exam on ideological understanding, the results of which will decide or influence the renewal of press cards. A manual for the exam lays down as a core principle that the relationship between the party and the news media is one of the leader and the led.

Foreign media operating in China came under pressure in a campaign of intimidation. Foreign journalists not infrequently find themselves prevented from undertaking assignments in China by visas being refused. Many journalists, including those of the *New York Times*, were held in suspense until the last days of the year as to whether or not their press credentials would be renewed for 2014 (one *Times* reporter in the end was forced to leave the country). In September 2014, the Foreign Correspondents Club of China issued a report on working conditions for foreign journalists outlining tighter controls and more difficult access. The issuing of temporary visas for journalists living outside of China is being tightened, depending, for example, on a prior 'visa notification' from an official host and prior signed approvals from intended interviewees. At the World Economic Forum in Davos in January 2014, the foreign minister, Wang Yi, took the opportunity, in an interview with the *Financial Times*, and with the display of power threat in relief, to say that 'we hope that media organisations will write about China with a great sense of responsibility and in a more objective light'.

Targeted organisations and foundations were shut down or banned from publishing in China, or continuing to publish. Under persecution or threat of persecution for 'rumour mongering', well-known and established netizens and micro-bloggers—anti-corruption campaigners, rights lawyers, whistleblowers, investigative journalists—shut down their accounts, or had them shut down, or lost their jobs, or were detained and put on trial, or phased back their activity. The writer and blogger Murong Xuecun has described how he was subjected to an orchestrated smear campaign on the Internet to destroy his name and reputation.[41] Activists can now (following a judicial interpretation issued by the Supreme People's Court) be prosecuted for posting 'rumours' if their postings are seen by more than 5,000 people or forwarded more than 500 times. By the end of 2013, the volume of Internet micro-blogging was noticeably down and debate forced into social media that spread information less easily and more slowly. The Chinese Internet had been if not silenced at least muted and tamed.

Controls do not prevent articles or postings or publications with critical content or comment from appearing, and do not hinder those who are determined and resourceful from accessing critical material from outside of the country. But the regime is able to keep unwanted information under control and prevent it from getting to the

41. *New York Times*, 21 September 2014.

level of general distribution. Information is not necessarily erased but is contained, and that is enough for the purpose. In the same way that the regime can live with and manage unrest as long as it is local, it can live with critical opinions being published as long as they are not easily and widely circulated and accessible. Discontent is manageable as long as it is contained and as long as discontents across the country remain localised and do not gel into broad networks and movements. Again, what is suppressed is rather organised activism than dissent as such.

(12) Academic censorship has been tightened. It is getting more difficult for Chinese academics to maintain research contacts abroad and, for example, to arrange international conferences, and more difficult for them to access non-Chinese sources of information. During a lecture tour to several cities in late 2014, I was told repeatedly as a matter of routine about work not being allowed to be published for political reasons: Some could not be published at all, some only with modifications, some published only by provincial outlets but not in Beijing, some being taken to Hong Kong or Taiwan for publication. To a question about censorship, the editor of a scholarly journal said, 'we try to avoid some politically sensitive issues, but there is no clear requirement'.

Towards the end of 2014, a campaign was launched of pressure being piled on universities and their staff. Xi Jinping gave a speech in which he called for greater party and ideological guidance and more intensive study of Marxism to fortify higher-learning institutions as 'socialist universities with Chinese characteristics'. Articles started to appear in official media to the same effect. On 13 November, *Liaoning Daily* published an 'open letter to university teachers': 'Please Don't Talk Like That About China.' The paper claimed to have sent reporters to schools and universities across the country and to have found that many university instructors were politically insensitive and critical. The open letter was subsequently spread on the net with obvious official backing. In January 2015, *Qiushi*, an online journal of the Central Committee, published an article on the need to distinguish between professors who provide 'reasonable criticism' and those who 'blacken China's name', with named delinquents. On 2 February, the minister of education, Yuan Guiren, published an article in the party journal *Seeking Truth* about the danger of foreign ideas and Western values on university campuses and how 'young teachers and students are key targets of infiltration by enemy forces.' On 6 February, the *People's Daily*, *Guangming Daily*, and *China Education Daily*, as well as the Xinhua website, published editorials on ideological indoctrination at China's institutions of higher learning. Meanwhile, on 19 January, the party's General Office published a document entitled 'Opinions on Further Strengthening and Improving Propaganda and Ideological Work in Higher Education under New Circumstances', and on 29 January the Ministry of Education and the party's Commission for Discipline Inspection convened a conference with leaders of education bureaus and universities on its implementation. We are unlikely to see a mass rounding up of deviant professors, although no doubt there is some of that, but these are signals that in the Chinese system, to put it carefully, are not trivial and do not go unnoticed. Discipline may be imposed with a light hand in leading universities with extensive international contacts and more capacity to resist, but even there, and more elsewhere, people will take care and there will be more self-censorship.

(13) Beyond the control of knowledge, the apparatus of control also works proactively to shape people's thinking and guide their views. This is done, firstly, by the standard method of propaganda. Newspapers, magazines, and broadcast media are stock full day in and day out with stories of achievement and progress, and in praise of the country's leaders and leadership. Museums are systematically propagandistic in the presentation of history. Propaganda placards litter the landscape. One hallmark of propaganda, as always, is lies and repeated lies. When the old city of Kashgar was flattened, 65,000 homes being erased, against the repressed resistance of local Uighur people, many of whom saw this as a symbol of the government's destruction of their culture, the official version by the Xinhua news agency (in 2010) was: 'The renovation of the old city in Kashgar is a project that complied with the wishes of the people.'

The propaganda stuff may seem bland and crude and one might wonder if anyone listens. However, the Chinese leaders are *very* serious about propaganda as a powerful tool, and we who look in from outside should also take it seriously. Our experience is from an environment of free information, and we may not fully grasp what the absence of something we take to be obvious means. Where information is controlled, what is repeated and repeated again gets believed, and what is not naysaid becomes truth.

(14) Thinking is influenced through educational campaigns. This method of work does not belong to a bygone past, such as the Cultural Revolution, but is alive and thriving in today's China and has been notched up in new 'mass' and 'rectification' campaigns by the new leadership. 'Mass line' is one of the main headings on the party's official home page, under which local officials are called to 'vigorously promote mass line education' in an effort that is said to be for the long duration. Schooling and education is under control and, from elementary through university levels, shot through with crude and sophisticated pro-system bias and propaganda. The school curriculum contains hours of monthly 'thought and politics' classes (still propagating Mao Zedong Thought). The political education of cadres at all levels goes on all through their careers, and receptiveness to political education is one among other criteria of promotion. In late 2014, the party launched an education campaign in the military services to strengthen political awareness and loyalty.

In April 2013, the party issued a communiqué (in principle secret but soon publicly known) from the Central Committee on 'the current state of the ideological sphere', known as Document 9. Here, cadres and officials were warned against 'Western' ideological influences that might undermine national unity and the authority of the party. They were reminded that 'struggles in the ideological sphere are perpetual' and admonished to 'make work in the ideological sphere a high priority in your daily agenda'. This was to be done by accepting ideological leadership from above, taking leadership guidance in distinguishing between true and false theories, adhering to the principle of the party's control of the media, and stronger management of the ideological battlefield. The document warned against seven false ideological trends: Western constitutional democracy, universal values, the promotion of civil society, the promotion of neo-liberalism, Western ideas of journalism, promotion of historical nihilism, and questioning the nature of socialism with Chinese characteristics.

The use of brainwashing campaigning came on conspicuous display after Xi Jinping launched his China Dream idea. In November 2012, shortly after the party leadership transition, in front of the new Politburo Standing Committee and against the backdrop of the National Rejuvenation exhibition in Beijing's National Museum, itself a propaganda display of the first order, Xi spoke about the great revival of the Chinese nation as 'the greatest dream of the Chinese nation in recent times' and of how 'each person's future and destiny is closely linked with the future and destiny of the country and nation'. As soon as it was clear that this was a signal that he had something in mind, the whole system swung into action to interpret and give content to the leader's slogan and flesh out its implications in ideology and practice. Study and discussion groups were organised throughout the party and government system. Research projects were launched in party schools and research institutes. The Chinese Academy of Social Sciences was encouraged to organise a research programme on the China Dream, aligned with 'deep research on socialism with Chinese characteristics'. Newspapers and magazines ran educational and commentary articles on the concept. State television, in both national and international services, staged learned debates. Bookstores mounted special displays with official handbooks for cadres and other relevant literature for the general public. Universities introduced the China Dream into their political training of young academics. On Children's Day, 1 June 2013, children and parents across the country were mobilised to praise, depict, and realise the China Dream. What is noteworthy here is how thoroughly and rapidly the system picked up a signal from the leader and turned it into a nationwide campaign to rally the population behind an expression of official propaganda.

(15) The controlling arm of the state reaches beyond the national borders. China tries to influence foreign reporting on itself by relentless criticism of what is seen as negativism. There appears to be not only blocking of foreign websites but also orchestrated interference and hacking. The media controllers are now developing, in addition to the Great Firewall to shut out undesirable sites, a new weapon in the form of a Great Cannon to shut them down. In Hong Kong, the book market is dominated by outlets owned by Sino United Publishing, which again is under the control of the Liaison Office of the (Beijing) central government. After the revolts in 2014, the distribution of China-critical literature has become much more difficult.

When China decided to establish what became known as Confucius Institutes around the world, they chose to do so inside established universities rather than independently on, for example, the British Council or German Goethe-Institut model. The Confucius Institutes are established in host universities with generous subsidies from the Chinese state and generally with a Chinese and China-appointed deputy director. The institutes are mainly for the teaching of Chinese language and culture, and there is in each case an understanding that there are topics in a broader agenda of Chinese affairs that will not be entertained, such as Tibetan autonomy, religious freedom, and the like. The institutes give official China a foothold in universities around the world and are constituted so that unavoidably host institutions are subjected to the pressure of self-censorship. A state-owned Chinese media organisation, Global CAMG, operates out of an office in Melbourne, masquerading as an Australian organisation, feeding pro-government news stories to other media organisations in Australia and beyond.[42] When Bloomberg published an article of brilliant investigative reporting on the wealth of the Xi Jinping family, state enterprises were instructed to not subscribe to Bloomberg's services, and the sale of its terminals in China declined. In a speech in Hong Kong in March 2014, Bloomberg's chairman repented, saying that the company should probably reconsider running articles that deviate from its core of business news. In April 2014, the Reader's Digest decided to drop the planned publication of a condensed version of the thriller *Thirst* by the Australian author L. A. Larkin. The book was being printed in China, in English and for distribution outside of China, when the printers noticed references in the text to 'torture' and to 'Falun Gong', and insisted that these references be removed for the printing to go ahead. The author refused to comply and the publisher, for reasons of cost, decided against moving the printing to outside of China. This was apparently a case of self-censorship at the printers rather than of demands from higher authorities.

Capacity

During reform and opening up, the Chinese state has lifted itself from bankruptcy to fiscal and administrative solidity. Since it was last challenged, in 1989, it has worked carefully on the double agenda of legitimacy and control so that it is now very difficult to see that a similar challenge could materialise again. Its history in this period is not one of inability but of getting done.

In assessments of state capacity, observers sometimes get two questions confused: Is the Chinese state a good state? Is it an effective state? Those who conclude that it is effective are sometimes seen to be in its praise, as if effectiveness makes a state worthy. Critics of the Chinese state are sometimes reluctant to concede its capacity,

42. A Reuters investigation, published on 2 November 2015, identified at least thirty-three radio stations in fourteen countries that are part of a network controlled by a state-run company called China Radio International.

as if so doing is to praise it as worthy. There may be an element in the critical camp of perverse wishful thinking that will have it that an unattractive state cannot be effective and that it for that reason cannot endure.

My conclusion is that the Chinese state has the capacity it needs to serve the regime's determinations. It is far from infallible and, again, more effective than efficient, but it has what it takes. My observations of the party-state and its machinery has brought me to the critical camp as far as intentions and methods are concerned but also made me immune to the wishful thinking that a state I see to be unattractive cannot be effective. If this regime is going to follow the experience of previous party-states and fail, that is not going to be because it is without capacity to deliver governance and maintain control.

Chapter 4
What They Produce

In Chapter 2, I have explored state intentions. The benevolent hypothesis is that the People's Republic is remaking itself into a state dedicated to the good of the common people, albeit in its own and convoluted way. In Chapter 3, I have explored the state's capacity and concluded that it has the administrative ability to get done, at least in broad terms, what it wants done. If the intention is a welfare state, we should by now be seeing the footprints of that kind of state in current public policy.

A welfare state is known by the services it provides to its population. Not by whether or not it delivers welfare services—under all my three hypotheses we would expect to see a state that is activist in service provision—but by the kind of services it provides and how it is done. It is therefore not enough to ask if there are welfare policies; it is necessary to look in some detail into how those policies are shaped.

But services are not only provided; they also have to be paid for. The state does that by extracting taxes from its population. A part of the welfare test must be to examine how the state treats its population in taxation, in addition to how it treats it with services. The combined examination of taxes and services is the standard model of welfare-state analysis. This is the 'narrow test' of the welfare hypothesis which I will pursue in the present chapter.

Taxes

How much do the Chinese people pay in taxes, and who pays what? As usual, we do not have an exact answer—the statistics are as always inadequate and unreliable—but we know more or less how it works out.

According to the Ministry of Finance and organisations like the International Monetary Fund, the World Bank and the OECD, the level of public revenue and expenditure is in the order of 25 to 30 percent of GDP. Public revenue is then defined as revenues from what is defined as taxation. If official GDP is overstated, as it without doubt is, then even the 30 percent estimate may be too low. Expenditures on this account are currently higher than revenues, out-of-control local government spending in recent years adding to the deficit, which is why public sector debt has risen to high, if unknown, levels (although the public sector, say, local governments, to some degree borrows from the public sector, say, state banks or their affiliated shadows). It is correct to say that we are here dealing with estimates. The government thinks, officially, that public sector deficit is about 2 percent of GDP, but the International Monetary Fund thinks it may be as much as 10 percent. The Ministry of Finance has (yet) no consolidated public accounts and does not know with precision how much goes in and out of the many public purses. But 25 to 30 percent of GDP is a reasonable baseline to start from.[1]

That is a much higher level than in the early years of reform and opening up, when state finances were depleted and the state effectively bankrupt, tax revenues reaching a low of about 10 percent of GDP. An important, and intended, consequence of economic reform was to rebuild the fiscal basis of the state. That took time and only picked up after comprehensive tax reforms in 1994, which included the introduction of the value added tax (VAT), since when tax revenues have risen sharply, lifting the Chinese state up to a level of economic solidity.

Revenues and expenditures thus estimated are still on the low side by international comparison, for example, 10 to 15 percentage points lower than the average in OECD countries.

However, public revenue and spending in China is only partially accounted for 'on-budget' in what is known as the 'general budget'. Additional 'off-budget' flows are recorded in various 'auxiliary budgets' and not included in the 25 to 30 percent baseline. By keeping some revenues and spending out of the general budget, China presents itself to the world as a moderately low-tax country. But that is false. Once off-budget finance is included (on which more later), public revenue and expenditure is on a level typical of high-income countries. In taxation, then, China, far from being a developing country, operates among the high-tax developed countries.

Taxes are levied by central and local governments on all levels, although technically not villages.[2] Some tax revenues go to central government coffers exclusively, such as customs duties, certain income and consumption taxes, and certain taxes collected from state-owned enterprises (which make some small contributions to the treasury even though most of these earnings stay with the enterprise). A second category is made up of revenues that are shared between central and local governments. The most important of these is VAT, of which the central government takes 75 percent and local governments get 25 percent. This is the most important single source of tax revenue, and the 75 percent share is the core tax base of the central state. Other shared taxes are on natural resource extraction, certain non-VAT consumption taxes, and certain industrial and commercial taxes. The third category is made up of

1. The revised Budget Law of 2014 aims to establish a framework for more rigorous and comprehensive public accounts.
2. But village authorities may still extract various 'fees', some legal and some illegal.

taxes that are entirely local and include certain business taxes, certain corporate and personal income taxes, an urban land use tax, market trading taxes, entertainment and slaughter taxes, property and vehicle taxes, stamp duty—and fines for tax delinquency. How many categories of taxes there are is a matter of definition; in one list it adds up to twenty-six, but many categories consist of several subcategories.[3]

Most of these taxes are indirect, such as VAT. Direct taxes on personal income are secondary and generate only small takings. Personal income taxes contribute only 5 to 6 percent of all tax revenue, and only a minority of households, probably 3 or 4 percent, pay such taxes. Formal rates are relatively high, but because of exemptions and evasions little revenue is raised. Employees and employers have a shared interest in evading taxes and often do, for example, by not formalising employment.

Local governments are mandated in detail by the centre to deliver services, and local leaders are pushed hard by assessment and reward systems to do so. That has left local governments with a huge shortfall in funds. This shortfall is filled in part by transfers from the central government, in part by local governments (and their agencies, including, for example, schools and the police) finding other revenues than government-allocated ones, and in part by deficits and borrowing.

Central transfers help local governments out, but with three problems. They are nowhere near filling the deficits in local budgets, they are inefficient, and they are poorly distributed. The remaining shortfall forces local governments to scramble for 'off-budget' finance. Inefficiencies arise because there are blank cheques in the transfer rules. For example, increases in civil service pay expenditures are generally covered from central funds, which means that local governments can hand out jobs and fill up their bloated bureaucracies at little or no cost to themselves. The intention has been that central transfers should shore up finances in poorer areas, but this has not worked, mainly because within-province distributions are not under central control but in the hands of provincial authorities. Revenue sharing has mainly been to the benefit of more affluent areas, adding to rather than subtracting from the already strongly unequal geographical distribution of public resources.

Almost all formal taxation is in the form of indirect taxes and taxes on productive activities, while income and property are taxed at low effective rates.[4] Indirect and activity taxes are either regressive to income or at best flat. VAT, for example, is regressive by the logic that the poor perforce use more of their income for consumption than the rich and therefore pay VAT out of more of their income. Personal and corporate income taxes are theoretically progressive but are relatively insignificant as sources of revenue and probably at least less progressive, if progressive at all, in practice than in theory because of a low level of compliance and a high level of avoid-

3. See Wong, 'Reforming China's public finances' and Shue and Wong, *Paying for Progress in China*.
4. The reform agenda of the current leadership includes a more effective wealth tax, mainly on housing property, which is supposed to come into effect from 2017.

ance and evasion. Professor Christine Wong describes the system of formal taxes as 'lacking progressiveness', which is an extreme understatement. Better to say it as it is: The Chinese tax system is harshly regressive.

All considered, then, the tax burden on the Chinese people is heavy. Actually, as we will see later on when we take into consideration non-tax extractions, the fiscal burden of the state is *very* heavy. As to who carries that burden, the rich and the middle class get off easily while those in the lower echelons of the income distribution and the poor pay more in proportion to their income. That is an uncomfortable relationship between state and people: a heavy tax burden unfairly distributed.

Welfare Services

Ever since Bismarck invented modern state-organised social protection in Germany in the 1880s, welfare policy has been recognised to be an instrument of state building, political rule, social order, and regime legitimacy. All modern states, democratic or dictatorial, even the vilest communist and fascist ones, have prided themselves on delivering social protection to their populations, and many dictatorial ones have been no less activist in this than are democratic ones. But not all states that deliver social protection are welfare states.

Although social control is always an aspect of social policy, it is not always the only purpose. Social policies can go beyond control and be dispensed for justice. What makes a state a welfare state is not that it provides protections but that it is in the welfare business for purposes beyond control, such as equality, fairness, or solidarity, and that its policies have the designs that are needed to promote these ends.

From Maoism to reform

Following the formation of the People's Republic in 1949, the new rulers set about establishing a socialist economy in which there would be no need for much of a separate welfare system. A lifelong employment policy was adopted in cities and in state-owned enterprises, state agencies, government departments, and other organizations in the public sector. Able-bodied adults were organized into 'work units'—*danwei*—through which comprehensive welfare packages were provided. Prior to the economic turnaround after 1978, more than 80 percent of the urban labour force was covered by the *danwei* system. In rural areas, peasants were organised into communes based on collective ownership of land, through which daily necessities were distributed. For those who fell outside of this system, both urban and rural, some rudimentary social relief was set up for basic needs. This model, though characterized by a sharp urban-rural divide and extremely rudimentary provision in poor areas, did provide a basic order of social protection for both workers and peasants.

As of 1978, China embarked on the great reforms towards the socialist market economy. The provision of security by way of guaranteed access to jobs or land was discontinued. Gradually, but slowly, it became accepted by the leadership that a market economy cannot function without the lubrication of some kind of social support. In a painful process of trial and error, new arrangements outside of work and production units started to emerge, although not until the late 1990s as systematic reforms. The interim was an awful period of policy neglect, social chaos, and misery.

In the first years after 1978, helpless measures were taken to restore some of the protections that had been destroyed during the Cultural Revolution.[5] That was counterproductive up against market reforms, and China in subsequent years found itself in social limbo with little of effective provision for those who did not float on the wave of economic growth. Many, very many, were eventually lifted out of poverty, but also many, very many, were left behind in destitution. In rural areas, the dismantling of collective structures meant that basic services such as health care evaporated for most peasants. In urban areas, the policy of full employment was dismantled and replaced with a system of individual contracts, and enterprises, including state-owned ones, relieved of employment and welfare responsibilities. By the 1990s, workers were massively laid off and many employers reneged on wage and social obligations, resulting in increasing poverty deep into the working population. Migrants gravitated to cities on subsistence wages and without access to any social support. Education, health care, and housing became widely unaffordable. Patients without money were rejected by hospitals and students in economic hardship by schools and colleges. The resulting misery gave rise to widespread and serious social unrest during the late 1980s and 1990s, including strike actions, on a scale beyond what has mostly been recognised outside of China.

The first phase of serious reform was to resurrect comprehensive measures for the traditionally privileged groups: public sector and urban formal sector workers. For these groups, health insurance and pensions were operational by the end of the 1990s. Social assistance, now under the name of a Minimum Subsistence Guarantee, started to be rolled out as a national policy in 1999. As of 2002, experimentation with rural pension insurance was stepped up and as of 2003 with rural medical insurance. In 2006, agricultural taxes were abolished. In 2007, free compulsory education was introduced for rural children and in 2008 extended to the whole country (although not to migrants' children). In 2007, the Minimum Subsistence Guarantee started to be extended to rural China. Migrant workers were, in principle, given access to pension insurance in 1999 and to work injury insurance in 2002.

These reforms have radically changed the support system. At the beginning of the reform period, urban households had upwards of 40 percent of their income from social benefits, the bulk being made up of food and housing support. By 2007, the

5. See Zheng, *China's Social Security during Thirty Years.*

share of social benefits in urban household income was down to 20 percent, and for rural households to 2 percent, the bulk now being made up of social insurance, housing and food benefits having been almost eliminated.[6]

In the early period, the People's Republic operated a functioning socialist social model. That fell apart with the restructuring of the economy. Then followed about twenty years of social anarchy. Out of that undignified neglect grew new reforms whereby, in about another twenty years, a new social model was constructed, compatible with the socialist market economy.

The new model emerged gradually and was eventually codified in the Social Insurance Law of 2010. The thinking represented by this act is that adequate provisions are now in place and that what remains is to get them implemented and operational in all parts of the country. That is to happen gradually, as economic advancement permits. It is not envisaged that there are remaining systemic innovations pending.

Public sector provisions

The new model stands on four main pillars: public sector provisions, social insurance, social assistance, and social services.[7]

State and party employees, including military personnel (but not most employees in state-owned enterprises) have pensions and health care provisions of their own, funded from taxes and provided by the state. Their pensions are fully covered from government budgets and arranged as final-salary defined benefit schemes. These are privileged entitlements compared to those of enterprise employees, for example at replacement levels after thirty-five years of service (thirty for military personnel) reaching up to 90 percent of the salary at retirement. Their medical allowances and services are again better and more comprehensive than for the rest of the population, in large measure amounting to free health care. Military personnel, veterans, and family members have access to 'special care and placement' with preferential social and medical care, housing, and other services for retired personnel.

The state, then, takes relatively good care of its own people, something the Chinese system has in common with the social systems in most other countries.

Social insurance

Outside of public sector provisions, two steering principles of the new model are *insurance* and *outsourcing*. The state is regulator and facilitator but in the main no longer provider.

6. Gao et al., 'The Chinese welfare state in transition'.
7. For a recent comprehensive analysis, see Saich, *Providing Public Goods in Transitional China.*

First, the state assists and regulates for the population to be included in various social insurance schemes. These provide income support in contingencies, such as old age and illness. The basic insurance schemes are state run, whereby the state is in control of the capital that is generated through insurance contributions.

Second, the state's insurance schemes provide income support, but most provisions come from other operators. Health care is provided by hospitals and clinics that are mostly run on a for-profit basis. Social services are increasingly outsourced to NGOs that are not directly a part of the state apparatus. Assistance to persons with disabilities, beyond that provided by families, is now largely a responsibility of ordinary businesses and the 120,000 full-time employees of the China Disabled Persons' Federation (which came to prominence under the able presidency from 1988 to 2008 of Deng Pufang, the son of Deng Xiaoping, who was confined to a wheelchair after having been beaten to disability during the Cultural Revolution). A system of state-run welfare factories which had provided employment for persons with disabilities was discontinued during the 1990s.

However, the state has not been able to shed all provision responsibilities outside of the public sector. Social assistance remains a state provision, and some forms of personal social care are local government provisions. Public housing was gradually discontinued during the reform period but has recently been reinstated in the face of mounting problems with the availability of affordable housing.

There are five main categories of social insurance: pensions, medical, work injury, unemployment, and maternity. The basic social insurance is and will remain state run and state owned. Citizens can purchase additional private insurance but not opt out of the state system. The general rule is that funding is through social pooling whereby employers, employees, the self-employed, and the state, in various combinations, contribute to building up funds, while entitlements are earned by contributions and, in the case of pensions and medical care, regulated by personal accounts.

There are three categories of *pension insurance*: for urban enterprise employees, for other urban residents, and for rural people. The pension age is normally sixty for men and fifty-five or fifty for women (for military personnel fifty-five for men and fifty for women). This is the age at which pensions start to be claimed but not necessarily the effective retirement age as some people continue to work beyond the technical retirement age.

Enterprise employees, mainly urban, have access to a basic pension insurance, which is obligatory, and may have access to a supplementary enterprise pension insurance. The basic pension is state run on the principle of social pooling and personal accounts. Supplementary pensions are additional to the basic pension and enterprise run, or run jointly by pools of enterprises, for the enterprises' own employees. Additional personal (commercial) pension insurance is encouraged (but not by tax incentives: contributions are not tax deductible). The aspiration is that basic, supplementary, and personal pensions for enterprise workers should add up to a replacement rate at about 60 percent of the wage at retirement, but that is unlikely to be achieved in any uniform manner in the foreseeable future. It would depend entirely on personal pensions which so far do not have wide take-up (although the international private insurance business sees it as a big potential market). Although coverage has widened and pension levels increased in nominal terms, replacement rates have fallen sharply, for urban enterprise workers from about 60 to about 40 percent of average local salaries since 2000, and for government and party employees from up to 90 down towards 60 percent. Replacement rates in urban non-enterprise pensions and in rural pensions are lower and also down.

The basic pension insurance is in principle obligatory for employing enterprises and employees. Contributions are paid by both employers and employees (20 percent of payroll and 8 percent of wages respectively, but with great variations between regions and sectors), the employer collecting the employee contributions. Employee contributions go into a personal account, the content of which is in principle personal property but which cannot be withdrawn until the pension age or used for other purposes.

Pension entitlements are estimated from employer and employee contributions, the local wage level, demographic (life expectancy) factors, and overtime indexing rules. Pensions are payable after a minimum of fifteen years of contributions, at a level such that members who have contributed for the minimum of fifteen years should receive a pension at approximately 15 percent of the average local salary, and with an additional 1 percentage point for every additional year of contribution.

The basic pension insurance is available, but not obligatory, to other categories than enterprise employees, for example, the self-employed, migrant workers, workers in part-time or irregular employment, and certain urban residents without work, all of whom, however, have to carry all contributions themselves. About 80 to 90 percent of local urban enterprise workers are now covered by the basic pension. The take-up by migrant urban workers is increasing slowly but as yet to no more than about 10 to 15 percent being covered.

Except for a small group with prior employment in state-owned or collective enterprises, pensions for rural residents lag behind provisions for urban residents. However, pension insurance for rural residents has been rolled out gradually since 2003, nationwide since 2009. It is set up on a similar structure to the basic enterprise pension insurance, including with personal payments into personal accounts, but with a 'collective and government subsidy' in the place of the employer contribution. Pensions from the rural system are at a lower level than those from the enterprise system. The rural pension scheme is (as for urban non-enterprise workers) voluntary, but the take-up has been good, coverage increasing to 330 million people by the end of 2011, up from 240 million in 2009.

A long-term aim is to 'integrate' urban and rural pensions, which seems to mean to reduce the differences between them. Early in 2014, the government announced an intention to merge the pension schemes for peasants and urban non-enterprise workers, as a first step towards more comprehensive integration.

The *medical insurance* is in three components: basic medical insurance for urban enterprise employees, basic medical insurance for other urban residents, and rural co-operative medical insurance for the peasant population. The enterprise medical insurance is obligatory for employing enterprises and employees, contributions paid by both parties, and available to others, such as the self-employed, who then pay all contributions themselves. The level of contributions in the enterprise scheme is generally 6 percent of payroll for employers and 2 percent of the salary for employees. Enterprises may set up supplementary medical insurance for their employees. In the non-enterprise medical insurance, contributions are paid by persons and the state. Contributions to be paid by the unemployed or those on social assistance are subsidised by the state.

The basic insurance is set up to cover a part of medical expenses for the insured—both working and (provided sufficient accumulated contributions) retired—but not all expenses or for all treatments. About half of the cost of hospital care is paid by patients although coverage varies across the country and the patient component may well often be higher. Dependents, including children, are not covered in the insurance. Patients pay a higher share of the cost in serious cases that require long treatment. Most medication beyond the very basic, as well as other 'extras', have to be paid for by patients. Hospital patients are usually dependent on families for food. Health care costs have risen sharply, and household spending on health care has not been reduced in spite of better insurance. The cost of health care remains prohibitively high for poor people. The portion of medical expenses covered from the insurance is supposed to be settled directly between the social insurance agency and the providing institution, but in practice patients often have to pay up front and then (try to) be compensated for some of their outlays later. Access to effective health care is patchy, and high-quality treatment is expensive and difficult to come by. Life expectancy is significantly different in different parts of the country.

Health care provision is through institutions and pharmacies which are 'designated service providers of medical insurance' and which may be private, and is, as is service provision generally, inefficient in delivery. Community health service centres are in operation in both urban and rural areas to provide some basic care and preventive health education and guidance, but health care all considered is hospital-centric and with poorly developed primary, general practice, and outpatient services, resulting in over-hospitalisation, both in frequency and length of stay. There is a heavy reliance on the use of pharmaceutics, partly because of perverse incentives which enable medical practitioners and institutions to profit from the prescription of (overpriced) medicine. Birth control 'services' are provided by separate family planning stations or centres.

The rural cooperative medical insurance started to operate in 2003 and is now implemented nationwide, almost all of the rural population now being covered. It is a voluntary scheme for rural residents, aimed to cover some medical costs for the treatment of serious ailments. Contributions are from central and local governments, rural collectives, and (low) premiums paid by participating persons. Reimbursements are very low compared with the basic medical insurance for urban enterprise employees.

Workers who are covered by the enterprise medical insurance are entitled to a fixed period of paid sick leave, based on their years of service. For others, the medical insurance does not cover the loss of income during illness.

The *work injury* insurance is obligatory for employing enterprises and funded fully by employer contributions (no employee contributions). The contributions are set at a level estimated to be adequate to cover local running expenses and are variable across regions, sectors, and enterprises according to work injury incidence, at between 0.5 and 2 percent of payroll. There are three main compensations: medical and nursing allowances, disability allowances, and allowances for work-related deaths, including funeral allowances and conditional allowances for family members. Wages during the treatment period (normally for up to twelve months) are to be carried by the employer. The insurance does not cover the consequences of permanent loss of working capacity, or of self-inflicted injuries, such as resulting from drunkenness.

The *unemployment insurance* is obligatory for employing enterprises and is funded by employer and employee contributions (2 percent of payroll and 1 percent of wages respectively). It covers urban workers (and, conditionally, the urban self-employed) and provides sustenance (living and, conditionally, medical expenses) for a duration of up to twenty-four months. Unemployment insurance for migrant workers who have labour contracts with urban enterprises covered by the unemployment insurance is under consideration. Non-employee residents are not included, such as peasants who have lost farmland due to, for example, local government expropriation.

In the *maternity insurance*, female employees have a right to compensation for the loss of salary and for medical expenses during childbirth (or undergoing abortion). The insurance is funded fully by employers at a regionally differentiated rate of no more than 1 percent of the employer's payroll costs. The birth allowance entitlement is at a local average salary level and for upwards of ninety days.

Social assistance

The main provision of social assistance is the Minimum Subsistence Guarantee (*dibao*). This gives access to a locally determined minimum subsistence level of cash support, conditional on family income. The relief is managed and funded locally.

Urban residents have in principle been covered since 1999 and rural residents gradually since 2006 (supplementing the existing rural 'five guarantees' provision of assistance to 'extremely needy' households). It is available only to people with a local *hukou*. Migrants are not eligible in their host localities. Some other forms of discretionary educational, medical, and housing assistance may be available for some 'needy' persons, depending on local practices, such as homeless people, people who are destitute ('vagabonds'), and disabled persons with 'disability certificates'.

The level of minimum subsistence is low and basic, generally about 20 to 30 percent of average local wages, and with huge local variations notably between (but also within) urban and rural areas. Both the right to support and the duty of provision are ambiguous.

Social services

Social services are a local responsibility and are provided for the most disadvantaged groups, such as orphans and the poorest elderly people. The trend, encouraged by central authorities but sometimes resisted by local bureaucracies, is to outsource social service provisions to non-government or non-bureaucracy organisations, which may or may not be for-profit and which may or may not be qualified for the work they take on.

Services for the elderly are targeted to the 'needy' or 'extremely needy'. They are marginal and mainly provided through institutions ('senior citizens' homes') which provide accommodation, in-house services, emergency aid, daytime care, health and rehabilitation services, and recreational services. For the overwhelming majority of elderly people, social services provided by the state play little or no role in their lives.

Services for children are targeted to orphans and abandoned children or those with disabilities and provided mainly through institutions ('children's welfare houses', boarding schools, and the like). Adoption and foster care is encouraged.

Public housing was a central component of social support in the pre-reform period, but was gradually discontinued, in-kind welfare housing being terminated by 1998. Public housing property was privatised through subsidised purchasing and housing policy limited to the injection of 'affordable housing' in the housing market. Housing was transformed from a public rental system to market-based owner-occupancy. Although successful in most urban centres in improved housing conditions and the creation of a new property-owning class, the retreat of policy came at the price of undermining poor people's access to affordable housing and of new inequalities and class divisions. This turned out to be too much policy retreat. In an attempt to tame the housing market, 'housing provident funds' were established in urban areas during the 1990s, as a mechanism for generating housing capital and improving access to the market. All employing enterprises are obliged to participate, both employers and employees paying fund contributions. The funds are in principle obligatory saving schemes on behalf of employees, but funded mainly by employers, in which employees hold accounts. Although not the intention, the capital was initially used (abused) mainly for housing construction. Gradually, employees have gained access to their accounts to use accumulated savings and additional loans for home purchase or to withdraw savings on retirement. The price of housing, however, continued to rise exponentially, swaths of the non-poor population finding decent housing beyond their reach. As of 2011, the government has re-entered the housing market as a provider with a renewed programme of public housing, including government-subsidised housing, joint-ownership housing, and public low-cost rental housing, to some degree reverting housing to a (subsidised) rental system.

Improvements in schooling and education, albeit substantial, have lagged behind what should have been expected given rapid economic growth. Enrolment in preschool education is at a low level, even in comparison with other middle-income countries, preschool education for rural children and children of migrants at notably low levels of reach and quality. Primary education is (in principle) free, as of 2008, but hidden fees and non-fee costs still represent a heavy burden on poor families. Secondary and further education is not free, and tuition fees are exceptionally high by international comparison. Public schools are segregated between 'regular' schools and higher-quality 'key' schools, the latter orchestrating selective intakes through various informal mechanisms, including 'selection fees'. Rural schooling is often substandard and has suffered deterioration in some areas of high-level outmigration. There is a growing sector of private for-profit schools, with no effective system of licensing and accreditation, which contribute to removing the children of affluent families from the public school system. Enrolment in secondary and senior secondary schools is at a comparatively low level and is for rural children stagnant (because of low-quality primary schooling and prohibitive fees and other costs). Schooling is strong on mechanical learning but weak on skills such as independent, creative, and critical thinking. On many indicators of quality and enrolment in schooling, the trend is towards widening inequalities and disparities. The children of migrants generally have restricted, if any, access to public schools and to sitting university entrance exams where they live.

Chinese schooling appears to be performing well in some international comparisons of educational quality, notably in the PISA study undertaken by OECD. Those results however, as so often with statistics from China, are bogus. In the PISA study, China is represented by Shanghai, its most advanced city, and Shanghai by a selection of schools that exclude those for migrant children.

Disclaimers

This description of the new social model must be accompanied by many and necessary qualifications. The components that are described above exist and are in operation, but there are divisions, differences, and shortcomings across the system in implementation on the ground. The description, therefore, should be read as reflecting in part operating policies and in part policy aspirations. What is actuality, what is aspiration, and what is serious aspiration cannot be stated in any precise manner.

The system of funded social insurance is in the making, with huge unresolved problems of implementation. The main aspirations are to move the management of social security from firms to state insurance agencies, to create more uniformity across sectors with more equitable provisions for workers in state-owned and private enterprises, and to start the building-up of funds to help finance future needs.

The collection of social insurance contributions and the distribution of benefits are in the hands of county social insurance bureaus, operating through local sub-offices. Both contributions and benefits are to some degree at the discretion of local authorities, and neither is uniform across the country.

The plan is to collect more in contributions than is paid out in claims, thereby to accumulate social insurance capital to underwrite future claims. The capital is to sit in funds, the management of which is gradually to be centralised to provincial governments, and in the case of pension funds to the central government. This centralisation is ongoing, against much local resistance, on an unspecified timetable.

The experience so far is that the system, in all components of social insurance, is shot through with irregularities, such as non-participation by enterprises, shortfalls in contributions, mispayment of benefits to non-eligible persons, excessive overhead costs, and misappropriation locally of social insurance funds, including by corrupt means. Although the system as a whole is running at a surplus, there is, as yet, only a moderate accumulation of capital, so that what on paper is becoming a system of funded social insurance, de facto continues to be run on a pay-as-you-go basis, so that by and large today's contributions go to paying for today's benefits. A National Social Security Fund was established in 2000 as a sovereign wealth fund for the management of some surplus social insurance capital.[8]

8. The government has indicated that from 2016 it will deploy some of the social insurance capital into the domestic stock market, another reason for its ill-fated stimulus of that market. That may or may not happen, both because the stock market after the 2015 crash looks less attractive and because it depends on local authorities on various levels relinquishing more of their control over locally collected social insurance capital, something they are apparently reluctant to do. They may instead wish to use the capital for purposes of their own, and they may not trust the relevant central authority, the National Council of Social Security Fund, to manage the capital well.

With the provisions that are now in place, China is moving towards near universal access to basic components of social protection. However, this statement needs to be qualified in five ways.

First, access is moving towards 'near universal' but not fully universal. The 2010 Social Insurance Law carefully envisages no more than 'wide' coverage. The main remaining and unresolved exclusion is of migrant workers, perhaps 250 million people, who are without most social entitlements where they work and massively discriminated against even in the entitlements they have. Non-migrant workers in irregular employment are at best marginally included.

Second, what is approaching near universality is access but not provision. For the self-employed and irregular workers, participation in social insurance is voluntary and expensive, since they have to pay all contributions themselves. Even where participation is compulsory in law, as it mostly is for enterprise workers, there is widespread non-compliance and failure by enterprises to sign up or to pay contributions in full. Social insurance entitlements are intended to be made portable so that workers retain them when changing jobs or relocating, but exactly what entitlements are portable is not clear, and the practicalities of portability are not in place.

Third, what there is access to is inadequate and not uniform. Social assistance has low efficiency in that the level of support is inadequate for protection against poverty, provisions are often poorly managed, and there are built-in work disincentives and poverty trap and dependency distortions. The Minimum Subsistence Guarantee is plagued by targeting errors and patronage, such as being given to friends and relatives of those who distribute it, limited anti-poverty results being achieved. Poverty rates have, as is well known, fallen dramatically, but social assistance specifically has contributed nothing or next to nothing to the reduction in poverty rates.[9] It was rolled out as a national policy in 1999, in part to respond with some level of support to mass unemployment resulting from economic restructurings in the state sector. Subsequently, through both central and local government re-regulations in 2012 and 2014, it has been pulled back to being more narrowly targeted to extremely disadvantaged people and those in need who are without work capacity and have no legal guardians. Welfare services are minimal. In social insurance, there are regional and occupational variations in provisions, including between government and enterprise employees and urban and rural residents, and to the exclusion of migrant workers. State, party, and military personnel form a privileged group in pension and health care provisions.

9. This has been demonstrated in studies in which the *dibao* has been subjected to the standard procedures of redistribution analysis, cf. Gao, 'Redistributive nature of the Chinese social benefit system'; Gao et al., 'Anti-poverty effectiveness of the minimum living standard'; and Gustafsson and Deng, 'Dibao receipt and its importance'.

Fourth, central government intentions may be mismanaged, ignored, or sabotaged locally. Local authorities have a great deal of autonomous power in the system. They have the power to interpret implementation duties and to regulate programme coverage and benefit levels. They can decide on the degree of inclusion or exclusion of migrant workers. They hold power over social insurance capital and have the power to divert these funds to uses of their own. Poor local authorities down to the village level have the power to be miserly and affluent ones to be generous, including through social provisions of their own. They have the power of disobedience. One example is in schooling. Although compulsory education is in principle free, schools and local authorities widely impose implicit fees on parents, which they may be coerced into declaring as 'voluntary contributions', and extract other forms of payments in 'a state-run education system overrun by bribery and cronyism'.[10] The result is a system with limited and unequal implementation and vast and complex inequalities of access and provision across localities.

Fifth, in so large and complex a country as China, provision—the bringing of benefits and services to claimants and clients—is extremely difficult. Social assistance and social services are provided by local agencies and organisations, often with low capacity and not always with good will. Social insurance cash benefits are provided through local social insurance bureaus, which may be inefficient or corrupt. In both social assistance and social insurance, the payment of benefits and entitlements is poorly targeted and widely misallocated. Social insurance benefits in kind, such as health care, are provided by service institutions and practitioners, which, private or public, operate on a fee-for-service basis. Access to even basic medical services is hard to come by, often depending on bribery, in a 'market of distrust'.[11] Hospitals and other health care institutions and medical practitioners have income from the sale of pharmaceutics, which are overpriced and pushed on patients, resulting in the cost of health care escalating and in massive overmedication. This complexity, along with that of government levels, contributes to the pattern of vastly differentiated provisions across the country.

All considered, then, China today operates an extensive system of social provision. This is in the main an insurance system, biased in favour of the urban population, and with minimal and disjointed other provisions, including for last resort poverty protection. It is without universality of coverage or provision and with deep differentiation of treatment between population groups. The great divide is between the urban and rural populations. Between these two groups is the large population of migrant and other irregular workers, who have notably inferior entitlements compared to regular urban residents.

10. *New York Times*, 22 November 2012.

11. As described by Cheris Shun-ching Chan, a sociologist at the University of Hong Kong. *New York Times*, 8 April 2015.

Welfare State?

A welfare state, in the narrow meaning considered so far, offers citizens fair taxation and adequate social protections. More precisely, in the most authoritative definition of the term, it is a state 'in which political and administrative power is used to modify the play of market forces in at least three ways: to guarantee individuals and families a minimum income irrespective of the market value of their work or property, to narrow the extent of insecurity in the ability of individuals and families to meet certain social contingencies which would otherwise lead to individual or family crisis, and to ensure that all citizens without distinction of status or class are offered the best standards in relation to a certain agreed range of health and social services.'[12]

It might be seen as not entirely fair to apply a somewhat idealistic British notion of welfare to the situation in China. However, this is not an after-the-fact definition formulated as an academic afterthought but one which reflects ideas and principles enshrined in the great British reforms from 1944 to 1948 (family and child allowances, social assistance as rights-based income support, consolidated social security, the National Health Service). This was Britain's wave of social policy modernisation not unlike one China has been through since the late 1990s. The reason these reforms could be carried forward as they were at the time was not that Britain was affluent enough to 'afford' generous social protections—Britain was then much less affluent than China is now—but that there was a political will manifested in a consensus coming out of the trials of the Second World War that British society should be transformed into one on a higher level of social justice. Far from being a luxury definition, it represents the kind of standard the Chinese model should answer to, and making it answer to that standard is in line with my approach of treating the Chinese state as a grown-up one. It is certainly a grown-up one in taxation, and it then makes sense to treat it as a grown-up one in delivery as well.

By this standard, and in spite of reforms that are in many ways impressive, China is not a welfare state. Even if we strip the definition down to basic principles and ask not for perfection but for tendencies and directions in the system, what is being achieved still falls short of a welfare-state threshold.

- Is there a tendency in the system to modify the play of market forces? The answer is no. On the tax side, the system is regressive in the extreme and rather worsens than modifies market inequalities. Crudely, the poor pay more. On the service side, the main body of provision is through social insurance, which by and large reproduces market inequalities. Main services such as health care and education remain costly and prohibitively expensive for poor people. The

12. Briggs, 'The welfare-state in historical perspective'.

middle class buys itself free from the strictures of social protection and lends the system no support.

- Is there a safety net to offer last resort protection against the risk of poverty? The answer is no. Social assistance is inadequate and ineffective. Social services for the poor are patchy, arbitrary, or non-existent.
- Is there a tendency in the system of access to the best standards of core services? The answer is no. For most people, services are mediocre. The only component in the system that has a genuine social quality in the sense of being a bit more generous than it needs to be for utilitarian purposes is maternity insurance. Otherwise, best standards, such as in health care and education, are only available to those who are connected or pay for it.
- Is there a tendency in the system of provision without distinction of status or class? The answer is no. The system is shot through with fragmentation and inequality of treatment, not only between public employees and other workers but also between enterprise and more or less irregular workers, between urban and rural populations, and always to the detriment of the millions of migrant workers and their families.

It is not only that these questions are answered in the negative in the meaning that this is where social protection has come so far. The system does not have designs that would enable it to mature in such a way that the answers to these questions might turn to the affirmative.

In the balance of what the state takes and what it gives, as considered so far, we see a state that takes a great deal in taxes and that takes proportionately more from the poor than from the rich, and that gives back a meagre package of welfare services—the kind of package that in the welfare-state literature would be described as 'marginal' and that would normally be associated with a low-tax regime—and a package that is without redistributive force in poverty protection or otherwise. This is not for want of capacity. China has more than enough affluence, more than enough tax capacity, and more than enough administrative capacity for better social provisions to be affordable and practically possible. A state that can keep 1.4 billion people under constant Orwellian control and that is perfectly capable of putting 2 million bureaucrats on the job of keeping bad information out of the Internet could give the poor and small in society more help and support than it does, if it wanted to. This regime has reluctantly accepted social protection as a necessary add-on but has little further interest in it.

The Chinese leaders have looked to other countries for experiences to build on—Singapore is often mentioned—but seem only to have learned what they have wanted to learn. Had they looked to South Korea they would have seen the successful experience of social protections being built up offensively from early on in the development process. The idea in China that the social side must wait to be developed until after the economy has developed is a lame excuse for non-action. In social protection, what does not start early on will never be done. This is precisely what is on display in China.

Had they looked to contemporary leaders in social inventiveness among middle-income countries, they might have learned about family support and conditionality. Conspicuously absent in the Chinese model is any articulated component of family support (except for what is euphemistically called 'family planning'). In one of the great recent innovations in social policy, Mexico and then Brazil found a way of spreading support to disadvantaged families and of designing that support to the benefit of children by tying conditions to it, such as children being taken to health control and school attendance. This way of using social support as an active policy instrument has subsequently spread through the developing world but not to China.

Had they looked to recent trends in Europe or America, they might have learned about 'activation,' about the integration of social and labour market policies to encourage dependents to work and self-reliance. In the Chinese model, however, any idea of social contributions to active labour market policies is as absent as any idea of family policy. In social assistance, the problem of work disincentives does not seem to matter. Welfare factories for the benefit of persons with disabilities are, as we have seen, no more. There was a flicker of initiative with 're-employment service centres' in the 1990s, but there was no determination in it, and the early experiments failed and have been abandoned.

In *China 2030*, the World Bank and the Development Research Center of the State Council review the social system in a way that is in line with my analysis here. The report finds provisions to be inadequate for the building in China of, in their language, a modern, harmonious, and creative society. This inadequacy is not for want of capacity but is explained rather by the absence of a vision for social policy and of a consensus on a common set of underlying values, including social equality and justice for all. They are probably right that there is no such vision. For example, the Social Insurance Law of 2010 is entirely pedestrian in ideas. But that is not to say that the leaders are necessarily in confusion about what they are doing. The reason no social vision has been offered is probably that the corresponding policy intention is not there. Social policies, to repeat, are always instruments of social control and regime legitimacy. They can also be instruments of social justice. In the Chinese case, they are not. The system is designed for the purchase of legitimacy and for no more. That it is not designed as an instrument of justice is policy, not lack of vision.

The components of social provision that have come into place during the last two decades are, although not insignificant, fragmented, haphazard and disjointed. Through this system, a great deal of attention flows from the state to the people in a way that enables people to see that the state is there and supportive. That is what the social provisions are for. But they add up to neither protection nor fairness. Nor do they need to for their purpose. There is no future of provision on a higher scale towards which the system is developing. Social insurance, for example, is broadening in scope and should be up to bringing basic securities to urban, regular enterprise workers (but hardly to dependents and family members), but is not designed to incorporate in any equitable way, even with time, rural people or migrant and other non-regular workers. Chinese society is organised by the principle of divide and rule. The urban, rural, and migrant populations have different forms of citizenship and with different entitlements. These divisions are enshrined in the *hukou*, the household registration system, as a barrier against broad and working-class solidarities. Rather than bridging such divisions, the system of social protection is so designed as to maintain them. Social provisions divide the population into manifold groups which are separated and treated differently and are not designed to bring the population together into a 'harmonious society'.

The best interpretation of social policies in China today is that they are designed to do what is necessary as seen from the needs of the regime. When necessity presents itself, provision materialises. When mass unemployment struck in the 1990s, social assistance was launched with some energy. When necessity recedes, provision is tempered. When the unemployment crisis was over, social assistance was pulled back rather than being developed further. When marketization resulted in a housing crisis for those who had not got on to the ladder of upwards prices early enough, some public housing provision was brought back.

It is to underestimate the Chinese leaders to suggest that they have forgotten about vision. They are doing in social policy what they are doing in all aspects of public policy, which is to do what they must do for their own sake. That may not be a vision but it is clear thinking. They are not in search of any broader consensus. Their social policy is exactly what it is intended to be: another instrument of stability and control, so much and no more.

Chapter 5
Who They Are

A recent conversation between two China watchers ran like this, condensed:

> Professor A: China is a dictatorship.
> Professor B: 500 million people have been lifted out of poverty.
> Silence.

This exchange and stalemate neatly captures the dilemma for anyone trying to understand China's political economy. Both professors are right. We might leave it at that. We might quibble about what matters most. Although there is much that is unpleasant about government in China, it delivers. Or, it is a dictatorship and it cannot buy itself free from condemnation with improvements in material conditions. Your opinion is as good as mine.

For my part, however, I am not content to leave it there. For one thing, that would not get me to where I want to go, to the soul of the Chinese state. This is a state with character and that character is not captured in a limp on-the-one-hand-and-on-the-other-hand indeterminacy. Also, although both A and B are right, neither captures the full truth. China is a dictatorship, but what kind of dictatorship? In what sense have 500 million people been lifted out of poverty, and in what sense has the state done the lifting? The Chinese leaders claim to have a model that is of solid timber, and my aim has been to tell you what kind of timber that is.

How It Works

Essentially, if not always efficiently, the regime works like this: The party decides, others do; the party controls, others stay in line.

Control

The regime's supreme determination is its own perpetuation. The leaders have many other concerns, but always stability has the final say. They have learned that confident self-preservation takes great effort. They must control their society, and that they do with force and in depth. But control, although never neglected, is not enough. They must also, as far as possible, distribute rewards and create willing compliance or connivance in the population. What is characteristic of Chinese rule now is that control and the purchase of legitimacy are not alternative strategies but complimentary ones. There is no turning away from controls in favour of more reliance on legitimisation. The leaders are perfecting and strengthening their system of control while always speaking to their people about their delivery of prosperity and governance. The two go hand in hand.

The leaders claim to have delivered, above all, economic growth. The meaning of that delivery I return to below. For now, it is worth noting that it needs not only growth but strong growth. At the first threat of contagion from the world economic downturn as of 2008, the government released a gigantic stimulus into its own economy to keep investment and growth up in the face of reduced demand for its products from the rest of the world. When the official GDP growth target for 2014 was published at 7.5 percent, there was already concern about slack growth. The reason people worry about a growth rate in China that most other countries could only dream of is political and not economic. Economically, 7.5 percent is ferocious. Even 5 or 4 percent would normally be seen as exceptionally strong growth but would in China get the alarm bells ringing incessantly. The Chinese regime needs an economic miracle. The state needs massive resources to fund itself, run its inefficient administration to effect, and feed its investment machine. The business class needs to be bought off by the access to making itself rich and by the promise of more riches down the road. The class of officials needs to be bought off by access to perks and corruption gains. There need to be resources left over to lift the standard of living of the masses of ordinary Chinese households. Economic growth is the regime's main instrument for the purchase of legitimacy. That purchase is expensive. For it to be effective, there needs to be enough growth to give everyone something, even when much is to be creamed off first to satisfy the appetites of the great bureaucracies, the state enterprises, and the political and economic classes that stand above the masses. The leaders know that what loyalty or acquiescence they have from their people, they have not because they are loved but because they bring them goods. The day the economy is no longer growing at a politically adequate rate, even if still growing at a good economic rate, there will not be enough to satisfy the manifold expectations the regime has itself created.

We who observe China from outside are keenly attentive to oppositional forces inside, as I am in these pages. We follow the doings of activists and the degree to which they are able to operate and when and how they are clamped down upon. We listen to oppositional voices among academics, journalists, and business people. We are alert to incidents of protest anywhere in the country. We know that China is not unified under the leadership of the party in the way the leaders would like it to be.

The truth, however, in the larger scheme of things, is that China *is* pretty unified. There is opposition and activism, of course, but not all that much. By and large, the press is loyal, the business middle class is loyal, the professoriat is loyal, cultural workers are loyal, students are loyal. Not fully, and many people push the boundaries of what they can do and say. Some go on from there and engage against the system and work in favour of human rights or the end to one-party rule. Representatives of ethnic minorities engage in revolt. These are courageous people, but in the end they are few and far between. Those able to take activism out of isolated action and into organised opposition are even fewer.

It is common among observers to think that the Chinese regime is stable because it enjoys a great deal of support from below, but that is a conclusion too far. It is not what the leaders themselves put their trust in. It may have had some success in making itself trusted, but that is not to say that it has won legitimacy in a safe or durable way. The forceful explanation is that the system of control works. For the most part, engagement in systemic opposition is so difficult, risky, and costly, and so unlikely to matter, that it is hardly worth the while. Nor is it generally encouraged from below. Sad as it may be, those who do are more likely to be seen by 'ordinary people' as foolish and as making trouble in vain than as heroes who stand up for principles and justice.

In some ways, the state has been in retreat in Chinese society. There is now a vast sector of private economic enterprise which operates outside of direct state command. Public administration and service delivery is being partially outsourced to agencies that are not directly a part of the state's administration.

But what has been less noted is that while the *state* may in some ways have retreated from directly running things, the *party* has extended its reach. In business organisations that operate 'freely', the party is present. In NGOs that are on the receiving end of outsourcing, the party is present. The retreat of the state, then, if that is what we are seeing, is not a retreat of the party-state. It represents a shift in the mode of control, from direct state command to a more subtle form of party control. The party is there, and everyone knows it is there. It does not tell everyone everything he or she must do. But it does control that people do not do what they must not, and it does so in great detail, from not having children that should not be had via not reading or seeing or hearing what should not be read or seen or heard, to not practising faiths that should not be practised—and above all to not organising.

This is a subtle system of indirect control that gets more of what it wants by working softly than by rough means. It knows that it does not need absolute obedience and that it would be counterproductive to demand it. It is a control system that does not control what does not need to be controlled and that relies extensively on managed self-control. Under Mao, people were expected not only to believe in the party and to obey the party line but also to show their devotion in their daily lives, for example in the way they dressed and the kind of entertainment they enjoyed. This nonsense the Chinese have been freed from. They can now live more as they wish. It is not that they are not controlled when it matters, only that they are not bossed around when it does not matter.

This modern (shall we say?) form of subtle control is contributing to the creation of a compliant population. The Chinese state is edging towards a dictatorship that is in some ways pain free, one in which controls run smoothly and in which people stay in line more or less by their own doing because it makes sense to do so. Various forms of brute control have been or are being rolled back, such as detention in education through labour. Subtle controls work well enough so that brute controls are less necessary.

However, all the while, how subtle the manifestation of control is generally, behind it all lies, always, the threat of punishment, harassment, detention, the loss of job or home, retribution against family and friends, violence, and ultimately death. The threat is always there, and is often enough shown to be real. No doubt, the authorities normally prefer not to have to act with brute repression, but they are not giving away their right and ability to do so when they have to, or their capacity to threaten or crush anyone who puts himself or herself in their way.

I have rejected the label of 'authoritarian' for the Chinese state. It is too accommodating. A state that demands obedience and controls to the extent the Chinese one does, that rules by fear and the force of armed power, that sends the police out at night to break down front doors and haul people away, and that in the last instance relies on violence, and on the demonstrable willingness to use violence when it sees that to be necessary or opportune, is not just an authoritarian state. It is a dictatorship. But I have also said that 'dictatorship' is not an adequate label. It is too unsophisticated. China is now a dictatorship in which dictate is restrained and in which, except in the last resort, indirect control is substituted for direct command. This mode of control, hard in effect but soft in execution, is being developed to perfection and makes the Chinese state a kind of dictatorship never seen before. That kind of dictatorship needs a name. It is not an autocracy; that is too benevolent. It is not a dictatorship like others; that is too primitive. I give it the name of *controlocracy*.

Totalitarian?

It is perfectly possible in China to live your own life—as long as you understand and accept the limits: that there are things you cannot do or say, that there are other things you have to do, or pretend to do, that there are things you are asked to believe and that you for many purposes must profess to believe, and things you must say and profess to believe in the right way, that there are beliefs you are not allowed to practise, that you cannot organise, that you are obliged to tolerate propaganda and mindless political education, that abuse by public officials is a fact of life you must accommodate to, that ultimately the party-state sets the rules and decides, that you do not have the right to question the party, or any other rights for that matter, including the right to have children, that you have to pay for what you are entitled to, that you are under observation and control, that if you break the rules, or what the authorities say are the rules, or if someone near to you does, you are in risk of being harassed, taken away, disappeared, beaten up, and possibly killed. In China's new capitalism, people do not have the right to do business; they can only go into business because the state, in its constitution, 'permits the private sector to exist'.

With these limitations and conditions, then, is the Chinese state totalitarian? It was that in Mao's time, but has reform and opening up modernised the system out of totalitarianism?

In *The Origins of Totalitarianism*, Hannah Arendt explained the nature of totalitarianism as a form of rule that goes beyond being merely dictatorial. Rule is totalitarian when it permeates society so deeply that 'the political' does not exist. There is no space between the ruled and the rulers in which citizens can speak and act in public with relative security and in which they can be themselves and express their views on social and political matters and on morality and governance, and where they can do so socially and together. Thinking and acting human beings have nowhere public to develop and act out their individuality, to work on their understanding of political life through deliberation, or to exercise even elementary exchange with others without control from above. Human beings as individuals do not have recognition, and ultimately do not matter. What remains of political life for the population is forced underground and into privacy, secrecy, and isolation.

Arendt went on to list the four main mechanisms by which rule makes itself totalitarian in a definition that has the strength of clarity and has stood the test of time:

- that rule is upheld by terror;
- that rule reaches into the regulation of natural human bonds and private spheres, including family bonds and practices, and even mindsets;
- that governing is exercised through an extensive and impersonal bureaucracy; and
- that the state operates under the authority of an ideology that explains its mission and justifies its hold on power and its means of governing.

In the modern and reformed People's Republic, is there rule by terror? The answer is yes. Everyone is watched, all public agencies are information gatherers, the party sees everything and knows everything. The security services and their hired thugs are on hand, as are the armed forces. Yang Maodong, the brave activist who in court compared China 'blow by blow' to Orwell's *1984* nightmare state, was right. Although the controlocracy is sophisticated and does not depend on the omnipresence of terror, the threat of terror is omnipresent, and that threat is backed up by a physical use of violence that is sufficient for citizens to know very well that the treat is not an idle one. There is so much those who want to get on with life must accept and so much uncertainty about the rules and where the limits are drawn, that life in China is stunted by connivance or infused with fear. One result of the tightening of controls under the current leadership is more uncertainty and deeper fear. No one knows the rules. Moderates get picked on, as if out of the blue and for inexplicable reasons. Within the public services, initiative and action has become dangerous because no one knows what might be seen to be subversive. All forms of expression are censored, be it in print or electronic media, down to the thought-work-induced self-censorship of every person among the common people who just want a normal life. It is true that the controlocracy uses terror with some economy, but it is also true that it holds the means of terror and is unhesitant in its use when necessary.

Does rule penetrate to the regulation of private spheres? The answer is yes. Thought work is integral to rule. What people know is controlled, what they are told is controlled, how they should think is influenced by omnipresent propaganda, political education, and mass campaigns. They live in an environment that is saturated by lies, half-truths, make-beliefs, and twisted language. Through its birth control policy, the state makes itself present and paramount for almost everyone in a formative life phase and in the most intimate aspect of what should be private life.

One of the consequences of headless GDP-growth-ism has been a shattering of family structures. Chinese culture is family-oriented. There is an anticipation and aspiration that life is lived in families, that family members take care of each other, and that family is your first resort for help and support. This expectation is, for example, basic to the design of social protection policies and enshrined in social legislation. The birth control policy, however, has aimed to reduce families in size, a consequence of which is to deprive them of the generational resources they need to meet social expectations. The result is too many elderly people who do not have necessary family support, too many children growing up as single children without a grounding in the robust family experience that comes from sibling relations, too many young adults who do not have brothers or sisters to call on, too many aspiring parents who do not have any children, and too many young men who cannot find wives and form families. Where those 'failed' men go with their frustrations and anger is perhaps not known; my spine-chilling guess is that many of them gravitate to the military and security services.

Economic growth has been and remains premised on the mobilisation of an army of migrant workers. This migration has resulted in a widespread uprooting of families. Many migrants have had to leave families behind, and innumerable families have been split up, leaving 'left-behind' children to be raised by a lone parent or by grandparents or relatives, or sometimes just left, 33 million of them in substandard boarding schools. When whole families migrate, often to inferior housing and living conditions, they make do as best they can in towns and cities where they do not have normal entitlements, including to health care and education, and where they often suffer disrespect, discrimination, and exclusion.

A further natural human bond that is held under state regulation is that of social networks. What all dictatorial states fear above all, more than individuals or small groups who are in opposition or in protest, is activism from below that can gel into networks or organisations beyond the very local. The Chinese state has dealt with this danger by, on the one hand, pulling as much of associational life as possible into the orbit of party control, and on the other hand by clamping down on anything that looks like grass-roots organisation. It does not matter if it is organisation for sanctioned causes; it is organisation itself that is dangerous. Any non-controlled organisation is a threat to the authority of the party. People can criticise the state; what they *cannot* do is engage in collective action. It is above all against this danger that the ultimate threat of terror gets unleashed. To the degree that natural human bonds are made up of people being able to meet up and deliberate freely and openly with each other, those bonds are eliminated.

Is governance by bureaucracy? The answer is obviously yes; there has never been a bureaucratic state like the Chinese one. This bureaucracy is not only big but also brutally impersonal. It is not a civil service but a party service. Public servants do not answer downwards to the people they serve but upwards to those they serve for. Abuse downwards is rampant.

As a result of these influences, where does 'the political', in Arendt's meaning, stand in China today? It obviously does not have much space. There is virtually no public space for free expression and development of political understanding and no public space at all for uncontrolled political organising or networking. How vibrant exchange is in private and under the radar is not clear. Perhaps ordinary Chinese take revenge in private ingenuity, but perhaps also the controlocracy denies them genuine space even for that.

One interpretation of the crackdown in 1989, which I have described as a decisive juncture in China's political development, is that a possible political opening was decisively closed. What happened, I have argued in Chapter 1, was that hope itself was killed and that overnight the only reality was accommodation with the fact of dictatorship. It is possible that the Chinese, or most of them, have adapted to that reality so that it with time has become obvious, in a silent victory for totalitarianism.

Evidence to that effect was offered in a beautiful and touching testimony by a brave mainland student in Hong Kong in the midst of the pro-democracy revolt there September–October 2014, published in the *Asia Literary Review* (under a pseudonym) under the title 'Letter to Hong Kong Students: Tonight I Picked a Side'. The writer starts by explaining her instinctive alienation from the 'immature' idea of political demonstration, but how she then came to see courage in political action and therefore to 'stand by you, because you are doing what I never dared to dream.' 'We mainland students,' she goes on to say, 'not only do we seldom care about Hong Kong issues, we barely understand our own. It is not even in our mindset to consider the legitimacy and integrity of [our political] process. We don't know that it's possible to ask, "What do *we* want?" Tonight, I saw a determination and solidarity that I have never experienced, and that has not been seen in China for a long time. Tonight, I saw you become brothers and sisters. Some say this is just not the way we deal with things, but seriously, how do we ever deal with anything? I cannot hide my jealousy of you for having the opportunity to fight. In my twenties . . . we never knew that there is such an option.' She acknowledges that the demonstrations may not achieve their goals, but nonetheless 'what you have now—your courage and hope, solidarity and discipline—are so precious. You have no idea how people in the dark corners of the world, me included, covet it.'

In my context, this extraordinary letter is from a young bright woman who through the events in Hong Kong discovers a community which she has not previously been able to see in which 'the political' exists and is being preserved with open action in the public arena. And thereby she also discovers, and is able to articulate, the reality of her own community in which 'the political' has ceased to exist, even down to political awareness, to 'our mindset'. And even if your mindset is not controlled, where is the space to cultivate it or for action? I am in a coffee shop in Shanghai with a young student who was preparing to go abroad for graduate studies. I ask if she felt she lives in a dictatorship. Thoughtfully, slowly, she answered 'no', but then added, after more thought, again softly, slowly, that 'life is not safe here'. The wife of Liu Jianshu, who was detained with others in a network of ten to fifteen likeminded young idealists in December 2014, said (to the *New York Times*): 'Now if I don't hear from a friend for three hours I get nervous. We are in touch every day to see who is missing. I'm worried that I'll disappear one of these days, too.'

By Arendt's first criteria, then, the Chinese state is totalitarian. The remaining question, yet again, is that of ideology. Totalitarian rule is hard. It takes serious and durable suppression. That takes motivation, determination, and justification. And that again takes the enforcement of ideology. An idea of totalitarian rule without a narrative that explains it both to those who exercise it and those it is exercised on does not make sense.

It would not be correct to describe the Chinese state as non-ideological. The party calls itself communist, it takes legitimacy from Marxism-Leninism, Mao Zedong Thought, Deng Xiaoping Theory, and so on. Stalin has not been denounced in China, and of course not Mao. Far from it, today's leaders are again basking in the continuity from Mao. Deng Xiaoping stressed propaganda and thought work and upheld the principle of the people's democratic dictatorship. Xi Jinping is nothing if not ideological in language and doing. The party remains the highest authority of history and truth, and by force of that authority commands allegiance. It controls, propagates, and educates on the merits of its truths. It represses other truths, beliefs, and practices because it has the right to decide what is right. It is not just that this state rules, but it rules by force of a narrative of history and destiny.

Up against the strong body of China analysis that rejects the proposition that the Chinese state is still an ideological one, I will continue to delay judgement. For now, I will only flag that I am sceptical. There is that inherent logic in the party-state that craves ideology: The justification of a party with authority above the state needs a powerful rationale. Reform and opening up never amounted to a questioning of the state's narrative; it 'only' rejected the method of constant revolution. Since then, rather than building down the state's ideological scaffolding, subsequent leaders have added new elements to it. Ideology is there and is being nurtured, developed, and reinvented. For a final assessment of the state, we do not escape the question of its real self-understanding.

China is without question a dictatorship. It is probably also correct to describe it as a totalitarian dictatorship. But as 'dictatorship' is too simple a term to capture the intricate nature of Chinese oppression, so also is unqualified 'totalitarianism' too simple. In this, as in all else, China is special. Its totalitarianism, like everything else, is with Chinese characteristics.

In *Democracy in America*, Alexis de Tocqueville, in his second and pessimistic volume, looked into the future and saw a possible evolution towards what he called 'soft despotism': a creeping erosion of freedom within a shell of democratic formality, gradually and hardly perceptively. This pioneer of political analysis taught us both to be aware that complex governance does not always work the way it seems to or is made to look and that the way to understand how things work is often to ask where they are moving. In China, too, there is obviously a big difference between surface presentation and underlying reality. The trend is towards ever tighter controlocracy. What is emerging is new brand of totalitarianism which looks less totalitarian than it is. This is not totalitarianism light, meaning less totalitarian than it could be. It is a totalitarianism with all the tools of the trade ready to be deployed but also of a kind in which those tools are not put to use when not needed. Not exactly soft totalitarianism but rather sophisticated totalitarianism.

Hannah Arendt, who drew on the experience of totalitarian rule in Europe, did not believe that China would fall into the category of totalitarian states. She thought it was too big and complicated a country to be brought under bureaucratic control. It has turned out that she underestimated the capacity that has been built up in the Chinese party-state. This is a state that in its enormous population knows those who oppose it by name, so that when a Tibetan activist who lives in Beijing gets a call on her mobile phone with an invitation to dinner in the American embassy, the state knows it and steps in to prevent so dangerous a person from attending so dangerous an event, and so that when a group of private citizens plan a quiet gathering at the grave of political martyr from the Maoist period, the security services know of it in advance. Its capacity of administration and control has been steadily improved so that now, as unlikely as it might seem in so big a country, the party is everywhere and sees and controls everything. We just do not quite know *why* it sees and controls everything, whether it is for self-preservation only or to serve a higher mission.

What It Gives

The welfare hypothesis goes to the big question of whether China has shed its persona of being a power state and is evolving into a benevolent autocracy. The answer to this question is to be found in an analysis of what the state gives and what it takes. Is what it takes fair and proportionate? If life is getting better for people in China, is that thanks to what the state has given them?

In Chapter 4, I concluded from a narrow test that China is not a welfare state by social and tax policy. It has built up a new system of social protection from scratch, in a conformation of state capacity, but the structure of the social state makes it entirely an instrument of regime legitimacy. It taxes its people heavily, and regressively, but returns to them less in social services than it should by the fiscal resources it takes in.

However, the narrow test is not conclusive. A welfare state is one in which the government, all considered, works for the cause of the common people. That needs to be tested more broadly. The broader test must consider not only taxes and social services but the whole range of services and disservices that flow from the state's governance, including, as we will see, extractions more broadly than taxation. We need a comprehensive balance sheet of what this state gives and what it takes. Actually, we need a balance sheet of what it gives, what it claims to give but does not quite do, what it should give but doesn't, and what it takes.

Stability

One thing the state now delivers is stability. I say 'now', because stability is not the work of the People's Republic but of the reformed People's Republic. China is now united and life in the mainstream is predictable. There is no foreign incursion or risk thereof, no occupation, no warlordism, no civil wars, no great leaps, no famine, no cultural revolution. Governance is steady and the country is developing. People have reasons to expect that development will continue.

Stability is no small matter in this country. The Chinese have not had it for a very long time and know full well that in its absence they get suffering and misery. The stability they now have is the work of the present regime. It is stability at a price, but still stability. I suspect that what the regime enjoys of genuine legitimacy in the eyes of ordinary Chinese it has thanks to the stability it has brought them.

However, the state may not have delivered quite the stability it boasts if we scratch under the surface. It is a stability grounded in control more than legitimacy and that can therefore snap if the controls fail. Because of the ubiquitous blight of corruption, much of the serious new wealth is unearned. These are matters that are strongly resented in the population and that may not continue to be tolerated when economic growth recedes and living conditions no longer improve. As the republican state disintegrated because of physical warlordism in the first half of the 20th century, the party-state may be threatened by economic warlordism in the 21st century. There is organised crime against the state from within the state, from the top of the state, on, in the true meaning of the term, a fantastic scale. This crime is in the hands of networks, gangs, complexes, fiefdoms—call it what you will—that challenge the power of the state, as did the physical warlords, and over which the state does not have control. The new leaders may be on a warpath to win that control, but the picture is not clear. The anti-corruption campaign is about many things, including internal party control, and there appears to be fiefdoms close to the new leaders that they cannot afford to turn on and that have protection. And Xi and Co. might lose the war they are waging and forfeit even the stability that has been achieved.

Growth

From 1990 to 2010, GDP growth was officially on average about 10 percent per year, and GDP per capita about 9 percent. Although these official rates probably overstate the pace of growth, China's growth has been impressive, to put it carefully. However, even this performance, which is at the heart of the world's awe of China and the regime's claim to admiration and loyalty, needs to be put in perspective with a dose of critical analysis.

First, China may have been the world leader in economic growth in a period but is still not unique in economic performance, certainly not in East Asia. My comparison is, again, with South Korea. That country was created in 1948, out of the ruins of Japanese colonisation and the Second World War, and was to suffer further destruction in the Korean War from 1950 to 1953. It started from a lower economic base than did the People's Republic. Yet from literally nothing, South Korea has lifted itself into the ranks of the world's high-income countries (as has Taiwan, which started from the same economic base as the People's Republic, and as did Japan in an earlier trajectory).

The People's Republic of China was established in 1949, like Korea on the ruins of war and civil war. This country, too, has lifted itself out of utter poverty, but in the same time as South Korea only into the ranks of the world's middle-income countries.

That is impressive, but it is not unique and is not an unbeaten performance. Even in raw GDP terms, the People's Republic of China has done less of a job than has the Republic of Korea. In recent years, Korea's growth has been slower than that of China, but that is because Korea reached the maturity of more moderate growth earlier, an adjustment that is only now happening in China.

The People's Republic got off to a good start in economic growth after 1949, but that was brought to a halt by Mao's disastrous policies. The current regime claims to be the one that came to power in 1949, and Mao's policies have not been denounced. If it wants to be thanked for the post-1978 growth, it must also take responsibility for the twenty or so wasted years of destruction and delayed growth.

In what sense have the twenty or so years of ultra-rapid growth been delivered by the state? The notion of government delivery is complicated. It refers to something noteworthy happening out there in society and to that happening on the behest of the government and as a result of its policies and interventions. Clearly, without reform and opening up, China would not have been growing as it has. But what is the counterfactual? What could otherwise have happened? The Great Leap Forward and the Cultural Revolution were both history and finished. Once Mao was gone, the continuation of Maoist policies was not possible and not an alternative. There were 'conservatives' within the regime who advocated some kind of continuity, and many in the regime were in confusion about what to do, but one way or other the economy had to be rebooted. No regime opts for going from disaster to continuing disaster. One of the reasons the economy had to be restarted was that the economic base had fallen out from under the party-state itself. The leaders were not going to sit passively and see their own edifice crumbling in bankruptcy.

The alternatives after Mao were not continued chaos or growth but different models of restructuring. What was chosen was a combination of economic opening up and political restitution. The alternative that might have been chosen was both economic and political opening up. There were voices within the regime for that alternative, but this faction did not prevail. Has China's performance in economic growth been thanks to the strategy that was chosen? The leaders who won the post-Mao power struggle obviously claim that it has. It was thanks to the stability they were able to deliver, which again was thanks to the dictatorial power they were able to muster. Whether that is true and whether the economy has grown more under the reconstituted dictatorship than it would have under political in addition to economic opening up is unknown. It can be argued both ways: The dictatorship has preserved necessary stability; democracy might have unleashed more energy and creativity. Political opening up might not have proved workable, but the claim that it could not have worked is not credible. It does not square with other experiences in the region. In South Korea, democracy was won as a result of revolt from below. In Taiwan, it was given as a gift from above. In both these neighbouring countries, the transition from autocracy to democracy was smooth and productive. Both these countries chose a path of political opening up, and both have outperformed China in economic development. China itself has probably done its best economically in periods when it has tilted towards political reform.[1] The claim that China has been able to grow thanks to dictatorial order cannot be disproved, but nor can it be proved and has to be left as only a postulate. It is probably the case that the regime is getting more thanks than it deserves for the growth it has presided over.

Poverty

In three decades, the rate of poverty fell from some 65 percent of the population down towards 10 percent—this is the lifting of 500 million people out of poverty, or now perhaps 600 million.[2] Again, an impressive performance, again to put it carefully. But again, we need perspective.

First, as usual we do not know the facts with any certainty. There are no official poverty statistics.[3] The United Nations Development Programme, in its 2014 *Human Development Report*, on the basis of survey data, sets the rate of income poverty to 12 percent of the population, measured by those living on less than the equivalent of US$1.25 per day. This is probably an underestimate. Semi-official estimates of rural poverty by the National Bureau of Statistics, and using a poverty line of US$1.70, find 120 million people in poverty in 2011 and 80 million in 2013. If the rural population is 600 million, that is 15 to 20 percent. There are no comparable statistics on urban poverty or poverty among migrants. Standards of living are higher in urban areas, but also inequality is wider. Urban and migrant poverty, measured by the poverty-line method, is probably not much lower than rural poverty, if lower at all. A national incidence of 15 to 20 percent is not unrealistic. That means somewhere between 200 and 300 million people living in strictly defined 'official' poverty.

Second, downward statistical trends in the incidence of poverty reflect movements across poverty lines which are set at a low level of cash income. Not all these movements are as impressive as the raw statistics might seem to suggest. Those who move most easily across the line are those who start just below it. They are out of poverty according to the official measure, but in real terms they may not have not moved much. Many who cross the line stay just above it. They are no longer officially poor but in reality about as poor as they were. Many of those who have been lifted out of poverty are migrant workers, who will be better off than they would otherwise have been (otherwise they would not have migrated) but still live in misery and

1. See Huang, *Capitalism with Chinese Characteristics*.
2. See, for example, Davis and Wang, *Creating Wealth and Poverty in Postsocialist China* and Li et al., *Rising Inequality in China*.
3. See Gustafsson et al., 'Data for studying earnings'.

degradation. Others who have been lifted out of poverty are previous peasants who have been driven off the land and 'urbanised' into non-agricultural lifestyles. They may have more cash income but will also be more dependent on cash income for their basic needs. Peasants who stay on the land continue to toil in China's low-productivity agriculture. In spite of achievements, then, China is still a country of massive and oppressive poverty.

Furthermore, if the lifting-out of poverty is to suggest that it is government policies that have done the lifting, this is a questionable proposition. All the reduction in official poverty has come on the back of economic growth and none of it as a result of redistribution through social policy. On the contrary, tax and social policy redistributions have been regressive and contributed to preventing growth from trickling down to lower rates of poverty. In much of the growth period, there was no social safety net in place, and the safety net that was eventually stretched out with the introduction of the Minimum Subsistence Guarantee at the end of the 1990s has been so inefficient that it has had next to no effect on poverty rates. As with growth, the regime is probably able to claim more thanks than it deserves for the reduction in poverty.

Public services

Compared to the early period of reform and opening up, the provision of public services has improved a great deal. Most of the Chinese now have some provision of public schooling, social security, and health insurance. There are limitations in what is provided, as we have seen in Chapter 4, in provision as such, in the quality of provision, and in equity, but the Chinese are mostly not left in total destitution when in need, and the state does invest in its people. It provides less in services and invests less in the people than it should by its economic capacity and the weight of taxation it imposes on the population, but public service provision is now in a different and better league than at any time previously in the People's Republic.

Modernity

Many Chinese, notably in the urban population and its middle and upper strata, can live distinctly modern lives. The state has invested in new infrastructures at all levels. Many people have regulated work and leisure and some or much discretionary income. They have property and are homeowners and consumers. They have household appliances and flat-screen TVs. They have smartphones, computers, and Internet access with a great deal of content. They can dress as they want and enjoy international music and entertainment. They have holidays. They travel the country and the world. They go to other cities on fast trains. Those lower on the ladder can aspire to move up.

As usual, there are limitations. China is a divided country, and one division is between the modern and the old, and the old remains the norm for nearly half the population, both the rural population and the downtrodden urban masses. If the hallmark of modernity is that people can live as rational beings in charge of their own lives, that remains beyond the reach of the Chinese. They, or many of them, may have joined the world of modern consumerism but not that of modern autonomy.

Quality of life

Life has got better for many in China in material terms, which is significant, but less so in qualitative terms. If the state has contributed to the delivery of economic growth (if less so than is often claimed), when we look beyond quantitative growth to such qualitative betterments that ought to follow, we see little of performance and much of non-delivery. It is a persistent pattern that China has achieved less quality from its growth and GDP wealth than it should have done. In the pursuit of headless growth, both old qualities have gone lost and new ones failed to materialise.

- Family life and generational and kinship patterns have been massively disrupted.
- Honesty and trust are now nearly non-existent commodities. Cheating and dishonesty is rampant in consumer markets, business, education, academia, policing, and public administration. For good reasons, people do not trust each other and do not trust governmental institutions.
- Corruption is everywhere, and people cannot count on getting what they are due without extracted and illegal payments.
- Air, water, and soil are contaminated and poisonous.
- Food is unsafe, even milk and baby food, consumer goods are unsafe, building work is unsafe.
- Cities are brutal and make for harsh human habitation. The heritage has been wasted, and possibly the sense of heritage, and replaced by imitations and kitsch.[4]
- And, of course, the quality of life that comes from living as free and autonomous agents, and as citizens with a say in public affairs, is unavailable.

China is one of the world's most unequal societies. That is true for the distribution of income, consumption, and property, but inequality sticks deeper. Urban and rural lives are different, urban ones, or many of them, modern, rural lives, or many of them, backwards. These differences go to everything from economic life to public goods, care, and schooling. In cities and development centres, migrant workers and their families are second-class citizens in their own country. *Always*, from daily affairs

4. On the loss of touch with tradition and the spread of copied kitsch, see Bosker, *Original Copies*.

to big business, system insiders and those with connections get better treatment and opportunities than others do. Children are made to suffer for the sins of their parents, migrants' children, and the children of those who have transgressed the rules of the birth control policy or other rules of the controlocracy. The children of detainees are no one's responsibility. China is a rigidly gendered society, and women are systematically disadvantaged. Young women carry the burdens of the birth control policy. A third of marriages end in divorce, in settlements in which the women are routinely deprived. Women are as good as absent from leadership positions in public life. Equality in the sharing of family and household duties is an unknown idea. Nowhere is there any sign of encouragement that China is moving in a direction of less inequity.

Happiness

In spite of economic growth, there has been no improvement in happiness in the Chinese population. From 1990 to about 2010, the period for which there are data, the proportion of the (urban) Chinese who describe themselves as happy or satisfied with life was constant, with no movement up or down. There was a moderate improvement in happiness in upper-income groups and a moderate drop in happiness in lower-income groups, balancing out to no improvement for the population as a whole.[5]

We know why the Chinese are not happier in spite of having it better. They know that they have it better in material terms, but they know equally well that there is an absence of quality of life. Survey evidence shows that when the Chinese are asked about their lives, their complaints go to bad air, unsafe food, the absence of say, and of trust, the burden of graft, and such matters.[6] They balance it up and make a realistic assessment of their lives and are not happy with what they are getting.

What It Takes

The Chinese state operates through two systems, economically through the socialist market economy and politically through the controlocracy. To make these operations work, it asks much of its people. It asks of them economically that they give up resources, and it asks of them politically that they give up freedoms.

I start here from a philosophical position that says that a country's resources belong to that country's people. Their government is entitled to tax them for necessary

5. As reported in Knight and Ding, *China's Remarkable Economic Growth* and in research by Richard Easterlin, summarised in a lecture of his at the University of Oxford on 17 October 2013. See also http://www.brookings.edu/blogs/future-development/posts/2015/06/16-happiness-china-graham.
6. For a review of relevant survey evidence, see World Bank, *China 2030*.

purposes and to take ownership of capital, but it should be recognised that it is the people's government that is putting to collective use some of the belongings of those same people. Governments as such genuinely own nothing; they are merely the custodians of values owned by the people. Whatever they take off them for the purpose of governance is extraction. My position is furthermore that people, individual human beings, own themselves and their freedom. The human being, by force of his or her existence as a human, is a free person. Governments have a duty to protect people's freedom, and such protection is necessary for people to be able to enjoy and exercise their freedoms, but governments are not the givers of freedom. They have the power to deprive people of freedom but not the authority to grant or deny it. As some of the people's resources need to be taxed in the interest of necessary governance, some of their freedoms need to be limited by laws and regulations in the interest of civilised coexistence. As with taxation, any limitation of freedom, valid or not, is extraction.

Resources

When we try to make sense of state extraction of resources, it becomes very clear that what we are dealing with is not a capitalist system in which state and economy are separate from each other with taxes and services flowing from one side to the other and back again. Instead, the state operates heavily inside the economy, and much of what it extracts to prop itself up does not flow out of the economy and into state coffers but does its work circulating inside the socialist market economy on the state's behest. For example, much of the state's enormous investment activity in building works and infrastructure is funded in ways in which formal taxes play no role.

States extract resources from their people both in cash and in kind. Extraction in cash is by direct and indirect monetary taxes on households and businesses. Extraction in kind is by goods and labour. Here, income is confiscated from workers and households before it reaches their pockets and becomes manifested as monetary income. It is taken out of their 'real income' in more or less invisible ways, resulting in their monetary income being lower than it 'should' be. This has been the dominant form of taxation through history. The pyramids of Egypt and the medieval cathedrals of Europe are testimony to the extractive powers of the pharaonic and monarchic regimes. The Soviet economies in Russia and Eastern Europe maintained vast state systems with very little of monetary taxation. Modern states extract labour through, for example, military conscription or a duty on employers to do tax collection work by collecting taxes from workers and passing the takings on to the state. In the early period of the People's Republic, the state relied heavily on the extraction of goods, principally agricultural produce. That is now phased out (state procurement of grain ended in 1985), but extraction in kind persists in various ways. Shanghai's monumental and mainly state-owned and state-built cityscape is modern China's equivalent of the ancient pyramids and cathedrals (if of lesser durability). Where does the state get that kind of investment capacity from?

In what goes under the name of taxation, the Chinese state, as we have seen, takes in about 25 to 30 percent of the national income. That, however, does not include off-budget revenues and hidden extractions inside the economy.

To get a fuller picture of taxation more comprehensively, I start by listing the various sources of state extraction and then turn to the questions of how much flows from each source and how the burden is distributed. This is an exercise in uncertainty. There is no objective or official definition of what counts as extraction, and there are no precise data for estimating the magnitudes. I will follow a 'minimalist principle'. I will include only obvious sources of extraction and not include possible but debatable sources. When we get to magnitudes, I will use conservative assumptions and systematically err on the side of underestimation.

(1) The baseline is again formal taxation—the 25 to 30 percent of GDP.

(2) The main acknowledged sources of off-budget revenues are from fees and land transactions. There is a wide range of fees and levies (some imposed by village authorities who officially are not engaged in taxation). Basic social insurance is compulsory and funded by compulsory contributions by members and, in the major programmes, employers. As with income taxes, there are vast evasions so that, although formal rates are relatively high, in the end the revenue that is actually raised is less that it should have been. The funds are in part under the control of local governments at various levels, principally county and provincial, and have been siphoned off extensively for non-social-security purposes. Local governments in addition levy fees for a range of services and do so with much imagination and generally a hard hand. Many social services, including education and health care, are subsidised but not free, and users have to pay a significant part of the cost. Providers, certainly in health care and to some degree in education, operate on a for-profit basis and use fees to compensate for inadequate budget finance, which leaves them to fend for themselves as best they can. Even detainees, such as prostitutes or drug addicts, are obliged to pay fees for accommodation, food, medical care, and other necessities (as well as bribes to officials), and to work without pay, sometimes enabling local governments to run a surplus in their detention facilities. The central government has tried to limit the ability of local authorities to levy fees, for example by converting off-budget fees into on-budget taxes and imposing a maximum level. That has been only partly effective since local governments and agencies continue to extract illegal fees. Consumers pay other fees, on toll roads, for example, and enterprises pay other social contributions, such as to housing provident funds and to the Disabled Persons' Association.

(3) Agricultural (rural) land is in collective ownership, which practically means under the control of state, local government, and village authorities. Rural land users have land-use rights, but these are not permanent and are poorly documented and protected.[7] Urban land (except for land in 'urban villages') is in state ownership. The government at various levels has unusually wide powers to convert land to urban or commercial use, with or without the acquiescence of those who have user rights to the land in question. China's economic growth over the last decades has been fuelled importantly by a transformation of agricultural land into commercial use. That has happened by land-use rights being removed from peasants and taken over by central or local authorities. Local authorities have either used land as a basis for business ventures of their own or leased land-use rights to other enterprises, usually for an extended period, say seventy years, often by auction. This flow of land and land rights from people to state has been continuous during the period of reform and is still ongoing, in both urban and rural areas, and thus represents a constant stream of resources into public control. Probably more than half of local government funds come from land transactions. Collectives are supposed to be compensated for the expropriation of land, but those compensations are low and may be withheld altogether. When expropriation is compensated, that is according to the agricultural value of the land, leaving the value added for enterprise use to the local government. Whether individual peasants who have to give up land are compensated is a matter for the collectives.

(4) Most states extract some resources through labour, the Chinese one massively. While most fees and land transactions are acknowledged in off-budget accounts, extraction through labour is neither acknowledged nor included in any account. The labour market is divided into three main components of about equal size: the peasantry, migrant and irregular workers, and regular market workers. There is mobility between these sub-markets, as manifested in migrant labour, but that mobility is regulated and restrained by various policies, most notably the *hukou*, in such a way that wages are repressed. Peasants can migrate to cities for work but not freely. They have to apply for and obtain a resident's permit. The regular market is not open to them. This keeps their wages down while their supply of cheap labour also serves to depress wages in the regular labour market. Outside of agriculture, wages have been and remain low relative to economic capacity, the flip side of which is high returns to capital, which in turn is part of what has enabled a consistently high level of investment. Wage increases, although rapid, have mostly been below the rate

7. There are ongoing experiments with improved land registration, with the aspiration of moving towards a better national system from 2017.

of economic growth, by say, one or two percentage points annually. The flip side, again, is an increase in returns to capital and to employers, including in the state sector, which in turn partly explains why state-owned enterprises have become more profitable. That wages and household income (and consumption) are lower than they 'should' be, and that they over time have become more so has been hidden behind the high rate of economic growth. That has enabled the paradox that there has been, on the one hand, a rapid increase in wages and in household income and, on the other hand and simultaneously, an increasing 'exploitation' of labour and an increasing subsidy by households of enterprises and investments. It is not easy to see that workers are squeezed more ruthlessly when pay packets become fuller by the year. An estimate by IMF staff suggests a subsidy by households to large corporations alone during the first decade of the century of about 4 percent of GDP annually.[8] How much of economic growth has gone back to labour and to capital respectively is not known with any precision, but there is a consensus that the return to labour is comparatively low and that 'a significant fall in labour income share has occurred'.[9] At least from the mid- or late 1990s, enterprise profitability has increased, in part as a result of over-time redistribution of income from wages to profits. As usual, we do not know the facts of these matters with precision, but there is every reason to think it is right that the relative return to labour is low and has been declining. Labour is compensated 'fairly' when wages are set in a fair labour market, possibly mediated by fair wage negotiations. These conditions are not present in China. The labour markets are politically rigged. Labour mobility is restricted by the *hukou* and now also by social insurance entitlements being non-portable, in fact if not in principle. The economy runs extensively on migrant labour and irregular workers, who are on low pay and do not have regular employment rights. Workers are without effective tools of wage bargaining. The nominal unions are a part of the state apparatus working downwards upon workers rather than upwards on behalf of workers. Although irregular labour wages are increasing relative to regular wages, migrant and irregular workers are still grossly underpaid, wages in the order of 25 to 50 percent less than regular urban wages. It is therefore safe to say that Chinese workers are underpaid and, in spite of rising wages, relatively safe to say that they have over time become more underpaid. This has not happened by chance but is a result of deliberate labour market and other policies which cause real wage income to be clawed back before it shows up in workers' budgets as monetary income. The benefit of underpayment flows, firstly, to public enterprises and employers and is then

8. As reported by Martin Wolf in the *Financial Times*, 2 April 2014.
9. According to World Bank, *China 2030*.

a direct extraction to the state. It obviously also flows to private enterprises and is then a state subsidy to businesses.

(5) Chinese households are big savers; the country has the world's highest household savings rate at about 50 percent of disposable income.[10] Some savings have gone into the housing boom and some into banks. Savers can choose between shadow banks, with decent returns but at high risk, and state banks. The state takes a 20 percent tax on the interest from bank savings.[11] However, before that the state takes a share of the 'real' interest on savings in state banks by paying artificially low interest rates. This helps the banks to provide subsidised credit to state-owned enterprises, a policy which the *Economist* has described as a 'cruel tax on ordinary people.'[12] The state has extractive power through other monopolies as well, one example being a 2,700-year-old state monopoly on the sale of salt that caused consumers to pay four times as much for salt as they would by market prices. This monopoly no longer matters much for state finances and is set to be scrapped in the current wave of reform. A state monopoly on the procurement of tobacco is also being phased out. Households are exploited also as a result of state regulations. One is from the policy of keeping the *yuan* exchange rate artificially low. That imposes a cost on consumers through high prices of imported goods, the flip side of which is an indirect subsidy to export businesses through low pricing. Another is to keep the price of pharmaceutics artificially high, giving health care providers an incentive to over-medication and representing a hidden tax on people with poor health and a subsidy to profit-minded providers. However, although these price riggings are exploitative on consumers, it would probably not be prudent to include this as an extraction to the state since it mainly involves the shifting of costs and benefits between households and businesses (although some of these 'businesses' are public service providers).

(6) Local governments have been encouraged to go into business and to compete with each other in generating and attracting enterprise, and have done so in a big way and used borrowings to fund both local enterprise and current expenditure. If expenditures funded from borrowing were added to the public accounts, the level of expenditure in those accounts would increase by about 5 percent of GDP.[13] Local authorities have technically not been allowed to borrow money except with central approval but have circumvented this restriction by setting

10. But official statistics may overestimate the level of household saving and underestimate consumption, partly because households, in particular in the increasingly affluent middle class, for tax reasons conceal a good deal of their income. For example, the sale of cars and luxury goods is higher than should be possible according to official statistics on household income.
11. A tax introduced in 1999, then abolished again in stages and totally by 2008, but subsequently reinstated.
12. *Economist*, 31 August 2013.
13. World Bank, *China 2030*.

up various 'vehicles' which have enabled them to borrow without supervision from above, usually at high cost from the shadow banking sector. As a result, local government debt has reached a very high level, generally thought to be between 30 and 50 percent of GDP, and rising.[14] Government borrowing from financial institutions is not, in the first instance, extraction from the population. But three costs follow. First, as with all borrowing, interest. Second, both interest and capital repayments when the debt is used, as it is extensively, to fund current expenditure rather than investment, or to cover old loans that have become unserviceable. And third, the repayment of debt on investments that are not profitable or go bad. Local government debt in China is a mystery, as is credit generally. Borrowing 'vehicles' are of many kinds and are not well known, whom they borrow from is not clear, where the money goes is not known, nor who finally picks up the tab. Costs arise in this circus which have to be paid for, and as with all government activity the bill eventually comes back to the population one way or other.

(7) An extraordinary kind of 'fee' on citizens is the extraction of money (or gifts) through graft. Corruption is, as we have seen, a complicated matter in China. There are traditions of gift giving and exchange of favours which are possibly seen to be normal by the Chinese although they may look corrupt from the outside. Economists sometimes reflect on 'optimal corruption', meaning the kind and level of corruption that is productive for economic growth. It is possible that some high-level corruption is conducive to economic enterprise and that, although there are big private gains, no one pays. Corruption and graft inside the public sector may be a necessary tool to compensate for low public compared to private salaries and for the state to be able to reward its officials and trust their loyalty. There is a grey zone between the extraction of illegal fees by authorities and straightforwardly corrupt payments to officials. We know something about corruption at the top through revelations of astonishing riches accumulated by top leaders and their families and friends, in part through excellent investigative reporting by the *New York Times*, Bloomberg, and others, and from big 'tigers' who have been taken to task in the recent anti-corruption drive. We also know from survey evidence that the burden of daily-life graft is a matter of great concern among Chinese people and a major

14. Some localities, such as the cities of Beijing and Shanghai, are now again being given the right to issue bonds under their own authority and thus to borrow without having to ask for central permission. The revised Budget Law of 2014 envisages the legalisation of local government borrowing, the view apparently being that legal and visible borrowing is better than illegal borrowing that cannot be scrutinised, a prospect, however, followed up by an explicit, if as ever unrealistic, warning in a State Council Opinion issued on 2 October 2014 that there will be no central government bailouts of irresponsible local borrowers.

source of dissatisfaction with living conditions and public services.[15] In any event, although the picture is complicated and mixed, corruption and graft are widespread and entrenched, from top to bottom in the system, and payments 'under the table' are for ordinary people and businesses a normal part of normal life. Citizens must count on having to cough up in encounters with officials, doctors, teachers, universities, examiners, bosses, courts, police officers, and others in order to get service or some quality of service, or to avoid harassment. Parents pay to get their children into the most sought-after schools and universities, or into kindergartens or schools associated with prestige universities, in the hope that that will eventually open their children's access to the university when the time comes. Public and party officials must count on having to cough up in order to advance to better jobs. Businesses must count on having to cough up for business licences, jobs, and contracts.

(8) China runs two state lotteries, introduced in 1987, a welfare lottery and a sports lottery. Gambling is otherwise illegal although widespread. State lottery ticket sales reportedly amount to up towards 1 percent of overall government revenue, and are growing.

(9) The Chinese are ruled by the double system of party and state and have to pay for both. The party apparatus is in the main paid for from state revenues, but there is also a contribution from membership fees. That's a tax. It is not exactly an obligatory tax, but nor is it exactly a voluntary fee. The CCP and its affiliates are not associations in the usual meaning of the term but instruments of the state. People join for reasons of insurance and of career and business advancement, and for many purposes party membership is a necessity. There are other (nominal) political parties in China which are nearer to being associations and which people join for other reasons and pay fees to voluntarily. What they pay to the CCP is in a different category. It goes into the funding of the party-state. In addition to the party itself, the core affiliates are the All-China Federation of Trade Unions, the Communist Youth League, the All-China Students' Federation, the All-China Women's Federation, and the All-China Federation of Industry and Commerce, not counting smaller ones such as of journalists and lawyers. Membership numbers are about as follows: Party 87 million, Trade Unions 230 million, and the Youth League 90 million (including about 45 million in the Students' Federation). The All-China Women's Federation is an umbrella organisation of some 6,000 associations and does not publish membership numbers of its own. How many members the 6,000 associations have is not known, but a guess of 100 million would be a careful figure. The

15. See Saich, *Governance and Politics in China*. It is therefore easy to understand that Xi's anti-corruption campaign is popular among the people, as Saich and colleagues have found in their most recent survey, cf. *New York Times*, 11 September 2015.

> Federation of Industry and Commerce has 3.7 million corporate, group, and individual members, organised in 3,000 local branches and 32,000 chambers of commerce. Membership numbers in all these organisations are rising. The number of party members, for example, is up from 60 million at the turn of the century and 75 million in 2008. The number of trade union members increased by 140 million in the decade up to 2010. The number of members in the Federation of Industry and Commerce increased by 45 percent from 2010 to 2014. If we take into consideration that available membership statistics are a bit out of date, and add a bit for smaller affiliates, we get, as a conservative estimate, a total of somewhere between 500 and 600 million memberships in the party system. That's an astonishing number, much more than half of the workforce and more than half of the adult population. The number of trade union memberships alone is close to the number of workers in the regular labour market. There are other quasi-official associations as well, such as the Family Planning Association (nearly 100 million members), the Chinese Red Cross (about 20 million members), the China Federation of Writer and Art Circles (a federation of five associations, including of writers—9,000 members—and artists—6,000 members), associations of lawyers and journalists, the China Bank Association, and so on endlessly.

If these are the sources of extraction, how much do they yield? As usual, there is no statistically precise answer. Even with better data than are available—and there is not much to go on—any answer would remain uncertain because any estimates would depend on assumptions that are flexible. Fortunately, precision is not necessary. It is enough to be able to suggest the order of magnitude. I will again follow the minimalist principle.

The starting point is the 25 to 30 percent. To this we need to add two other forms of extraction: pre-tax extraction from real income and non-tax extraction from monetary income.

The Ministry of Finance produces estimates of off-budget revenues in three auxiliary budgets (additional budgets outside of the 'general budget'): on 'government funds', on 'state capital operations', and on 'social insurance funds'. According to the ministry's reports to the National People's Congress in the last three years, these budgets generate about the following revenues.

The weighty component under 'government funds' is revenue from land transactions, which amounts to 6 to 7 percent of GDP. That is based on local information, which is likely to underreport actual revenues and which would not include compensations withheld. Other components in this category add only marginally to this estimate. Revenue from 'state capital operations' is the remitted profit from the biggest state-owned conglomerates and amounts to less than half a percent of

GDP (not including, obviously, profits that stay with the conglomerates and are used through them). Reported revenues from social insurance fees amount to between 5 and 6 percent of GDP.[16]

That covers my two first sources on top of formal taxes, land transactions and fees. I include only acknowledged revenues in the official off-budget accounts, which then understates rather than overstates the extraction from these sources. Not included, for example, are employer and employee contributions to housing provident funds (generally 5 percent or more of the salary for both employers and employees). Nor are enterprise disability contributions included. The policy here is that enterprises either employ workers with disabilities or pay into an 'employment security fund' operated by the Disabled Persons' Federation to the effect of 1.5 percent of the average local wage multiplied by the number of employees, adjusted downwards for the number of employees with disabilities. I would personally consider these fees to be taxation since they are obligatory payments into the funding of public policies, but it is debatable so I leave them out.

Adding this to the on-budget revenues—the 25 to 30 percent—brings acknowledged public revenues up to between 35 and 40, possibly 45 percent of GDP. This correction alone, then—and we are still dealing only with officially acknowledged and accounted revenues—puts China into the family of high-tax countries with a level of public revenues, as noted in Chapter 4, on a par with OECD countries.

The big additional extraction on top of on-budget and official off-budget revenues is from labour. What that may amount to, we again cannot know for certain but we can make a reasonably educated guess. First, the large peasantry is kept working publicly owned land for low earnings. That is clearly exploitative but not necessarily extractive. I prefer to consider it a structural backdrop to keeping non-agricultural wages lower than they 'should' be and hence conservatively to include no estimate of independent extraction from agricultural labour. Second, if migrant and irregular wages are 25 percent below regular urban wages (which is a conservative assumption), let us say that 10 percent is underpayment, the rest being because of lower qualifications. That spreads out to between 2 and 3 percent on the entire workforce (given the share of migrant and irregular workers in the workforce). Third, if underpayment in regular wages, because of market riggings and other policies, is also to the effect of 10 percent, that spreads out to another 2 or 3 percent on the entire workforce. This would then add up to a general level of underpayment to labour of about 5 percent. To that we should add the likely increase in the level of underpayment that has occurred over the last couple of decades (at least). What that might be we again do not know. The World Bank and the Development Research Center of the State Council, in *China 2030*,

16. These estimates are from the government's budget reports to the National People's Congress.

suggest a decline in the share of GDP to labour in two decades from the early 1990s from 60 to 40 percent, but also warn that these figures are not trustworthy if taken as a trend. On the other hand, if wages have lagged behind growth by one or two percent per year, or even less than that, it inevitably adds up over time to a very considerable aggregate lag. One half of the higher estimate would be 10 percent and a quarter 5 percent. These guesstimates bring us to an indicative current level of underpayment to labour of between 10 and 15 percent of real income.

On first sight, this estimated extraction through labour might seem extraordinary, that 10 to 15 percent of Chinese workers' labour is expropriated for state use and not paid for, but on reflection it is not at all high. It does not include any extraction from agricultural labour. The rest of the labour market is *hukou* regulated with restricted mobility and not by any stretch of imagination fair. Up against an economy of big conglomerates, workers do not have the collective power of union representation. What is incredible in China's political economy is not that workers are exploited but the persistently high level of investment. Maintaining an economy of growth driven by investments is not possible without the inflow of huge resources into those investments. One way—the only way?—of securing an unusual level of resources for investment is to exploit labour.

In total, then, the real taxation of labour is threefold: income taxes, social security contributions and other fees, and extraction through underpayment. The weight of this burden can by any standard only be described as extremely heavy.

The remaining sources of extraction are each of lesser magnitude but still add up quite significantly. If local expenditures funded from borrowing add up to 5 percent of GDP, and if half of that are expenditures that do not repay themselves, we have another 2 to 3 percent in extraction. What local (illegal) fees and levies, and misuse of social insurance funds, add up to is again unknown, but let's prudently say another 1 percent of GDP.

If we assume conservatively that Chinese households save upwards of 30 percent of their income, that at least half of that goes into low-interest state bank accounts, and that interest in these accounts is 2 to 3 percent 'too low', this cruel tax on ordinary people (not counting the 20 percent formal tax) is between one-third and two-thirds of a percent of household income, again probably an underestimate.

The cost of graft is obviously unknown but is again considerable. People routinely have to cough up for want they are entitled to. Businesses need a licence to operate, which can be difficult to obtain and can be removed. If they are entitled to tax exemptions, these may not be easily forthcoming. The assistance of 'contacts' may be necessary in order to manoeuvre bureaucratic mazes and hurdles. And many of those they depend on may expect to be entertained, lavishly so. In one account, a business operator estimates expenses for maintaining connections—*guanxi*—to 3 to 5 percent of operating costs. The problem of corruption is endemic and reaches into every niche of economic and social life. Again, considering only low-level corruption, let's say as a prudent guesstimate yet another 1 percent of income. High-level embezzlement also in the end comes out of the people's income, but this is better seen as theft than as state extraction.

If lottery sales amount to 1 percent of public expenditure (conventionally estimated), that puts an additional 0.25 percent of GDP on to the tax burden.

If members of the party and its affiliates pay an average fee of 2 percent of income, and if the number of memberships are half the number of taxpayers, that represents an additional 1 percent of income extraction. This is probably, again, an underestimate. Party members pay, or are supposed to pay, a fee of 1, 3 or 5 percent of their income; the higher the income, the more they pay. In the All-China Federation of Trade Unions, members' contributions are 0.5 percent of gross income while companies with unions pay a union levy of 2 percent of their total payroll.

So it adds up. We start from 25 to 30 percent of GDP in formal taxes. Official off-budget revenue brings that up to between 35 and 45 percent. Extraction through labour, conservatively estimated, adds another 10 to 15 percent, and the additional smaller sources of taxation together at least another 5 to 7 percent.

All together, then, the state costs the Chinese people between 55 and 67 percent of their real income.

This, astonishingly, is a cautious and conservative estimate, based systematically on the minimalist principle in both what is included as extraction and in the estimates of yield. It is also, to repeat yet again, a guesstimate with many uncertainties. None of the estimates are precise. There is an additional margin of error in the adding-up of the various percentages in that that they are not all from the same denominator, some being from GDP, some from household monetary income, and some from the higher 'real' income. In the estimated extraction through labour, it is probable, but not established fact, that the share of income returned to labour has declined over the last couple of decades. But for all the uncertainty and all necessary qualifications, what we have here is a reasonable and conservative guestimate that shows the order of magnitude.

The state that officially runs on a quarter or so of GDP in reality absorbs about two-thirds. Of course, some of that goes back to the population in services, but that's for the other side of the account. The state's invoice to its people for the governance it provides them is for two out of every three *yuan* of their real income.

Finally, who pays? In the same way that we do not know with precision how much is paid, we do not know with precision who pays what. But we know enough to easily say what the distributive profile of extraction is.

Formal taxes are, as we have seen, regressive in their distribution. Extractions through labour and land are strongly regressive. Underpayment falls disproportionally on migrant and irregular workers who are poor because they are underpaid. Land is extracted from peasants, who are at the very bottom of the income scale. These misdistributions are compounded by many underpaid migrant labourers being precisely the peasants who have been driven off the land.

The remaining sources of revenue, except for fees to the party and affiliates, are in distribution akin to indirect taxes and hence regressive to income. Fees to the party and affiliates are possibly progressive in the aggregate in that members may be disproportionally from higher social and income strata and formally progressive internally (although it would seem unlikely that millionaire and billionaire party members pay a fee in proportion to their income). In any event, these flows are insignificant in the bigger picture and do not noticeably affect the overall distribution of the burden.

Although no precise answer can be given to the question of who pays, we can conclude with certainty that the burden of paying for the Chinese state is shared not only in a regressive way but in a strongly regressive way. Disproportionally, those on lower-income levels pay and those higher up are let off more easily.

This government is of course not alone in extracting resources from its population in other ways than through formal taxes, but state extraction with Chinese characteristics is nevertheless in a league of its own. There is no other socialist market economy in which the state operates on a similar scale inside the economy through its own banks and enterprises and subsidises those enterprises with cheap labour and credit, which are cheap because the state holds back from workers and savers some of the compensations they should have had. There is no other economy in which labour markets are similarly segregated and rigged with an instrument such as the *hukou*. There is no other economy in which all land is in public ownership in such a way that local governments can extract a continuous flow of resources through expropriations which are compensated, if at all, at an artificially low rate. There is no other economy in which local governments operate on the basis of illegal borrowing on a scale in which debt cannot be serviced. There is no other economy in which corruption is institutionalised in such a way as to be an informal tax on common people in their ordinary dealings with public services. There is no other party-state in which people are pulled into the controlling embrace of the party and its many affiliates and for which privilege they are obliged to pay. There is no other economy in which these manifold pre-tax and non-tax extractions combine as they do in the Chinese one. There is no other economy in which, during the last couple of decades, the state's level of extraction of economic resources from its population has been hidden behind extraordinary rates of economic growth. The Chinese socialist market economy is like no other economy. There is no other economy anywhere in the world, except possibly in pure kleptocracies, in which an account like this one would add up in burden and regressivity as it does in the Chinese case.

Freedom

In addition to its extraction of economic resources, the second great extraction by the state from citizens is in their freedoms. Chinese people do not have standard human rights, such as freedom of expression and to peaceful assembly and association, do not have an institutionalised say in public affairs, and do not have the freedom to live their lives as they wish.

Everyone knows that China is a dictatorship in which people are without basic rights and freedoms, but this is still knowledge that sometimes gets skirted over and that therefore bears being stressed and repeated. In his otherwise excellent book *The Party*, Richard McGregor writes; 'In place of Mao's totalitarian terror, the Party has substituted a kind of take-it-or-leave-it compact with society. If you play by the Party's rules, which means eschewing competitive politics, you and your families can get on with your lives and maybe get rich.' Likewise the *Economist*: 'After the 1989 protests in Tiananmen Square, and their subsequent bloody put-down, the deal China's leaders offered the country changed: stay out of politics and you can do almost anything else you want.'[17] This benevolent view of the regime enables liberal-minded observers to admire China for becoming less dictatorial. But that is a perverse logic. A colleague put it thus: 'Personally, I don't think the party can take much credit for taking their boot off the windpipe of a suffocating man, and then saying they have saved his life.'

It is also totally mistaken. There is no do-as-you-want pact, or any other pact or deal between state, society, and people for that matter. The party-state does not make pacts; it decides. To suggest that there is a pact is not only wrong but also offensive. When Mr. McGregor wrote that 'you and your families can get on with your lives', the birth control policy was still in its one-child incarnation, and still now that it is edging towards a two-child policy, families can only have legal children by first obtaining a permission document from the state. The *Economist* gets it wrong not only by reducing the nationwide uprisings of 1989 to 'protests' and to 'Tiananmen Square' but also by further reducing the dictatorship to a playground where the Chinese can do 'almost anything else you want'. They cannot. What they are limited from is not only 'politics' but the whole range of rights and daily-life opportunities the deep infringements of which I have rehearsed at various parts of this book.

The Balance

States give and states take. A state that works for the cause of the common people gives in a way that adds to their security and well-being and takes what is proportionate and

17. In a report on China's NGOs. *Economist*, 12 April 2014.

justified for that purpose. What it gives is a broad range of services which includes social protections but is not limited to that alone. All states take from their people and thereby inevitably reduce not only their disposable income but also their freedoms. In these respects, the Chinese state is like any state. The question is whether it is effective, fair, and proportionate. Does it give its people what it should relative to what it takes from them? Is what it takes necessary for what it gives back?

The reformed Chinese state has given the country stability, economic growth, less poverty, more social protection, and more modernity. Of these services, stability, of sorts, is the only one the regime can claim to have genuinely delivered. To the others it has contributed rather than delivered, and it has contributed less than it should by its economic and other capacities, less than it generally claims, and less than it is often given credit for. What it has failed to deliver is quality of life and happiness. Indeed, it has contributed to its flagship performance of economic growth in a way that has come at the price of increasing quality-of-life burdens.

What the state takes is a heavy combination of economic resources and freedom. Its taking cannot in any reasonable meaning be summed up as proportionate and for the public good. This is a state that takes not primarily to serve its people but to maintain itself. Some of what it takes it returns to the people in the form of services, but compared to what it takes, not much. And even what little it gives is mainly self-serving and to prop itself up. What it takes in freedom is grossly out of proportion with anything that can be justified morally, or even in stability.

In its taking, the Chinese state is a highly developed one and second to none in its extraction and taxation. In its giving, it is underdeveloped up against its fiscal and administrative capacity.

If it were right that the Chinese state had struck a deal of benevolent autocracy with its people, it would not need to be as dictatorial as it is. But this is a regime that needs very much to be in dictatorial control. The claim that it needs to be dictatorial for the purpose of stability is not tenable. It needs to be dictatorial because it is the kind of state it is, because of its greediness in what it takes and how it takes it, and because of its stinginess in what it gives and how it gives it. A regime of this kind would not be possible if it were to depend on the consent of the people.

What Kind of State?

There is a way of looking at China which is near instinctive to the 'Western' observer. It is thought that as China opens up and grows economically, it will also inevitably modernise in other ways, meaning becoming more like us, perhaps even democratic. We have been looking at China in this way since Deng Xiaoping released China from Maoism. This was also the inside view of China in the optimistic 1980s.

This has been called 'the liberal myth' (a term coined by the sociologist Richard Madsen). One might have thought that myth had been dispelled with the reaffirmation of party-state dictatorship in 1989, but it was not. At a dinner in Hong Kong, hosted by then Chief Executive C. H. Tung at the end of an official visit to China in July 1998, US President Bill Clinton reassured the anxious during the evening's conversation that China was on its way to becoming an open society. Economic growth was breeding a new middle class which would not tolerate a life of dictatorship. In a speech ahead of his visit he had argued that 'the more we bring China into the world, the more the world will bring freedom to China.'

We continue to want to see China in this way, both because it is convenient and because it is intellectually difficult to absorb that a country that grows economically and becomes, as it is thought, capitalist, could continue to be Leninist politically. This also remains the outlook of many inside China. In a recent conversation with a distinguished academic, who is not at all naïve about the blemishes of the regime, he replied to remarks of mine about dictatorship that 'some colleagues are too anxious; it will come right'.

This line leads to a certain interpretation of political developments. It leads the observer to think that 'reforms' are changes for, in our eyes, the better. They are seen as 'steps in the right direction'. Administrative reforms are steps towards in some meaning democratisation. Penal reforms are steps towards a fair judicial system. Relaxations on the one-child policy are steps towards its abolition. *Hukou* reform is a step towards an open labour market. Legal reform is a step towards rule of law. And so on.

This paradigm is, however, misguided. It does not square with the empirical reality. Opening up was never said to mean political opening up. Since then, the regime has perfected itself into a controlocracy of an entirely unique kind.

Furthermore, there is no explanation in the liberal myth of why it should be expected that China should open up more comprehensively. President Clinton and many with him have thought that the middle class would demand freedom, but it has instead become another pillar of the regime. The economic and intellectual middle classes, as well as the modern working class, are of the party-state's making and are co-opted into its corporatist designs. Others have hoped the Internet would become a force of liberalisation from below, but it has instead become another instrument of control from above.

The liberal view is a myth because it ignores the basic truth that the Chinese state is not just a state but a party-state. In China, nothing is 'inevitable', and everything depends on the men in Beijing. They have never though that their country should be open and democratic, and as a result it isn't and isn't on its way in that direction.

The alternative way of looking at China is to try to understand it as it is and on its own terms, as a state-led country, a party-led state, and a socialist market economy. That is exactly what the men in Beijing have been saying and are saying, and the rest of us should by now have learned to listen to what they say.

In this paradigm, 'reform' looks different. It is not about copying 'the West' but about the regime shoring up and perfecting itself. Administrative reform is not to change it but to improve its effectiveness. Penal reform is to get rid of embarrassing retributions that are no longer necessary. And so on. When the party's Central Committee adopts an agenda of 'socialist rule of law with Chinese characteristics', that is not a 'step in the right direction' according to a normal concept of rule of law but a tightening up of the instruments of central control and command within the party-state.

I started this exercise from the state's view of itself and by giving the regime the benefit of the doubt. I followed through from there to a welfare hypothesis: that the reformed People's Republic is in its way governing for the good of the common people. I have tested that hypothesis twice over, both in a narrow and in a broad test. By both these tests, the welfare hypothesis falls. My first conclusion is that the People's Republic of China is not a welfare state for the people. That is not the kind of state it is.

The Chinese leadership sometimes present their country modestly as still being a developing one. There is some truth to that; China remains in many ways underdeveloped. But politically, it belongs to the family of developed countries. Developing countries are short of resources for adequate public policies. That is not China's situation. The state has ample administrative capacity and is fiscally solid and ferociously extractive. A second conclusion is that my determination at the start to treat China as a grown-up country has been vindicated. What this state does or could do for its people is not limited primarily, if at all, by incapacity or unaffordability. It does less for its people than it would be able to and could afford to do because it has other determinations and priorities than to work for the good of the common people.

A third conclusion is that China has been overestimated. It is overestimated for economic growth; there has been remarkable economic growth but not as remarkable as has been officially said, and mega-growth is now a thing of the past. It is overestimated for the size of the economy; it is a very big economy but not as big as the world has come to think. It is overestimated for its economic dynamism; there is development but development fuelled by wasteful investment bubbles fuelled by excessive debt. It is overestimated for poverty reduction; millions have escaped raw destitution, but China is still a country of massive and oppressive poverty. It is overestimated for standards of living; standards have risen but at less than the pace of economic growth and without commensurate, if any, improvement in quality of life and happiness. It is overestimated for its turning to capitalism; there is a great deal of private enterprise, but China maintains a state-controlled command economy. It is overestimated for cohesion; the country is unified but socially divided by inequalities and exclusions, with a social fabric that is fragile and weakened by family disruption, distrust, and the demoralisation of oppression. It is overestimated for stability; there is stability but one that depends on near-totalitarian oppression. It is overestimated for order; there is order but one that sits on lawlessness, criminality, corruption, and organised crime. It is overestimated for modernisation; the country is modernising but also increasingly riven by deep social and economic divisions.

And as China is overestimated, so is the Chinese state. It is overestimated for its delivery; it has contributed more than delivered. It is overestimated for its opening up; there has been economic but not political opening. It is overestimated for its relaxation of dictatorship; there is a different dictatorship but not a lessening of dictatorship into mere authoritarianism, never mind benevolent authoritarianism. It is overestimated for legitimacy; it does have some support from below but relies mainly on controls and on the buying of support with rewards. It is overestimated for power; its international presence is commanding but based on weight more than on respect and diplomatic skill. It is overestimated militarily; the PLA is a formidable force but a second-rate fighting machine. China's great weakness is to be a state-dependent country with a state that rules without the consent of the ruled. The state's great weakness is that it runs a system that depends on extreme levels of extraction from the population and that it is unable to maintain itself without dictatorship.

With the welfare hypothesis disproved, the two alternative hypotheses remain strengthened. Which is it, then? Is the Chinese state trivial, a state that is for itself only, or is it a power state, a state that rules for an ideological mission? To answer, we need the statistician's tools of stocks and flows, of distinguishing between where a system stands and how it is moving. If we for a moment stop history and look at the Chinese state as a snapshot, we see a state that is in my terminology trivial. Not only trivial in being overestimated but also trivial in having no purpose beyond itself.

During the reform period, the state has consolidated itself as one dedicated to self-preservation, stability, and economic growth. The reign of Hu and Wen from 2002 to 2012 was entirely devoted to keeping the wheels moving. They did try to lift their gaze from the economic statistics and took to the flowering language of 'harmonious society', but there was no determination in it. They left to their successors a state that is in control and fiscally solid and that is presiding over an economically strong nation, but also one that is a bit of a bluff in strength and that maintains stability at the cost of an epidemic of organised crime.

As to where the state might be moving with the post-2012–13 leadership, it is in the balance. We cannot yet say that Xi Jinping has discontinued the trivial state consolidation. He has brought in a new style of leadership, concentrated power in his own hands, and displayed much energy and determination in the centralisation of power, the cleaning-up of the party, and the purging of competing elements in the establishment. But it is as expected of a new leadership team to start off with the display of energy and then entirely possible for it to gradually settle down to the art of the possible. That may well be the pattern the new regime will follow. If so, the Chinese state will continue to be what it now is, a state that is forceful but still trivial.

Whether that will prove a prescient prediction is, however, an open question. The new leadership may turn out to be of a new kind and with a different ambition, and China may break away from the reformist continuity and take some or other new path. That, however, is in the realm of speculation. We can say something with some authority about where things stand but nothing with certainly about where things may move. That speculation I prefer to deal with separately and relegate to the postscript.

Postscript

A Better Regime?

As the Chinese leaders are haunted by ghosts from their past, so are some China watchers, myself included. My ghost is the sometimes inability of outsiders to recognise totalitarian regimes for what they were until too late. Even Nazi Germany was widely respected until it took Europe and the world to war. We do not like to remember it today, but this respect was strongly present in all the countries that subsequently fought Germany, including among intellectuals. That admiration survived astonishing odds: the ever more vile, brutal, and racist dictatorship, the ranting madness of Hitler whenever he spoke. Many observers of the Soviet Union saw there a credible alternative to democracy, and way into and beyond the Stalinist period a regime that was in many ways superior, sometimes morally superior. This admiration again survived what should have made it impossible: collectivisation and famine, political murder as an instrument of rule, the pact of collaboration with Hitler to annex parts of Poland and the Baltic states, the gulag, the invasions of Hungary and Czechoslovakia. Even when I was a student in the 1970s, in, of all places the University of Oslo in Norway, it was good teaching that the East European regimes, East Germany in particular, were in many ways superior to our own systems.

Today, it is the People's Republic of China that attracts admiration, an admiration that again has survived adversity: the brutality of Maoist dictatorship and its catastrophic consequences, the failure at the junction after Mao to choose the route of political opening up, the resort to political murder in 1989. Philosophers praise China as a civilisation state. Business people around the world, and academics, are falling over each other to get in on the China act. China is of course far from universally admired, as also previous totalitarian systems were not, but it is as if some have a need to see the regime as more benevolent than it is. In the 1980s, the world failed to listen to Deng and chose to believe he was moving China in a liberal direction. But he never said he would and never did. When Xi Jinping came to power in 2012, the man the world again thought would be a reformer instead lurched to the Maoist left, tightened all the screws of dictatorship, and turned to an ideology of aggressive nationalism. Against the odds, both inside and outside of China, people persist in believing and expecting that China is moving towards a more socially and politically open society, in what was once, hopefully, called a 'slow-motion revolution'.[1]

Two fallacies are behind these inabilities. One is an uncritical admiration of delivery, in particular delivery by autocratic order and strength. While the Soviet Union looked its strongest, and while Maoist China looked to be the vanguard of world revolution, the democratic world was immersed in self-doubt. The force and determination of authoritarianism looked good because the alternative looked bad. This caused many observers both to admire the dictatorial regimes for their prowess and to disregard or downplay the human costs behind their delivery. It also caused them to overestimate what was actually delivered. The Soviet regime in fact never delivered although for a while it looked as if it did. It kept a state economy afloat on the backs of a population that was exploited and kept in poverty. The true story of Maoist China was not delivery but destruction. Now the reformed economy is said to be on the way to becoming the world's largest, a story told by prettied-up statistics and repetition.

The other fallacy is ideological. Both the Soviet Union and Maoist China used the weapon of ideology to great effect. They offered the world belief systems that promised paradise once the struggle was won, and many outsiders bought into those powerful narratives, some fully and some to a great degree. Those who did made themselves disposed to seeing the good in the regimes they admired and to excusing the ugliness as necessary sacrifices now for the greater good tomorrow.

In the case of contemporary China, there is also the size factor. China is big and strong, not least economically. It is opportune to make oneself believe that a regime one has to deal with and with which there are many benefits to being on good terms is a laudable regime, or at least another regime among regimes.

But China is *different*. Its state is different—a party-state; its polity is different—a controlocracy; its economy is different—a socialist market economy. The complacent view that contemporary China is just a regime that happens to be economically successful and effective in delivery is to not take China as it is seriously. If it was a plausible hope after the dawn of reform and opening up that China would open up politically, that hope has subsequently been extinguished, most recently under the Xi Jinping leadership that has consolidated the dictatorial regime. On this, there can now be no doubt; the question is only how radical that consolidation will be.

The journalist Evan Osnos, on leaving China in 2013 after years as a correspondent for the *New Yorker*, drew his experiences together in a book entitled *Age of Ambition*. That is an appropriate title. China is rising, the leaders are assertive, neighbours and others are uneasy. But just how ambitious is the Chinese state and, as the leaders look forward, what is the nature of their ambition?

1. Johnson, *Wild Grass*.

We cannot know. The model may or may not be at a watershed. Those who previously have been most eager to predict have more often than not got it wrong. The best I can do is to suggest some possible scenarios and speculate on their probabilities.

Scenario 1: Steady on. The reformist continuity may persist. The economy may continue to grow, at least enough. The state may continue to be in control, at least enough. There may be the familiar path of step-by-step administrative reform. There may be continued collective leadership. The socialist market economy may be twigged as necessary. The population may stay reasonably compliant. The rest of the world may continue to engage. China may avoid international adventurism and pull back from the brink of confrontation with neighbours. The leaders may continue to value stability above all. If they can rely less on legitimacy, they have the means and will to deploy more severe controls, as we have seen in the last two or three years. The regime has done well from reform and opening up, and the leaders may not want to put at risk what has been gained. They may remain cautious and hold ambition under control.

I classify this as a high-probability scenario. China has muddled through for years and continued muddling-through might be the regime's best bet. The new leadership may turn out to be less ambitious than it first made itself look and may, as have previous leaders, settle down to doing what is necessary rather than what might be desirable. The shock of the stock market crash in 2015 may shift the pendulum of economic management back from marketisation towards more control.

However, in the final process of completing this book, and as our understanding of the new leadership is improving, I have come to think of this scenario as a bit less than high probability. Xi Jinping has gathered unprecedented, since Mao, powers in his own hands and is presenting himself as an ambitious and activist leader who may not have in mind a legacy of simply having kept the ship on steady keel. It seems he might be a man with a mission, and if so he may have concentrated enough power in his hands to pursue it and may be determined or trapped into imposing his own will to the bitter end.

Scenario 2: Demise. Although much seems to suggest that the economy will continue to grow and that the controlocracy will persist and improve, the much-lauded stability rests on many a fine balance. There is no end to what could go wrong. Contradictions in the socialist market economy may not continue to be manageable. Growth may not only slow but stop. The oligarchic class may continue to rob a state that can no longer afford to be robbed. The bubble of debt-infused investment may burst, as the stock market part of it did in 2015. Too many of those who can may leave for the free world and take too much money with them. Latent conflicts in the leadership may not be suppressed. Xi may be seen as an emperor in the making and find colleagues turning on him—or he may succeed in making himself supreme, suspend collective leadership and, like Mao, steer the party-state off the rails. He may prove to be a true believer in the purity of the party and drive his effort to clean it up to ultimate and self-defeating collapse. The military could intervene. The anti-corruption campaign may backfire and bring on administrative paralysis. Social forces may assert themselves. The new economic and intellectual middle classes may not remain content to obey, nor students, nor journalists. Internet control could break. Ethnic minorities may revolt. Democracy contagion from Taiwan and Hong Kong may not be containable. Neighbouring countries may collaborate in alliance. Foreign powers could take on China. War could break out.

All this and more is possible—but I do not classify this as a high-probability scenario, although the crash of 2015 must be taken as evidence that stability is fragile. Still, contrary to the view that the Chinese model is riven by contradictions and cannot hold, I have concluded that the party-state is one of high capacity. It is effective in administration and control. It is fiscally solid. It is able to reform and adapt, and to deploy more repression as needed. It is more likely that controlocracy holds at home and that rationality prevails abroad. But not certain: Things may get out of hand and much could go wrong.

Scenario 3: Utopia. The regime claims to be on a socialist path and currently in a transition phase of capital accumulation and dictatorship of the proletariat before, when the time is right, it turns to using its accumulated resources and stability for the creating of a socialist utopia of security, harmony, and freedom. That view is written into the party's constitution. Something along these lines could happen. The time may come for equality in the 'growth first equality second' programme. Xi and his associates may succeed in crushing the counter-powers of the oligarchic class. Inequalities could be reined in. The embryonic system of social protection could evolve into a genuine welfare state. Rule by law could evolve into rule of law. Public administration could be made honest and responsive. Corruption could be pushed back to no longer being unbearable in daily life. Core structures of the controlocracy, such as the *hukou* and the birth control policy, could be seriously relaxed or abolished. Civil society, for example, around the emergence of non-official NGOs, could take on force and make itself a partner with the state in a peaceful transition to balanced state-society relations.

This also is possible, but is also, in my judgement, a low probability scenario. Inequalities and divisions on many dimensions are entrenched. There is nothing to suggest that the regime is intent on anything like a serious policy of social protection and justice or that it would be able to embark on that kind of policy even if the leaders wanted to. The war on the oligarchic class might end in a truce when the leaders are content that they have eliminated their opponents within the system, or be long drawn out, brutal, and possibly destructive. The state is not trusted and autonomous social forces, if allowed to take life, would more likely establish themselves in opposition to the state than in partnership with it. All previous movements towards open and balanced social relations have turned to a demand for democracy, have then been seen as a threat, and have been crushed before having been able to consolidate into any kind of autonomy. The new regime has been determined to fortify the controlocracy and has shown no sign of wishing to relax it.

Scenario 4: Democracy. The leaders also claim that their model is or is on the way to becoming a democracy with Chinese characteristics. Although China today is very much a dictatorship, and looks to remain a dictatorship, the emergence of a democracy of its own kind is not impossible. There is democracy of sorts on the village level which could be a basis for further evolution. There have been experiments with extending democracy up the hierarchy although so far not successful ones. China has proved to be a pressure cooker in which the desire for democracy has been brewing and the democratic aspiration is without doubt alive in the population. America invented a new kind of democracy in its day; China could do the same now.

A possible trajectory could be to make village democracy real by allowing genuinely competitive elections, then extending local democracy to urban areas, and then building upwards with a system of indirect elections so that officials on any level are elected competitively by and among lower-level officials.[2] That would create a structure within existing state institutions in which officials would answer downwards, ultimately to the lowest level of directly elected officials, very different from the current system where officials answer upwards. The common people would have a say, and a feeling of say, in public affairs. Theoretically, one could imagine this implemented in both the state and in the party so that the party apparatus could be maintained within a framework of democratic indirect elections.

The method of indirect elections has not had much attention in recent democratic theory, a sign perhaps of resistance among political scientists against thinking of other kinds of democracy than the now conventional model, and might be underestimated as a way of solving the problem of scale in so large a country as China.

But, although something like this may not be impossible, no one with insight into the Chinese system would be likely to take this as a scenario with much probability. What China has reinvented is dictatorship, not democracy. If there is one thing there seems to be solid agreement about at the top, it is that anything that resembles real democracy is a danger to that all-important stability and not permissible given the regime's determination to self-preserve.

---

2. In *The China Model*, Bell suggests that democracy at the local level could be enough to secure the regime genuine legitimacy, provided the rest of the system was made effective and honest with the help of a well-functioning and open 'meritocratic' system for the selection and promotion of leaders.

Scenario 5: The perfect fascist state. Following on from my discussion under 'the power hypothesis' in Chapter 2, the leadership could cast caution aside, embrace ambition, and reconstitute China as an ideological power state. Deng advised the country to 'hide its capacities and bide its time'. Perhaps the time is coming to step out of that restraint.

The architecture of a power state is there: the party-state structure, the unity of party and military, the bureaucracy of propaganda and control, the omnipresent security forces. Under the post-2012 leadership, the pendulum of governance has swung from trust in its ability to purchase legitimacy towards more reliance on its capacity to control. Central political command is being strengthened. The top leader is concentrating power to himself. Business and civil society are co-opted into corporatist institutions under party guidance. Censorship and stability management is being tightened. Propaganda, political education, and thought work is being made more assertive. Mass-line campaigns and mass organisation work are back in pride and use. The top leader is giving himself a patina of person cult and making his power felt. He is admonishing cadres to 'make work in the ideological sphere a high priority in your daily agenda' and to 'embrace the spirit of Mao Zedong'. One day he convenes authors and artists and instructs them about the duty of cultural workers to serve the nation and party. One day he lectures architects to steer away from the design of 'weird buildings', and one day think-tanks to heed party guidance in their work. And one day a leading paper publishes an article about his busy workday which starts before breakfast with clearing away the paperwork that has come in after midnight and ends late in the evening when he 'finds happiness in exhaustion'.[3] His works and thoughts are being published in multivolume editions and in many languages. The Chinese Academy of Social Sciences is organising a massive programme of multiple research projects on Xi Jinping thought. In April 2015, an app was launched, created at the Central Party School, with Xi Jinping's remarks and works, immediately branded 'the little red app' by netizens. On 23 September 2015, the *People's Daily* released a (frankly nauseating) Youtube clip, part of a series, called 'Who Is Xi Dada?' with foreign students praising the great man, in everything from strength and wisdom to concern and charm.

I have concluded that the Chinese controlocracy is the perfect dictatorship. It does not depend on commanding most people in their daily lives and is able to mostly rely on their acquiescence and self-censorship. But behind that façade of softness is the hard reality of as perfect control as is possible when control is needed, of ruthlessness, and of a totalitarian system's care to let its capacity of control and unforgivingness be known to all. Xi Jinping has moved governance away from apparent softness and towards more undisguised hardness.

3. All this was in a four-week period in October–November 2014.

However, a power state needs ideological in addition to administrative grounding. Totalitarian use of state power needs more than the excuse of stability; it needs the justification that comes from higher ideas and principles. A resurrection of classical communist ideology would not be credible. A new power state in China would need a new ideology. That ideology may be in the making in Xi Jinping's China Dream.

It is possible that the China Dream will turn out to be hot air of little substance, as have previous ideology-like signals. Perhaps that it all it is—but it could also become the new narrative for a revived China, a narrative that draws on Chinese history more than on Marxist theory and that goes to nation, nationalism, strength, unity, and patriotism. When Mao declared the People's Republic in 1949, his message was that China had risen again. He slotted the revolution into a tradition of nation and greatness. He got himself lost in a fantasy of revolution, but those who have followed him have reverted to nation building. The unifying idea has been China the great. This may now be in the process of finding its ideological articulation.

The narrative of national greatness has the resonance in Chinese imagination and tradition to make that possible, the resonance that 'harmonious society' failed to find. There are signs that Xi's promotion of it is taking hold. No sooner had he said 'dream' than the whole system swung into action to give his signal content and meaning. Overnight it became the story that party, state, educational, and other agencies and institutions took to as giving purpose and direction to their activities. It became the object of study in the party system at all levels, and in schools, colleges, and universities, and discussed in official media and through the Internet. When the party issued an instruction in early 2015 on strengthening ideological work in higher education, the China Dream was to be at the core of enhanced political training for faculty. Professors and students, it was reported from the late January conference on the implementation of the instruction, 'wholeheartedly support the party's leadership . . . and the great resolve of the Chinese nation through the China Dream.' It is flagged up front on websites of the party, of party affiliates, and of the state system as the idea those wishing to display their loyalty have to pay lip service to. The slogan on the poster in front of government headquarters in Shanghai to celebrate the 65th anniversary of the revolution in 2014 read 'The East Is Red. Chinese Dream.' It was the crescendo with which Premier Li Keqiang concluded his reports on the work of the government to the 2014 and 2015 National People's Congresses.

If the China Dream is ideology, of what kind is it? Xi himself, on its launch, presented it as 'the greatest dream of the Chinese nation in recent times' and 'the great rejuvenation of the Chinese nation', and added that 'each person's future and destiny is closely linked with the future and destiny of the country and nation.' The sting is in the tail of this exhortation, is in the idea of unity of nation and person.

Xi presented his dream as a double narrative, not just of nation and greatness but also of a relationship between state and people. That double meaning was quickly picked up in subsequent interpretations and has constantly been repeated. An early and long first-page article on 5 April 2013 in *Beijing Daily*, the capital's party newspaper, was remarkable:

> Use the China Dream to gather consensus and unify strength. . . . Extensively promulgate and realise that the China Dream of the great rejuvenation of the Chinese nation is precisely what will strengthen the nation, revive its ethnic groups, and bless its people. . . . Extensively promulgate that the future and destiny of every person is inseparably linked to the future and destiny of the country and the nation. . . . Extensively promulgate that patriotism is the nucleus of the national spirit. . . . Promote patriotism as the soul of a powerful and invigorated country which joins minds and gathers strength, and as the spiritual force which strengthens and unites the Chinese people. . . . Extensively promulgate that realizing the China Dream requires the consolidation of Chinese power. Extensively promulgate that the China Dream is the dream of the nation, and is also the dream of every Chinese person.

This is not just a celebration of national greatness. It is in addition an idea that national greatness and individual happiness are one and the same and inseparable, and conversely that there is no individual happiness without national greatness.

This is a very different idea from what one might think its inspiration, the American Dream. That term was minted by the historian James Truslow Adams in 1931, in his *The Epic of America*. This was a dream of a social order in which every man and woman can realise his or her capabilities to the fullest and be recognised by others as equals. It was a dream of personal aspirations and fairness. The China Dream is a dream of national aspiration and for the nation ahead of the people who make it up. Their aspiration is said to be fulfilled if the national aspiration is fulfilled.

Ideologies are dangerous. What we are seeing in the China Dream is the embryo of an ideology that is ultra-dangerous. It is that because it sits on a rhetoric of power and national greatness and because, ultimately, it is an ideology in which the person ceases to exist as an autonomous being and is subsumed in the nation. If individual happiness comes from national greatness, then the pursuit of national greatness is an undivided good. If national greatness is the making of individual happiness—because the destiny of every person is inseparably linked to the destiny of the nation—then there is no autonomous good for individual women and men that might restrain the national project or the policies of the party-state that is the custodian of that project. There is no independent good of persons that can stand in the way of and limit what is seen as the good of the nation or the strength of its state. If repression, aggression, and ultimately war are in the national interest, then these policies are by ideological fiat also for the good of 'each person's future and destiny'.

At its core, the idea of unity between nation and person is a fascist idea, *the* fascist idea. Even communist ideology (if of course not practice) has been built in the enlightenment spirit that persons are objectives and that systems are for their good, and that they prove themselves by promoting the good of individual women and men. The final horror of fascist ideology as it arose in Europe was its rejection of enlightenment modernity by the elimination of individual autonomy. Governments are to serve the cause of national greatness, nation and people are one, national greatness is for the good of the people, there is no other way that persons can prosper than that their nation prospers. Ultimately, if war is in the national interest, it is for the good of the persons who are the building blocks of the nation. This is not abstract theorising. In fascist Europe there was no limit to repression, no limit to aggression, no limit to evil, no limit to political murder, and no limit to sacrifice that was not for the good of the people. It was by this ideology that European fascism was able to worship war as an arena of national glory and a cleansing experience for a people.

The new Chinese state has been described elsewhere as fascist. For example, Yu Jie, the author of *Xi Jinping: China's Godfather* (a critical biography published in Chinese in Taiwan and Hong Kong) has in interviews described the regime as fascist for being aggressive, nationalistic, and militaristic. But that is a misunderstanding. A state is not fascist for being nationalistic; it is fascist if its nationalism is grounded in a fascist ideology. A nationalistic state is one thing, a nationalistic state that eggs itself on by ideology something else.

It is too early to tell. After Mao and until Xi Jinping, the Chinese state was in my schema a trivial one, successful and increasingly strong but with a regime carefully dedicated to self-preservation and ready to accept almost any price for stability. That may endure. The Chinese state is a sophisticated dictatorship but, as things stand today, possibly not yet an ideological one. It is a near-totalitarian regime but not fully totalitarian.

But it is also a regime still in the making. Its present remaking is not a pretty sight. The current leadership has step by step tightened dictatorial controls. The year 2015 was a bad one for them. It hit home, domestically and abroad, that economic growth is on a downwards slide. The stock market crash, the decline in the value of the currency, a deadly explosion (death toll: 173, hundreds more injured) in a chemical warehouse in Tianjin that was not an accident but the result of rules having been flaunted through political corruption—all this conspired to undermine the credibility of a regime that has built its clam to legitimacy on safe management and economic performance. The logic is convoluted. There is more dictatorship, hence more need for justification. There is less justification to be found in the legitimacy of good governance, therefore yet more reliance on controls. Its reputation for steady economic management in shatters, the regime must turn elsewhere for justification, to narrative and ideology. Hence the increasing prominence of propaganda, political education, and mass campaigns, and the new rhetoric of national greatness, nationalism, and chauvinism, and the super-rhetoric of the China Dream.

The leaders now speak a new and assertive ideological language, and it is, as usual, unwise not to listen to what they say. When powerful leaders turn to ideology, there is *always* danger and others *must* pay attention. Theirs could be a state that has risen so that it is no longer possible for it to bide its time. Economic growth may not be narrative enough when the real underlying project is national greatness. The party-state and its controlocracy may no longer have *raison d'être* enough without more forceful ideological justification. Ideology is in the remaking and might become inevitable. The balance could tip to fully fledged totalitarianism. It could be that China is rising not only economically but irresistibly also as a power state.

For all we know, Xi Jinping may not deliberately be embracing ideology at all and may just be experimenting with slogans that work. But to play with ideology is to play with fire and he may, even if inadvertently, be releasing a force that is not only strong but also repugnant and that takes on a life of its own and becomes its author's master on terms the author may not have fully anticipated. A big and powerful country, a strong state, an ambitious and shrewd leader—that adds up to a force to be reckoned with. A big and powerful country, a strong state, an ambitious and shrewd leader, a commanding ideology—that adds up to a force to be feared.

This, in my judgement, is a second high-probability scenario. If the Chinese state is to be a power state it must be ideological. There seems to be no other serviceable ideology in the offering than one with fascistoid characteristics. The tug of war between my two high-probability scenarios comes down to ideology. If the Chinese state continues to operate as a custodian of economic growth and political control, and does so effectively, it is likely to remain dictatorial but pragmatic. If it becomes dependent on ideology and embraces a narrative in which persons are subsumed in the nation, it will have made itself a totalitarian state of the most sinister kind, the kind in which persons are only 'the masses' and do not matter individually. An ideological strong state is by historical experience dangerous. If it takes to basking in a story of its own making of national glory, pragmatism is unlikely to prevail, and no one can tell what might follow. As I have been following the sayings and doings of the new leadership and have come to thinking of my first scenario as high probability minus, my instinct on completing this exploration is to classify my final scenario as high probability plus.

Bibliography

Adams, James Truslow. *The Epic of America*. New York, 1931.

Arendt, Hannah. *The Origins of Totalitarianism*. New York, 1951.

Asian Development Bank. *People's Republic of China: Toward Establishing a Rural Health Protection Scheme*. Manila: ADB, 2002.

Beardson, Timothy. *Stumbling Giant: The Threats to China's Future*. New Haven: Yale University Press, 2014.

Bell, Daniel A. *The China Model: Political Meritocracy and the Limits of Democracy*. Princeton: Princeton University Press, 2015.

———. *China's New Confucianism: Politics and Everyday Life in a Changing Society*. Princeton: Princeton University Press, 2008.

Berlin, Isaiah. *The Crooked Timber of Humanity*. London: John Murray, 1990.

Bosker, Bianca. *Original Copies: Architectural Mimicry in Contemporary China*. Honolulu: University of Hawai'i Press, 2013.

Briggs, Asa. 'The welfare-state in historical perspective.' *Archives européennes de Sociologie* 2, no. 2 (1961): 221–59.

Callahan, William A. *China Dreams: 20 Visions of the Future*. Oxford: Oxford University Press, 2013.

———. *China: The Pessoptimistic Nation*. Oxford: Oxford University Press, 2010.

Callick, Rowan. *The Party Forever: Inside China's Modern Communist Elite*. New York: Palgrave Macmillan, 2013.

Cardenal, Juan Pablo, and Heriberto Araújo. *China's Silent Army: The Pioneers, Traders, Fixers and Workers Who Are Remaking the World in Beijing's Image*. London: Allen Lane, 2013.

Carillo, Beatrice, and Jane Duckett, eds. *China's Changing Welfare Mix: Local Perspectives*. London: Routledge, 2011.

CCP. *Decision on Several Key Issues Concerning the Establishment of the Socialist Market Economy System*. Third Plenum of the 14th Central Committee of the Chinese Communist Party, Beijing, 14 November 1993.

Chan, C. K., K. L. Ngok, and D. Phillips. *Social Policy in China: Development and Wellbeing*. Bristol: Policy Press, 2008.

Chang, Jung. *Empress Dowager Cixi: The Concubine Who Launched Modern China*. London: Vintage, 2014.

Chang, Jung, and Jon Halliday. *Mao: The Unknown Story*. London: Vintage, 2006.

Christensen, Thomas J. *The China Challenge: Shaping the Choices of a Rising Power*. New York: Norton, 2015.

Coase, Ronald, and Ning Wang. *How China Became Capitalist.* New York: Palgrave Macmillan, 2013.

Cook, S., N. Kabeer, and G. Suwannarat, eds. *Social Protection in Asia.* Delhi: Har-Anand Publications, 2003.

Davis, D., and F. Wang, eds. *Creating Wealth and Poverty in Postsocialist China.* Stanford: Stanford University Press, 2009.

Dickson, Bruce J., and Jie Chen. *Allies of the State: Democratic Support and Regime Support among China's Private Entrepreneurs.* Cambridge, MA: Harvard University Press, 2010.

Dikötter, Frank. *The Tragedy of Liberation: A History of the Chinese Revolution 1945–1957.* London: Bloomsbury, 2013.

Dorfman, Mark C., Robert Holzmann, Philip O'Keefe, Dewen Wang, Yvonne Sin, and Richard Hinz. *China's Pension System: A Vision.* Washington, DC: World Bank, 2013.

Eimer, David. *The Emperor Far Away: Travels at the Edge of China.* New York: Bloomsbury, 2014.

Fenby, Jonathan. *Tiger Head, Snake Tails: China Today, How It Got There and Where It Is Heading.* New York: Simon & Schuster, 2012.

———. *Will China Dominate the 21st Century*? London: Polity Press, 2014.

Fewsmith, Joseph. *The Logic and Limits of Political Reform in China.* Cambridge: Cambridge University Press, 2013.

Finer, S. E. *The History of Government.* Vols. 1–3. Oxford: Oxford University Press, 1997.

Gao, Qin. 'Redistributive nature of the Chinese social benefit system: Progressive or regressive?' *China Quarterly* 2 (2010): 1–19.

Gao, Qin, Sui Yang, and Shi Li. 'The Chinese welfare-state in transition: 1988–2007.' *Journal of Social Policy* 42 (2013): 743–62.

Gao, Q., I. Garfinkel, and F. Zhai. 'Anti-poverty effectiveness of the minimum living standard assistance policy in Urban China.' *Review of Income and Wealth* 55 (2009): 630–55.

Garnaut, Ross, Cai Fang, and Ligang Song, eds. *China: A New Model for Growth and Development.* Canberra: Australian National University Press, 2013.

Givens, John Wagner. 'Suing dragons? Taking the Chinese state to court.' DPhil thesis. St. Antony's College, University of Oxford, 2012.

Greenhalgh, Susan. *Just One Child: Science and Policy in Deng's China.* Berkeley: University of California Press, 2008.

Gustafsson, Björn, Li Shi, and Hiroshi Sato. 'Data for studying earnings, the distribution of household income and poverty in China.' *China Economic Review* 30 (2014): 419–31.

Gustafsson, Björn, Li Shi, and Terry Sicular, eds. *Inequality and Public Policy in China.* Cambridge: Cambridge University Press, 2008.

Gustafsson, B., and Q. Deng. 'Dibao receipt and its importance for combating poverty in urban China.' *Poverty & Public Policy* 3 (2011): 1–32.

Holdstock, Nick. *China's Forgotten People: Xinjiang Terror and the Chinese State.* London: I. B. Tauris, 2015.

Holliday, I., and P. Wilding, eds. *Welfare Capitalism in East Asia.* Basingstoke: Palgrave Macmillan, 2004.

Hsu, Jennifer Y. J., and Reza Hasmath, eds. *The Chinese Corporatist State: Adaptation, Survival and Resistance.* London: Routledge, 2013.

Huang, Yasheng. *Capitalism with Chinese Characteristics: Entrepreneurship and the State.* Cambridge: Cambridge University Press, 2008.

Jacques, Martin. *When China Rules the World.* London: Penguin, 2012.

Johnson, Ian. *Wild Grass: China's Revolution From Below.* New York: Penguin, 2015.

Joseph, William A., ed. *Politics in China: An Introduction.* New York: Oxford University Press, 2010.

Keynes, John Maynard. *The General Theory of Employment, Interest and Money.* London, 1936.

Kinkel, Jonathan, and William Hurst. 'Access to justice in post-Mao China: Assessing the politics of criminal and administrative law.' *Journal of East Asian Studies* 11 (2011): 467–99.

Kissinger, Henry. *On China.* New York: Penguin, 2011.

Knight, John, and Sai Ding. *China's Remarkable Economic Growth.* Oxford: Oxford University Press, 2012.

Knight, John, and Lina Song. *Towards a Labour Market in China.* Oxford: Oxford University Press, 2005.

Kwon Huck-ju. 'The reform of the developmental Welfare-state in East Asia.' *International Journal of Social Welfare* 18 (2009): 12–21.

———, ed. *Transforming the Developmental Welfare State in East Asia.* Basingstoke: Palgrave Macmillan, 2005.

Kwong, Julia. *The Political Economy of Corruption in China.* New York: M. E. Sharpe, 1997.

Lam, Willy Wo-Lap. *Chinese Politics in the Era of Xi Jinping: Renaissance, Reform, or Retrogression?* London: Routledge, 2015.

Lampton, David M. *Following the Leader: Ruling China, From Deng Xiaoping to Xi Jinping.* Berkeley: University of California Press, 2014.

Laruelle, Marlène, and Sebastian Peyrouse. *The Chinese Question in Central Asia: Domestic Order, Social Change and the Chinese Factor.* New York: Herst, 2012.

Lee, Il Houng, Murtaza Syed, and Liu Xueyan. 'Is China over-investing and does it matter?' IMF Working Paper, Asia and Pacific Department, November 2012.

Leibold, James, and Chen Yangbin, eds. *Minority Education in China: Balancing Unity and Diversity in an Era of Critical Pluralism.* Hong Kong: Hong Kong University Press, 2014.

Leonard, Mark. *What Does China Think?* London: Fourth Estate, 2008.

Leung, J. C. B., and R. Nann. *Authority and Benevolence: Social Welfare in China.* Hong Kong: Chinese University Press, 1995.

Li Shi, Hiroshi Sato, and Terry Sicular, eds. *Rising Inequality in China: Challenges to a Harmonious Society.* Cambridge: Cambridge University Press, 2013.

Lieberthal, Kenneth. *Governing China: From Revolution through Reform.* 2nd ed. New York: Norton, 2004.

Lieberthal, Kenneth G., Cheng Li, and Yu Keping, eds. *China's Political Development: Chinese and American Perspectives.* Washington, DC: Brookings Institution Press, 2014.

Lim, Louisa. *The People's Republic of Amnesia: Tiananmen Revisited.* New York: Oxford University Press, 2014.

Link, Perry. 'Politics and the Chinese language.' *ChinaFile*, 24 December 2012.

Loh, Christine. *Underground Front: The Chinese Communist Party in Hong Kong.* Hong Kong: Hong Kong University Press, 2010.

Lora-Wainwright, Anna. *Fighting for Breath: Living Morally and Dying of Cancer in a Chinese Village.* Honolulu: University of Hawai'i Press, 2013.

Luttwak, Edward N. *The Rise of China Vs. The Logic of Strategy.* Cambridge, MA: Harvard University Press, 2012.

Madsen, Richard. *China and the American Dream: A Moral Inquiry.* Berkeley: University of California Press, 1995.

McGregor, Richard. *The Party: The Secret World of China's Communist Rulers.* London: Penguin, 2012.

Miller, Tom. *China's Urban Billion: The Story behind the Biggest Migration in Human History.* London: Palgrave Macmillan, 2012.

Mitter, Rana. *A Bitter Revolution: China's Struggle with the Modern World.* Oxford: Oxford University Press, 2004.

———. *China's War with Japan, 1937–1945: The Struggle for Survival.* London: Allen Lane, 2013.

———. *Modern China.* Oxford: Oxford University Press, 2008.

Murphy, Rachel. *How Migrant Labour Is Changing Rural China.* Cambridge: Cambridge University Press, 2002.

Nathan, Andrew J., and Andrew Scobell. *China's Search for Security.* New York: Columbia University Press, 2012.

O'Brien, Kevin J., ed. *Popular Protest in China.* Cambridge, MA: Harvard University Press, 2008.

Orwell, George. *Orwell in Spain*, edited by Peter Davison. London: Penguin, 2001.

Osburg, John. *Anxious Wealth: Money and Morality among China's New Rich.* Stanford: Stanford University Press, 2013.

Osnos, Evan. *Age of Ambition: Chasing Fortune, Truth, and Faith in the New China.* New York: Ferrar, Straus and Giroux, 2014.

Pantsov, Alexander V., with Steven I. Levine. *Deng Xiaoping: A Revolutionary Life.* Oxford: Oxford University Press, 2015.

Paulson, Henry M., Jr. *Dealing with China: An Insider Unmasks the New Economic Superpower.* New York: Twelve, 2015.

Pei Minxin. *China's Trapped Transition: The Limits of Developmental Autocracy.* Cambridge, MA: Harvard University Press, 2006.

Pettis, Michael. *The Great Rebalancing: Trade, Conflict, and the Perilous Road Ahead for the World Economy.* Princeton: Princeton University Press, 2013.

Read, Benjamin L. *Roots of the State: Neighborhood Organization and Social Networks in Beijing and Taipei.* Stanford: Stanford University Press, 2012.

Ringen, Stein. *Nation of Devils: Democratic Leadership and the Problem of Obedience.* New Haven: Yale University Press, 2013.

———. *What Democracy Is For: On Freedom and Moral Government.* Princeton: Princeton University Press, 2007.

Ringen, S., Huck-ju Kwon, Ilcheong Yi, Taekyoon Kim, and Jooha Lee. *The Korean State and Social Policy: How South Korea Lifted Itself from Poverty and Dictatorship to Affluence and Democracy.* New York: Oxford University Press, 2011.

Rose-Ackerman, Susan, and Paul Lagunes, eds. *Greed, Corruption, and the Modern State: Essays in Political Economy.* Cheltenham: Edward Elgar, 2015.

Rosen, Daniel H., and Beibei Bao. *A Better Abacus for China.* New York: Rhodium Group, 2015.

Saich, Tony. *Governance and Politics of China.* 3rd ed. New York: Palgrave Macmillan, 2011.

———. *Providing Public Goods in Transitional China.* New York: Palgrave Macmillan, 2008.

Saich, Tony, and Biliang Hu. *Chinese Village, Global Market: New Collectives and Rural Development.* New York: Palgrave Macmillan, 2011.

Schell, Orville, and John Delury. *Wealth and Power: China's Long March to the Twenty-First Century.* New York: Random House, 2013.

Shambaugh, David. *China Goes Global: The Partial Power.* New York: Oxford University Press, 2013.

———. *China's Communist Party: Atrophy and Adaptation.* Berkeley: University of California Press, 2008.

———. *The Modern Chinese State.* Cambridge: Cambridge University Press, 2000.

Shirk, Susan L. *China: Fragile Superpower.* New York: Oxford University Press, 2008.

Shue, Vivienne, and Christine Wong, eds. *Paying for Progress in China: Public Finance, Human Welfare and Changing Patterns of Inequality.* London: Routledge, 2008.

Simon, Karla W. *Civil Society in China.* New York: Oxford University Press, 2013.

Sicular, Terry, Yue Ximing, Björn Gustafsson, and Li Shi. 'The urban-rural income gap and inequality in China.' *Review of Income and Wealth* 53 (2007): 93–126.

Snow, Edgar. *Red Star over China.* New York, 1938.

Solinger, Dorothy J. *Contesting Citizenship in Urban China: Peasant Migration, the State, and the Logic of Market.* Berkeley: University of California, 1999.

———. 'Social assistance under capitalist, authoritarian rule: Two management models in Chinese municipalities.' *Journal of Contemporary Asia* 44 (2014): 500–520.

Temple, William. *Citizen and Churchman.* London, 1941.

Thornton, Patricia M. *Disciplining the State: Virtue, Violence and State-Making in Modern China.* Cambridge, MA: Harvard University Asia Center, 2007.

Tocqueville, Alexis de. *Democracy in America.* Paris, 1835, 1840.

Tsai, Kellee. *Capitalism without Democracy: The Private Sector in Contemporary China.* Ithaca: Cornell University Press, 2007.

Tsang, Steve. 'Consultative Leninism: China's new political framework.' *Journal of Contemporary China* 18, no. 62 (2009): 865–80.

Vogel, Ezra F. *Deng Xiaoping and the Transformation of China.* Cambridge, MA: Harvard University Press, 2011.

Walder, Andrew G. *China under Mao: A Revolution Derailed.* Cambridge, MA: Harvard University Press, 2015.

Wasserstrom, Jeff. *China in the 21st Century: What Everyone Needs to Know.* New York: Oxford University Press, 2010.

Wedeman, Andrew. *Double Paradox: Rapid Growth and Rising Corruption in China.* Ithaca: Cornell University Press, 2012.

Westad, Odd Arne. *Restless Empire: China and the World since 1750.* London: Bodley Head, 2012.

Whyte, Martin K. *One Country, Two Societies: Rural-Urban Inequality in Contemporary China.* Cambridge, MA: Harvard University Press, 2010.

Whyte, Martin King, Wang Feng, and Yong Cai. 'Challenging myths about China's one-child policy.' *The China Journal* 74 (July 2015): 144–59.

Wong, Christine. 'Reforming China's public finances for long-term growth.' In Ross Garnaut, Cai Fang, and Ligang Song, eds., *China: A New Model for Growth and Development*, 199–219. Canberra: Australian National University Press, 2013.

Wong, Linda. *Marginalization and Social Welfare in China.* London: Taylor & Francis, 1998.

World Bank and Development Research Center of the State Council. *China 2030: Building a Modern, Harmonious, and Creative China.* Washington, DC: World Bank, 2013.

Wu, Harry. *Re-estimating Chinese Growth.* New York: Conference Board, China Center Special Briefing Paper, 2014.

Xi Chen. *Social Protest and Contentious Authoritarianism in China.* Cambridge: Cambridge University Press, 2014.

Yang Dali. *Remaking the Chinese Leviathan: Market Transition and the Politics of Governance in China.* Stanford: Stanford University Press, 2006.

Yang Jisheng. *Tombstone: The Great Chinese Famine, 1958–1962.* New York: Ferrar, Straus and Giroux, 2013.

Yongshun Cai. *Collective Resistance in China: Why Popular Protests Succeed or Fail.* Stanford: Stanford University Press, 2010.

Zhang Weiwei. *The China Horizon: Glory and Dream of a Civilization State.* London: World Scientific, 2015.

Zheng Gongcheng. *China's Social Security during Thirty Years.* Beijing: Renmin University, 2008 (in Chinese).

Zhu Yapeng. 'Housing policy in China at the crossroads: Trends and prospects.' *China Journal of Social Work* 7 (2014): 189–201.

Index

About the Author

Stein Ringen, a Norwegian political scientist, is emeritus professor at Green Templeton College, University of Oxford, where he from 1990 held the chair in sociology and social policy, and an affiliate of St Antony's College, Oxford. He started his academic career as a junior fellow at the International Peace Research Institute in Oslo and was subsequently project director of the Norwegian Level of Living Study, fellow of the Institute of Social Research and of FAFO, both in Oslo, professor of welfare studies at the University of Stockholm, senior research scientist at the Norwegian Central Bureau of Statistics, and adjunct professor at Lillehammer University College. He has held visiting professorships and fellowships in Paris, Berlin, Prague, Brno, Barbados, Jerusalem, Sydney, Hong Kong, and at Harvard University. He has been head of research in the Norwegian Ministry of Public Administration, Assistant Director General in the Norwegian Ministry of Justice, a consultant to the United Nations, and a news and feature reporter with the Norwegian Broadcasting Corporation. He is a visiting professor at Richmond, the American International University in London.

His books include *What Democracy Is For* (Princeton University Press, 2007; Chinese version published by Xinhua in 2012), *The Korean State and Social Policy* (co-authored, Oxford University Press, 2011), *The Possibility of Politics* (Oxford University Press, 1987 and Transaction, 2006), and *Nation of Devils: Democracy and the Problem of Obedience* (Yale University Press, 2013, the Chinese version of which, by CITIC Publishers, is currently 'suspended' by the censors).

He lives in London with his wife, the novelist and historian Mary Chamberlain.

CPSIA information can be obtained
at www.ICGtesting.com
Printed in the USA
LVHW050922210122
708252LV00003B/18

9 789888 208944